The Meetings, Incentives, Conferences, and Exhibitions (MICE) Industry in China: Residents' Perceptions

中国会展产业发展：居民的感知研究

Zhou Chao

周　超◎著

ZHEJIANG UNIVERSITY PRESS
浙江大学出版社

Preface

This book is based on the doctoral thesis on residents' perceptions of general impacts of meetings, incentives, conferences, and exhibitions (MICE) development. As in other Chinese cities, Hangzhou's MICE policies are primarily determined by the municipal government with comparatively less reference to residents. The research was conducted respectively in 2007 and 2012 after two world leisure expositions were hosted in Hangzhou. However, during the publishing process of the book, the 2016 G20 Hangzhou Summit was also hosted, which brought enormous effects to the MICE industry in the city.

The researcher has found very little prior research into the subject of residents' perceptions of MICE. Nevertheless, as described in the book, there has been increasing competition among cities as each seeks to build conference centres and attract business. Much of the literature reviewed is based on the research into Western cases, but reference is also made to potential differences between China and other places.

Given the lack of previous research in China, the main focus of this book is descriptive and exploratory in nature, but the initial results permit the development of a potential set of causal relationships that are summarised in the main text. This permits a series of four propositions to be examined. It is to be noted that the term 'proposition' is used rather than 'hypothesis'. The latter term implies quantifiable relationships that are thought to exist and that can be tested. The literature review reveals a general deficiency about residents' perceptions of MICE and the Chinese situation, so at this stage it is proposed that a relationship between residents and MICE should be tested.

The propositions include:

Proposition One

Socio-demographic variables have an impact on residents' perceptions of MICE at the city and personal levels, and on evaluations of Hangzhou's MICE policies. In this respect, generally, it was found that socio-demographics were not discriminating variables, and only employment status and a past experience of MICE attendance had some role of significance.

Proposition Two

There will be differences between residents' perceptions of the impacts of MICE policies when the residents' were asked to consider (a) impacts on Hangzhou generally, and (b) impacts on personal daily life. This was found to be generally true, and generally respondents were supportive of MICE policies that generated benefits for the city as a whole.

Proposition Three

There will be differences in perceptions that can be caught in psychometric measurements that will enable different clusters to be discerned, whereby some will be supportive of MICE policies and others less so—such differences being determined by the evaluations of social and environmental costs as against economic gains. In short, there is an inherent tension of the economic, social, and environmental aspects within the current state of Hangzhou as a fast developing city in a fast developing nation. This has proved to be the case.

Proposition Four

A history of past attendance at MICE will be a variable that shapes support for MICE development and evaluations of MICE policies. This was partially supported.

While distinct factors, clusters and the role of past attendance were found, the overall model proposed in Chapter Three, whereby a mix of civic advantages and personal impacts were thought to generate evaluations of MICE policies, was not wholly supported by path analysis.

Contents

Chapter Three   Methodology

Chapter Four   Pilot Study: Qualitative Research Analysis

Chapter Five   Sample Characteristics and Overall Results

Chapter Six   Data Reliability and Exploratory Factor Analysis

List of Figures

List of Tables

Chapter One

Introduction

➡ 1.1 Background

Event tourism is currently a significant sector in the tourism industry and a force in the economic regeneration or micro-modernisation of both the tourism industry and regional economies. Ritchie (1984) wrote that event tourism involves either major one-time or recurring events of limited duration, developed primarily to enhance the awareness, appeal and profitability of a tourism destination in the short and/or long term. The success of these events relies on uniqueness, status, or timely significance to arouse interest and attract attention. Raybould and Fredline (2012) mentioned that one of the most extensively researched areas of special events is their economic impact. Canniffe (1998) and Ryan (1998) also agreed that the nature and impact of events rely on whether the destination is a country as a whole or a particular region, city or town within it. For his part Getz (1989) added that although the majority of events have probably arisen for non-tourist reasons, there is clearly a trend to exploit them for tourism and to create new events deliberately as tourist attractions. Consequently, the significance and success of meetings, incentives, conferences, and exhibitions (MICE) tourism are not unanticipated, for MICE is deliberately engineered by the local, regional and national government as a means of prestige and economic regeneration. As Getz (1991) said, the growing interest in festival and special events is based on events' profitable activities in the community.

According to the International Congress and Convention Association (ICCA) (2013), the number of meetings of international associations between 1963 and 2012 was 173,432; the current ratio of association members to meetings is 1 : 13 compared to 1 : 3 in the 1970s; the estimated total expenditure on all meetings in the ICCA database taking place in the last five years is 56.4 billion USD. The position of international events and especially event tourism is becoming important in the world economy. The ICCA (2013) stated that each year the ICCA figures are anxiously awaited by destinations around the world, all of which compete fiercely for a larger share of this lucrative market. These figures have subsequently increased and in 2008, ICCA estimated that, in 2007, there had been, globally, a total of 6,500 conference sessions, an increase of 800 sessions over the previous year 2006. International event tourism also possesses significant potential for growth. Because of worldwide economic integration, and in spite of the growing use of the Internet, commercial, academic, and governmental needs dictate a growing demand for frequent face-to-face MICE. This need has enabled the industry to get less impact and survive recessions during economic downturns.

Due to the economic impacts brought by MICE, MICE tourism has played a very important role in tourism and economic policy development by regional and national governments. The creation of special events and attractions is increasingly playing an important role in attracting tourists to a local region or community (UNWTO, 2012). Kim, Uysal and Chen (2002) agreed, stating earlier that one of the fastest growing sectors of the tourism industry has been 'event tourism'. As Hall (1992) said, events are being viewed as an integral part of tourism development and marketing plans. Again, to further cite Hall (1992), international events are an opportunity for nations to improve their image in an increasingly market and brand image conscious world. Yet this is not new. According to Armstrong (1986, p. 11), '... the first international exhibition, the Great Exposition of the Works of Industry of All Nations, held in Hyde Park, London, in 1851 was held because, as Prince Albert stated, "It was the only way to out-do the French".'

It has thus become commonplace that events are important success factors for the marketing of tourism and its development (Getz, 1997; Peters & Weiermair, 2000). Consequently, event tourism and MICE management have also become an important issue. Getz (1997) stated whether an event is organised by professionals or volunteers, corporations or non-profit associations, event management is both an art and a science. According to Yeoman, Robertson, Ali-Knight, Drummond and McMahon-Beattie (2004), the components involved in event management are varied such as financial support, volunteers' motivation, theme selection, and the ability to identify market segments and their needs.

It is therefore not uncommon for the public sector to be responsible for a large proportion of the special events provided for the community, and many local governments now have a substantial and varied events program (Thomas & Wood, 2004). Indeed, in many countries local authorities have someone within their organisation who has the specific role of devising a portfolio of events and conferences and who seeks to encourage the private sector to initiate conferences, conventions and meetings. Yet despite the growth in the importance of such activities and the increasing role of the public sector in providing special events (Shone & Parry, 2001), the public service provision for entertainment, culture, and arts remains a non-mandatory requirement (Borrett, 1991). Furthermore, because of the interest in economic regeneration, research has been dominated by economic impact assessment. Many researchers have focused on the residents' reactions to or a relationship between mega events and the local community. Warnick, Bojanic and Xu (2015) mentioned that most economic impact (EI) studies focus on tourist destinations and long-term seasonal tourism attractions and special events, which by nature are different from permanent attractions. However, there are still gaps in the research such as studies of residents' perceptions of event-related policies and financial and social benefits related to hosting events. This lack of interest specifically exists in the Chinese MICE research area, partly due to the very recent emergence of MICE development in this country. Thus it can be stated that the Chinese MICE industry has been less studied than that of the West. This book attempts to go beyond a narrow economic approach and explore a wider resident perception of MICE tourism with specific reference to a regional centre located in the People's Republic of China.

Visitors attending a convention or exhibition often look for elements beyond the core of the event to complement their experiences. It is common to draw upon local cultures to provide these attractions because these are specific to an area, and are thereby unique and are thus thought to attract out-of-region visitors (Kim, Uysal & Chen, 2002). Robinson and Phipps (2003) defined what are termed 'pockets of opportunity' whereby convention and exhibition delegates increasingly seek to touch, at different levels, the essence of 'otherness' communicated through various intercultural mediators such as food, outdoor music, objects, aesthetic signs, and narration.

1.2 MICE Development

MICE tourism has developed well in the US, Canada, UK, Spain, France and Germany. According to Xinhua News Agency (2003), many international MICE events are held in a few Western economies such as the US, which has the world's biggest passenger transportation demand and 33.8% of the demand for hotel accommodation (ICCA, 2006). This is also certainly true for Canada, Australia, etc. Whilst Western countries have made large profits from the international MICE tourism market, at present the industry is embryonic in Asian countries. The gap between Western countries and Asian countries is obvious.

Although there is an obvious disparity between Western and Asian countries, the growth of MICE tourism in the Asian tourism market cannot be ignored with its rapid development. According to ICCA (2013), there were two major Asian cities in the ranking of the top ten popular event-hosting cities in 2012 (see Table 1.1)—Singapore and Seoul, while Hong Kong was not on the list.

Table 1.1   Ranking of Top ICCA Event-hosting Cities in 2012

Ranking	City	Number of Meetings
1	Paris	204
2	Madrid	186
3	Vienna	182
4	Barcelona	179
5	Berlin	178
6	Singapore	175
7	London	166
8	Istanbul	146

(continued)

Ranking	City	Number of Meetings
9	Lisbon	125
10	Seoul	125

Source: ICCA. (2013).

The Asian Association of Convention and Visitor Bureaus (AACVB, 2014) noted that the Asian business events market achieved an impressive growth of 133% in the six years between 2008 and 2013, substantially outpacing the global growth of just 19.9% over the same period. Building on this, it also shows that Asia now occupies the top three positions for holding international meetings. For example, Hong Kong and Singapore have pursued this market for the past 20 years in recognition of its high yield. Singapore, as the most 'Western' place in Southeast Asia, can be considered as the capital of Asian MICE tourism market. 'One of the markets which has been targeted is the meetings, incentives, conventions, and exhibitions trade which produces S$300 million (187.5 million US dollars) worth of business a year for Singapore' (Hall, 1994, p. 132). Not only Singapore, but also Hong Kong and Seoul have seen a dramatic development in the event industry. The Global Association of the Exhibition Industry (UFI, 2004) additionally noted that the event industry is important in Thailand's tourism market. Thailand has potential as a prime destination for trade exhibitions and trade fairs; these events in Thailand represent revenues of over 7.5 million baht. Also by 2000, China ranked 34th in terms of the number of MICE attendees (Chinese International Airline Agency, 2000). The vitality of the sector in Asia is evident in the growth of these individual markets, with the Chinese business events industry experiencing an annual growth of 20%, the government of the Republic of Korea prioritizing business events in its '2013 Direction on Economic Policy', and Thailand marking an important milestone in 2013 by welcoming more than one million business events visitors, among other examples. So recognized as true growth drivers and backed by strong government support, key markets such as China, the Republic of Korea, the Republic of Singapore, Thailand, and other AACVB members continue to accelerate their business events offerings and position themselves as top business events destinations.

The prosperous development of the MICE industry in the Asian tourism market enforces the level of high competition between several tourism countries including China. The

Commonwealth Department of Tourism (1995) noted at an early stage that the Australian National Convention Strategy identified the Asia-Pacific region as the major competitive MICE destination to Australia in terms of both location and development of world-class convention facilities. Rod (2003) found that competition is high as Malaysia, the Republic of Korea, China, the Philippines, and Indonesia move to increase their brand recognition and marketing power. Rod (2003) also emphasised that the last decade has seen major competitive development between those Asian tourism countries including the building of new convention centres such as those in Manila and New Delhi.

As already noted, many countries and regions have written event tourism as a major promotional method into their tourism strategies. Chinese mainland has to 'compete for the same market with counterparts in the Asia-Pacific region, most of which are well established and have a sophisticated tourism industry for example, Singapore, Hong Kong…, with similar products but better service and cheaper price' (Zhang, 1989, p. 64). Hing, McCabe, Lewis and Leiper (1998) described Singapore, Kuala Lumpur and Hong Kong as establishing purpose-built convention centres and noted that their governments have also funded their respective international convention business. Hall (1994) also mentioned that, like other countries, Indonesia has also used a combination of events such as cultural festivals and 'visitor years' to raise its profile in the overseas tourism market. Hall (1994) compared a 'visitor year' to a 'mingled' event group that provides a large range of festivals and events. He noted that in the 1990 'Visit Malaysia Year', a total of 107 events ranging from festivals, sports tournaments, and cultural shows were held. 'Visitor year' is not a newly-emerged concept; it has become a model for ASEAN (Association of Southeast Asian Nations) countries to promote their tourism industry. Rurakdee (1991) noted the success of the 'visitor year' held in Thailand in 1987. The Malaysian Tourist Development Corporation likewise designated 1990 as 'Visit Malaysia Year', and the Japanese government held 'Visit Japan 2010' campaign. In Thailand's tourism development plan, event tourism takes on a very important role. Corben (1990) identified four priority areas for the development of Thai tourism, which are: conventions and meetings, family-oriented leisure travel, sports travel, and incentive travel. Estimates indicated that, in 2007, Thailand hosted 95 international conferences and created more than 41 billion baht, and so ranked 29th in global terms by the criterion of the number of events held

(ICCA, 2008). ICCA (2004) reported that in Asia, the biggest event-hosting country was indeed the Republic of Singapore. Thus, for example, it hosted the International Olympic Committee in 2005 when the latter selected London as the host city of the 2012 Olympic Games. However, the trend of MICE development in China is fast and even unbelievable. According to the ICCA (2013) report, among new destinations, Beijing ranked the 18th in terms of hosting international conferences with a total of 105 international conferences. In part, this was thought to be due to an 'Olympic effect' and one might surmise the same effect would have influenced the number of such conferences for 2008.

However, from late 2007 until the time that most of this book was completed (early 2012), the world economy has suffered a 'cold winter' due to the global financial crisis. Starting as problems in the US housing and subprime mortgage market, this financial crisis swept the whole world rapidly with a strong negative impact on the economy due to inter-bank lending practices that had bundled poor debt into a number of trading instruments including derivatives. This affected currency values, and the world economy slipped from a financial crisis into a downturn, adversely affecting the non-monetary economy in manufacturing and employment in different parts of the world. Due to its strong impacts, this world financial crisis has been entitled 'the Wall Street tsunami'. As Bedford (2008) stated in a research article:

> Starting in the middle of 2007, deteriorating credit quality in the US residential mortgage market served as the catalyst for a systemic financial crisis that has spread far beyond its original source... Strains in international financial markets have also affected New Zealand's financial system and real economy. (p. 18)

Another commentator, Egypt (2009) noted that although the crisis was triggered by events in the US housing market, it has spread to all regions of the world with dire consequences for global trade, investment, and growth.

This recession exposed several weaknesses in the function of the global economy. Indeed, trade and capital flows are the key factors of business cycles (Fidrmuc & Korhonen, 2010). For example, the size of the financial markets in the originating country is an important determinant of cross-border outbound investments (Di Giovanni, 2005). Similarly, Chor and Manova (2012) suggested that 'adverse credit conditions play a significant role in the conduction of the effect of the crisis on trade flows across the world economy'. The MICE industry is not immune to these economic influences. Some researchers have stated that the MICE industry acts as a sensitive barometer of the economy, accurately reflecting the status of economic development trends for the forthcoming period. Many countries' MICE industry faced problems. For example, Zhang (2009) referred to data derived from the Las Vegas Convention and Visitors Authority, stating Vegas's exhibition industry received a total of 5.9 million people who participated in various exhibitions in 2008, a figure five percent lower than that of the previous year. Additionally, forecasts based on bookings predicted a continued drop of four to five percent in 2009. According to statistics from the China Council for the Promotion of International Trade (CCPIT, 2009), while a total of 1,800 organisers were approved to hold international economic and trade exhibitions, in fact only 1,000 exhibitions were held in 2009: a total that was five percent lower than in 2008.

However, while the world has suffered and struggled to recover from the wave of the economic crisis, some countries have maintained a strong MICE industry momentum. The Association of Corporate Travel Executives (ACTE, 2010) reported that during the 2008/2009 economic crisis, while the US and UK economies were battered, China, India, and Australia generally remained 'steady'. Although China's MICE industry was impacted by the financial crisis, the demand for MICE remained high or even increased. According to the 2015 China's Exhibition Industry Development Analysis Report, in 2014, there were a total of 7,851 exhibitions hosted nationally, an increase of 0.5% over 2013; the total exhibition area reached over 103 million square metres, an increase of 13.7% over 2013 (China Convention and Exhibition Economy, 2016). This situation was based on the twin pillars of strong MICE development and general economic growth in China.

1.3 MICE Development in China

It is evident from the above that competition for event tourism in Asia is high; China with its possibly unexpected tourism development in the MICE industry now also challenges other Asian countries, including the Republic of Singapore. Based on its fast tourism development, China has already changed the 'one branch of the tree is particularly thriving' situation in the Asian tourism market and has become an important tourism destination, and 'ranks fourth in the number of tourist arrivals in the world' (UNWTO, 2006). Compared with others, China also has its own advantages: richness in tourism resources, a stable policy structure, one of the longest history in the civilised world, the vastness of the land and thus topographical and climatic variety, rapid economic growth, and more capacity in tourism employee recruitment. China maintains stability in government policy and economic direction. 'China's population of approximately 1.2 billion, its fifty-six distinct nationalities... its territory of 9.6 million square kilometres all contribute to a cultural and natural resource base that provides the country singular [advantages] with enormous potential for tourism development.' (Zhang, Jenkin & Qu, 2003, p. 277). Furthermore, when China is compared with other countries, a long history is also a significant advantage. Zhang, Pine and Lam (2005) argued that a history of over 5,000 years provides China with brilliant cultures comparable to India, Egypt, and other ancient countries.

The Republic of Singapore, when compared to China, is little more than a city-state with a small resource and land base. Other countries like Thailand and Indonesia possess similar cultural backgrounds, but with more threats of external or internal conflicts and some diseases like AIDS. So, although China is currently at a disadvantage, given its size, it seems realistic to assume it still has huge potential to grow in the international MICE market and achieve a significant share of that market.

The development of the MICE industry in China is based on the Chinese tourism boom. In the past decades since the implementation of some opening-up policies and under the influence of fast economic growth, China has been 'going all out' to make tourism a pillar industry in its national economy. According to AsianInfo.org (2000, p. 1), 'In 1998, the number of tourists entering China reached 63.48 million, 35 times the figure for 1978 and the foreign exchange income from this industry reached 12.6 billion US dollars, 48 times that of 1978'. Tourism revenue has already become a significant contributor to the national GDP increase and a major tool in regional economic development and regeneration (Ryan & Gu, 2009). According to Research and Markets (2006), the total revenue of China's tourism industry reached 67.3 billion US dollars in 2002, accounting for 5.44% of the GDP. This astonishing development is not a 'flash in the pan'; it will maintain such growth rates for some time, and by 2015 China achieved the second place in the contribution of travel and tourism economy to GDP among the countries (Ennew, 2005; WTTC, 2017. See Table 1.2 below).

Table 1.2   Rankings of Countries by Contribution of Travel and Tourism Economy to GDP

Contribution of Travel and Tourism Economy to GDP (2005)	Contribution of Travel and Tourism Economy to GDP (2015)
1. US	1. US
2. Japan	2. China
3. Germany	3. Japan
4. France	4. France
5. UK	5. Spain
6. China	6. Germany
7. Italy	7. UK
8. Spain	8. Italy
9. Canada	9. Canada
10. Mexico	10. Mexico

Source: Ennew. (2005).; WTTC. (2017).

'Possibly few, if any, countries in the world have experienced as fast a rate of growth in tourism as China.' (Wen & Tisdell, 2001, p. 15) With this, tourism has become a main source of tax revenue and a key industry for economic development, and as UNWTO (2006) estimated, China will be the first nation that will secure the first position as both a tourism generating and tourism receiving country by 2020.

This growth in tourism has benefited from profound changes in Chinese society, which are transforming a traditional society to a modern one and an agricultural society to an industrial one. This huge social change has had an unprecedented impact all over the Chinese mainland and has caused a huge growth in domestic tourism demand from more and more Chinese people. Lew, Yu, Ap and Zhang (2003) also noticed that by 2020

Chinese domestic tourism revenue will reach 2,100 billion RMB, 6.6 to 9.4 times that of 2000. It is well known that China has the largest population in the world with over 1.3 billion people currently, so if the domestic tourism industry can be stimulated enough, the subsequent growth may be well beyond imagination. Although domestic tourism is currently growing vigorously, it still has more potential to grow.

Currently there appears to be an uneven, slow development of domestic tourism compared to that of international tourism. As Zhang et al. (2005) noticed, more detailed statistics are usually available about international tourism when compared to those about domestic tourism. Yet Jafari (1986) said almost all travel through the world is domestic. The potential growth of domestic visitors to experience MICE tourism products is large. Therefore one purpose of this research is to explore the demand of MICE products in the Chinese domestic market by examining resident propensities and perceptions of MICE events and those of attendees.

There are many statistics that show China is fast becoming a popular venue for international MICE groups. In 2012, the total of events held in China increased to 7,333 (CCTV News, 2012). The growth of MICE tourism is obvious according to Xinhua News Agency (2003) and the rate of events being held in China has increased progressively by 20% every year, most of which are domestic in nature. In China, the use of international events is perceived as an effective means of exciting and attracting not only international but also domestic tourists. China is still a developing country and started its reform and opening-up only about 40 years ago; so many people still have but a small chance to travel overseas due to both economic and other reasons. But people want to know more about the outside world and these international events are seen as one way to help add more knowledge of foreign locations and as a means of doing business and meeting people. Additionally, due to China's large population, the potential for domestic MICE tourism is significant.

Although the MICE market in China is thriving and prosperous, competition for the MICE market in different cities that have the capacity to hold events is severe. Many Chinese cities have seen the potential advantages offered by event tourism, such as high consumer spending and subsequent profits. In recent years, many cities have focused on 'event tourism' and have engaged in 'branding their event city' according to their regional characteristics and advantages. Xinhua News Agency (2003) noted that, due to the popularity of the event industry, China has been engaged in building exhibition halls, and many event operators and tourism organisations have striven to join international event organisations. Every tourism city that has the capacity wants to share and seize this potential market. The 'event tourism' competition among Chinese cities has aided China's event industry to progress, which provides both experience and development opportunities such as the 2008 Beijing Olympics, 2010 Shanghai World Expo and 2016 G20 Hangzhou Summit.

Event development is a 'new shining spot' for the tourism industry combining different industries and socio-economic elements. According to Xinhua News Agency (2003), the coefficient of event development is 1 : 8: the '1' means event industry, and the '8' means its impact on transportation, accommodation, food, shopping, entertainment, and travel, etc. This is akin to an event consuming chain and the tourism consuming chain. These link the event and tourism industry into a tight relationship, which means if the event industry grows, so do other components of the tourism industry. To further develop event tourism, the capacity of a city is important, which includes its geography, economy, security, cultural and social attractions, and scenic values. Li (2004) stated that when applying for an international event, both the tourism environment and natural resources are important factors in the choice of an event destination. China is still a developing country, although many cities have developed well, the above factors are still limited in some cities.

1.4　Hangzhou's General Information

Hangzhou is known as a 'paradise on earth'. The West Lake is like a 'back garden' and the city is in the middle of the 'fish and rice' land as well as a production base for silk (Zhang, 2002). Hangzhou has more than 40 scenic spots around the West Lake, a specific feature of this city. Hangzhou is not a very big city, but its economy has attained high status in China. According to China-Window.com (2015), in 2014, the GDP of Hangzhou amounted to 9,201 billion RMB, which ranked second among all provincial capitals, second only to Guangzhou. Hangzhou is a historical city with many cultural resources.

Zhang (2002) noted that during the Southern Song Dynasty, Hangzhou was the world's most prosperous city, and the Hangzhou residents' leisure traditions originated from that wealthy era. Hangzhou is one of the more suitable cities with the capacity to hold major international conferences and events.

Hangzhou is the capital city of Zhejiang Province with a city area of 16,596 square kilometres and an urban population of about 6.79 million (Hangzhou.gov.cn, 2016a). The city is located in the southeast of China, which is one of the main economically developed areas in China and it lies among the top in Chinese cities in terms of comprehensive strength. One of its main scenic spots is the West Lake, which is largely artificial and is surrounded by mountains. Not only that, its unique gardening art has integrated cultural and natural landscapes as a key attraction. Recently more than 100 scenic spots have been renovated in Hangzhou, which in 2013 attracted 'more than three million foreign tourists and ninety million domestic tourists' (Zhejiang Online, 2014).

Hangzhou has long been regarded as a desirable travel and tourism destination in China and it possesses notable historical and cultural features. Marco Polo had praised Hangzhou as 'the most beautiful and elegant city in the world'. In his travel notes *The Travels of Marco Polo* first published in 1298, he meticulously described Hangzhou as the follows: a total of 1.6 million houses, spacious streets with the canal traffic, stone discharge sewage drain; the city's main street has ten big markets, lanes and streets glutted with countless small markets; Hangzhou people treat outside people very kindly, they provide good treatment, support and advice; Hangzhou's citizens like hot water bath services, the city has 3,000 public bathhouses;… people cruising on the West Lake accompanied with many beautiful women, drinking and singing… it is paradise (Polo, 1913). Historically many poets and authors have written thousands of poems to praise Hangzhou. Along with the changes made in China since the late 1970s, the tourism industry has been improved year by year. The West Lake is the heart and soul of Hangzhou's tourism. It has helped brand Hangzhou as a famous tourism city, which has achieved recognition in the honorable verse 'In heaven there is paradise; on earth, there are Suzhou and Hangzhou'.

The city's history is a long one, and dates back to the Neolithic Hemudu culture 7,000 years ago. According to *Chinese Brief History* by Du Hongyi (2006), during the Southern Song Dynasty, Hangzhou was the national capital, which made it one of the seven ancient cities in China that have served as capital cities throughout the Chinese history. The West Lake itself still possesses as a feature a causeway built in 1090 by Su Shi (one of China's most famous poets). And when Marco Polo visited Hangzhou, he hailed it as one of the finest cities in the world as noted above. A long history in China is always coupled with a profound culture. Hangzhou thus has marketed itself for both domestic and international tourism as a city of leisure based on cultural and heritage assets (Zheng & Liu, 2005). According to Zhou (2006), Hangzhou has a rich religious culture, especially that of 'Zen Buddhism'. Many temples were built in Hangzhou and still have high status in Chinese Buddhism. Hangzhou is also one of the world's main cradles of tea culture. It has a conventional tea drinking atmosphere with many teahouses, some even several hundreds of years old. Zhou (2006) also mentioned that the city not only possesses its traditional culture, but has also gained many modern descriptions such as 'paradise', 'capital of love', 'capital of beauty', 'leisure city', and 'happy Hangzhou'.

1.5　Hangzhou's Tourism Development

Crouch (2000) noted that places are but one pervasive component of leisure and tourism, nonetheless they are an important component. Hangzhou is a tourism-based city through its inheritance of lake, mountains and other scenic resources. Hangzhou has two designated state-level scenic spots—the West Lake Scenic Area, and the Two Rivers and Two Lakes (Fuchun River, Xin'an River, Qiandao Lake and Xianghu Lake) Scenic Area; two state-level nature reserves—Mount Tianmu, Qingliang Peak Nature Reserve; seven state-level forest parks—Qiandao Lake, Mount Wuchao, Fuchun River, Mount Daqi, Mount Banshan, Yaolin Forest and Qingshan Lake parks; a state-level tourist resort—Zhijiang National Tourist Resort Area and the country's first state-level wetland park—Xixi National Wetland Park. Hangzhou also has 25 national conservation sites of cultural heritage and 9 national museums. As a result, Hangzhou has been regarded as 'China's best tourist city' by the China National Tourism Administration (CNTA) and the United Nations World Tourism Organisation (UNWTO), and won the award of the 'Oriental Leisure City' by the World Leisure Organisation. The West Lake was also inscribed on the World Heritage List by

UNESCO in 2011. Hangzhou's economy is increasing dramatically, and one positive effect is that having residents with more real income has also aided the tourism economy to develop.

As one of the key national scenic tourism cities, Hangzhou takes tourism as a key to its prosperity. In recent years, with an increasing emphasis on the tourism industry at all levels, Hangzhou has improved its tourism infrastructure, undertaken new promotions and initiatives, and with its historical and cultural attractions, Hangzhou has started to catch the world's attention. In order to stimulate its tourism industry, many coordinated statutes have been promulgated by the local government. The most representative policy is the 'free West Lake', which is also perhaps one of the more contentious policies executed by the Hangzhou government. According to Shao (2004), since 2002 when Hangzhou began the comprehensive West Lake protection project called 'return the lake to the people', under which various attractions around the lake have been opened for free. The policy has attracted some criticism. By 2004, the entire West Lake had been opened for free. Because of inflation and increasing costs, this policy has been challenged and on many occasions has been in conflict with local public opinion, but the policy has brought a positive image to the city and gained good economic returns. According to the statistics from Hangzhou.com.cn (2010), for the national day holiday in 2010, hotel prices of the Yangtze River Delta increased, and Hangzhou increased the most. Also, budget hotel prices increased by 30%. It is obvious that the policy forgoes revenue from the sale of entry tickets to the lake, but it has attracted more tourists to come and extend their stay, which brings an impetus for the development of the restaurants, hotels, retail business, and other related industries.

There are many new and future tourism developments. Just two will be briefly covered as indicative of the developments in Hangzhou. Xixi is China's only nationally accredited wetland and covers an area of over 11 square kilometres. Being one of the three 'Xi's along with the West Lake (*Xihu*) and Xiling Seal Engravers' Society, the wetland offers not only scenic beauty but also cultural resources with the Persimmon and Plum Festivals, dragon boat racing events and others taking place. Some of the new initiatives are also based on historical precedents—the earliest dragon boat races date back to 1465 there and the Persimmon and Plum Festivals back to the period of the 1600s. The ponds of the wetland have a long history as a source of aquaculture and festivals within the history of Hangzhou, and are being used for purposes of modern recreation, leisure, and tourism as well as environmental restoration and conservation.

The Beijing–Hangzhou Grand Canal district is like many such walks in other parts of the world which is being developed as a hub of restaurants and cafes that creates an outdoor meeting and dining area. The canal itself links Hangzhou with Beijing and dates from the 7th century.

There are a large number of tourists coming to Hangzhou every year. According to statistics, from 2010 to 2015, the city enjoyed obvious tourists growth (see Table 1.3).

Table 1.3　Number of Tourists to Hangzhou from 2010 to 2015

Year	Number of Tourists/million
2010	65.75
2011	75.06
2012	85.31
2013	97.16
2014	109.26
2015	123.42

Source: Hangzhou.gov.cn. (2016b).

Although foreign tourists have started to visit Hangzhou in an increasing number, the main tourism business in Hangzhou is still from its domestic visitors and the majority of tourists in recent years are domestic tourists.

➡ 1.6　Hangzhou's MICE Development

The MICE industry in Hangzhou has a long history. In 1929, from June to October, one of China's earliest international expositions—'West Lake Expo' was hosted in Hangzhou. This exposition lasted about four months and attracted 20 million visitors, and more than

147.6 thousand items were shown during the exposition. This exposition was a landmark in the Chinese MICE development history. In 2000, Hangzhou government decided to resume the West Lake Expo annually, for which it has done successfully. The West Lake Expo and the MICE industry have thus become an important factor in Hangzhou's economic development strategy. According to Fu (2005), in 2001, Hangzhou hosted 109 exhibitions in total, among which 25% were accounted for by the West Lake Expo which has become the leading MICE business in Hangzhou. Based on the success of the West Lake Expo, in 2006 and 2011 the World Leisure Expo were held in Hangzhou. According to World Leisure Expo (2006), there were more than 100 events, exhibitions or festivals during the exposition period in 2006, and the expo received 15 million domestic tourists and one million international tourists. The G20 Summit was also hosted in Hangzhou in 2016. More international events will be held in Hangzhou such as the 2018 FINA World Short Course Swimming Championships, the 2022 Asian Games, etc.

Destination's capability to successfully host MICE has long been a prerequisite for long-term success, and a key factor is the role of local government and its MICE planners. To make MICE more sustainable, many appropriate policy instruments were enacted by Hangzhou's local government. The following are five international conference centres in Hangzhou: Hangzhou International Conference Center, Hangzhou International Expo Center, Zhejiang World Trade International Exhibition Center, Hangzhou Peace International Conference and Exhibition Center, and Hangzhou Baima Lake International Convention and Exhibition Center. These large conference centres intend to lead the Hangzhou MICE industry into a new stage of development.

The conference centre fits alongside various events and festivals that take place on the Labour Day, National Day, and Spring Festival vacations. Hangzhou is thus developing a portfolio of tourism events which potentially yields many benefits for the city's residents. However, while economic data generally point to increases in visitor numbers and expenditure, and hence job creation, of importance too are whether soft gains are being perceived by Hangzhou's residents. Do they feel that Hangzhou is gaining additional prestige, not only in China, but on the world stage? Do they take pride in such developments? To what extent will they tolerate the disruptions caused by the construction work in the city? Do they directly benefit from these developments, or do they feel that others benefit, but perhaps not themselves? These are the types of questions that the research is directed to.

Due to Hangzhou's rapid economic and tourism development, the MICE industry plays an important role in the city's economy. This book uses Hangzhou as the 'base' example and case to explore the local residents' perceptions of and demand for Chinese MICE events.

In the research, it was found that international event development is a challenging but strategically important segment for the local economy. Previous studies on the events' impact analysis suggest that they have favourable effects on the local economy, society, and the sustainable development. Nearing the end to completing the book, lots of research on events have started to focus on the less-researched areas like residents' perception, local cultural protection, etc. For example, in the study of Kim, Prideaux and Chon (2010), they concluded five basic event research classifications: motivation and goals for the event participants' arrival; residents' and non-residents' participation in the events; the economic impact of festivals or other similar special events; evaluation of the effectiveness of methods used in the economic impact analysis; and the impact of socio-demographic and cultural factors on the expenses of the events' participants. It should be noted that apart from the assessment of the economic impact of the organised events, studies of assessment of the socio-cultural (Deery & Jago, 2010; Walker et al., 2013), environmental (Sherwood, 2007), and the altogether economic-social-environmental factors (Andersson & Lundberg, 2013) of the organised events were undertaken. Thus the relationships occurring between the quality of events and their value and the experienced satisfaction and loyalty (Kim et al., 2010), satisfaction with participation in the event, the experienced satisfaction and, consequently, the creation of loyalty (Yoon, Lee & Lee, 2010) were also be examined.

In addition, the 2016 G20 Summit of the world's major economies was hosted in Hangzhou. This magnificent conference not only enhanced Hangzhou's image to a higher international level, but also increased local residents' pride in the city. In this situation, local residents' perceptions may have changed, which provides room for the future research. The author will focus on the local residents' perceptions of mega events in the future.

1.7 Main Questions of the Book

Following the above description, the research questions for this book are:

- What is the relationship between local residents and the MICE-hosting city?
- What motivations attract local residents to attend MICE?
- Are there any effects for destinations' physical environment, natural environment, social environment, and government involvement from MICE hosting?
- Do these effects influence local residents' life?

These issues form the basic questions, which are based on the tourism academic literature. More important features also emerged through an examination of the MICE literature as presented in Chapter Two.

Chapter Two

Literature Review

➡ 2.1 Introduction

The purposes of this chapter are to both conceptualise and systematise the major factors, and provide an overview of event development and competition in the tourism market by a review of the concepts. The literature will also examine research on residents' perceptions of the impacts of MICE to provide a foundation for the analysis.

Several important features have emerged from an examination of the literature on MICE. First, there is no unified definition and classification of events. Many definitions of different event types are mixed. For example, MICE in some studies belong to hallmark events, in others, they are categorised differently. Some literature classifies festivals under the mega events or special events; some others identify festivals as one of the phenomena of MICE. Second, there is a huge range of event tourism impacts, but the majority are based on economic orientation with relatively little attention being paid to the important psychological, social, and physical impacts. Third, it can be observed that much of the research is pragmatic and descriptive in nature and an absence of conceptualisation exists other than in the use of economic modelling based on multipliers and input-output methods of economic assessment.

⇒ 2.2 General Concepts of Event

An 'event' seems simple to explain but actually is complex. Getz (1997) defined an 'event' as a temporary occurrence, either planned or unplanned. There are some basic dictionary definitions of event, which are:

- something that happens at a given place and time;
- a special set of circumstances;
- a phenomenon located at a single point in space-time; the fundamental observational entity in relativity theory; and
- a consequence: a phenomenon that follows and is caused by some previous phenomenon.

From these definitions, it can be seen that 'event' has a wide and complex meaning with reference to its myriad implications. It can embrace many different occurrences from the static to the intense. It is impossible to list all events here. Watt (1998) said the event area is so large that it would be impossible to detail all the possibilities. Getz (1997) also considered the same universe of the 'event' to be so diverse that any classification is bound to be incomplete. Jago and Shaw (1998) also discussed the diversity of event and associated different features to create a hierarchical framework (see Figure 2.1).

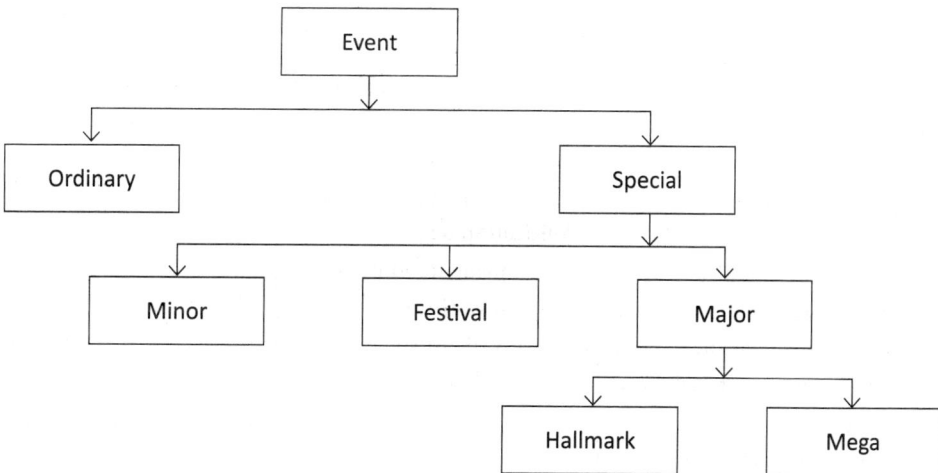

Figure 2.1 Categorisation of Events

Source: Jago & Shaw. (1998).

From this framework, 'event' is divided into 'ordinary' and 'special' events, and then special events can be divided into three other categories—'minor', 'festival', and 'major'. 'Hallmark' and 'mega' events are the two elements comprising major events. Another framework by Getz (1997) looked at a content-based conceptualisation of events. Getz treated most events as planned and sorted them into major taxonomic categories.

2.3 Typologies of Events

Watt (1998) suggested that it is important to recognise the diversity of events and treat every event as different; each event has its own characteristics and requirements to be identified and met. On the basis of there being a wide range of events, it is better to specify some common types (see Table 2.1). Due to the multiple definitions of MICE in the industry, it is also difficult to categorise MICE types.

Table 2.1   Typologies of Events

Cultural celebration:	Sports competitions:	Private events:
● festivals	● professional	Personal celebrations:
● carnivals	● amateur	● anniversaries
● religious events	**Educational and scientific:**	● family holidays
● parades	● seminars, workshops	● rites of passage
● heritage	● congresses	Social events:
● commemorations	● interpretive events	● parties
Art/Entertainment:	**Recreational:**	● reunions
● concerts	● games and sports	
● other performances	● amusement events	
● exhibits	**Political/State:**	
● award ceremonies	● inaugurations	
Business/Trade:	● investitures	
● fairs, markets, sales	● VIP visits	
● consumer and trade shows	● rallies	
● expositions		
● meetings/conferences		
● publicity events		
● fund-raising events		

Source: Getz. (1997).

Different countries classified different types of events into different areas. Generally this book only lists some common event types as below.

>> Hallmark Events

Hallmark events are found in many places but by definition are infrequent in occurrence. Ritchie (1984) defined hallmark events as:

> Major one time or recurring events of limited duration, developed primarily to enhance the awareness, appeal and profitability of a tourism destination in the short and/or long term. Such events rely for their success on uniqueness, status, or timely significance to create interest and attract attention. (p. 2)

Hall (1989) thinks hallmark tourist events are a major type that contains fairs, expositions, and cultural and sporting events of international status, which are held on either a regular or a one-off basis. Ritchie (1984) understood hallmark events to be major events, which have an 'ability' to draw national and international attention to the destination. A similar notion arises from Bowdin, McDonnell, Allen and O'Toole (2001, p. 17): '…the term hallmark events refers to those events that become so identified with the spirit or ethos of a town, city or region that they become synonymous with the name of the place, and gain widespread recognition and awareness.' Because of the embracing nature of hallmark events, the primary function of the hallmark events is also expected to be providing the host community with an opportunity to secure a position of prominence in the tourism market for a short and well-defined period of time (Ritchie & Beliveau, 1974; Buck, 1977; Della Bitta, Loudon, Booth & Weeks, 1977; Ritchie, 1984; Hall & Selwood, 1987). Burns and Mules (1986, pp. 6-7) also noted the importance of scale in 'special events', sometimes called 'hallmark' events… which are events that are expected to generate large external benefits, or where the external benefits are so widely distributed and the event costs are so substantial that they are funded, either partially or wholly, with public monies. Examples of such events include the Edinburgh Festival or the Calgary Stampede inasmuch as these major events come to symbolise a destination and help 'hallmark' a place. Others might be said to 'hallmark' a sport or culture, and can include major sporting events not associated with a specific place but with specific associations: the World Student Games or the Commonwealth Games, etc.

>> Festivals

Festival is another of the more popular events in the recent event industry. According to Rolfe (1992), festivals are a type of event that share a number of characteristics including intense output and a clear time-specific programme delivered with a clear purpose and direction. Bowdin et al. (2001) underlined the fact that the term 'festival' has been used for hundreds of years and can be used to cover a multitude of events. With its attractive and inclusive features, and mature operational experience, a 'festival' has been chosen frequently to promote a destination in tourism strategies. Cousineau (1991) noted that the festival has been seen as 'a good medicine for the soul'; it is the soul that glues and galvanises communities together, or it can be a tourist attraction that generates all sorts of economic benefits.

The Policy Studies Institute (PSI, 1992) from London defined a festival as:

> traditionally a time of celebration, relaxation and recuperation, which often followed a period of hard physical labour, sowing or harvesting of crops, for example. The essential feature of these festivals was the celebration or reaffirmation of community or culture. The artistic content of such events was variable and many had a religious or ritualistic aspect, but music, dance and drama were important features of the celebration. (p. 1)

Turner (1969) noted festivals are commonly thought of as occasions that bring together and reinterpret various symbolic elements of recreating social relations and the symbolic foundations underpinning everyday life. In the contemporary world, old and traditional things have become a new fashion framework in people's minds, so tourists are more likely to experience some historic events. Festival, with its long history, has its own advantages. The term 'festival' as commonly understood today was first used in England in 1655, when the Festival of the Sons of the Clergy was first delivered at St Paul's Cathedral, London. Bowdin et al. (2001) enumerated several early festivals such as Three Choirs Festival (1731), the Norfolk and Norwich Festival (1989) and the Royal National Eisteddfod of Wales (1980). Although festivals have a long history, some precious and old events are fading from people's sight. Wood (1982) observed that due to the dual forces of industrialisation and 'muscular' Christianity of the mid-19th century, many of the traditional festivities that developed alongside folklore were lost.

>> MICE (Meetings, Incentives, Conferences, and Exhibitions), Weddings, etc.

The acronym 'MICE' is not used globally but it is not a new word. It came into being in the middle 1990s and has been generally adopted by the industry. MICE industry is said to be one of the fastest-growing and most lucrative areas of the tourism industry. According to the Commonwealth Department of Tourism (1995), the MICE industry and the products from MICE events have been recognised as an effective communication medium. According to McCabe, Poole, Weeks and Leiper (2000), the MICE industry, as the name suggests, includes a number of different and diverse areas such as conferences, meetings, incentives, exhibitions, some festivals, trade shows, and group weddings, etc.

◆ Meetings/Conferences

Similar concepts such as meetings and conferences as Getz (1997) noted, are assemblies for the purpose of conferring and discussion, and 'meetings' should be small enough to facilitate interaction, whereas 'conventions' are generally large assemblies of people from associations, political parties, and clubs. Conferences cannot be described by a specific concept, but are diverse. Mills (1991) defined conventions as events in which members of a professional organisation, political party, civic group, or business group meet to exchange views, and are an important class of convention centre activity. Bowdin et al. (2001) described the meeting/ conference sector as being largely characterised by its business and trade focus though there is a strong public and tourism aspect to many of its activities. Wagen and Carlos (2005) suggested the meetings and conferences industry is highly competitive. Many conventions attract thousands of people, whereas some meetings include only a handful of high-profile participants.

◆ Incentives

According to WebFinance Inc. (2005), incentives are a reward for a specific behaviour, and are designed to encourage that behaviour. Swarbrook and Horner (2001) defined incentives as a global management tool that use an exceptional travel experience in support of organisational goals.

◆ Exhibitions

Exhibition is another type of event that also has a long history and is a growing part of the industry. Bowdin et al. (2001) cited the research undertaken by RS & M on behalf of event agency McMenemy Hill, which estimated that in the UK, 77 companies found that exhibitions were the most frequently held event. Bowdin et al. (2001) continued to say that exhibitions bring suppliers of goods and services together with buyers, usually in a particular industry sector. The Exhibition Liaison Committee (1995) noted the present UK exhibition industry could trace its origin back to the first industrial exhibitions held in London in 1760 and 1791.

◆ Wedding Groups and Celebrations

A wedding group is a newly emerged commercialised market segment. Shone and Parry (2004) argued that wedding tourism can be complicated to organise, involving friends and family and a whole range of related service activities, from catering to entertainment, as well as the formal aspect of the marriage ceremony itself. It has thus elicited a specialist sub-group of companies or organisations within wider companies that concentrate on this market segment.

➡ 2.4   Event Tourism (MICE)

Consequently, as shown above, the definitions of MICE cover many different activities with many event researchers failing to achieve consensus. In this book, the MICE industry is, for pragmatic reasons, identified as the same with event tourism, as it largely depends on the same functions and purposes, which includes meetings, incentives, conferences, exhibitions and events. Additionally the term 'event tourism' is an independent definition with its own development and operation features; it cannot be viewed as a phrase that simply adds 'tourism' after 'event' (Getz, 1997).

The defining characteristic of MICE is their transience but it would be difficult to induce and sustain the same sense of occasion and excitement if such an event was to be held more frequently. So Getz (1997) divided event tourism into two types:

- The systematic planning, development, and marketing of events as tourist attractions, catalysts for other developments, image builders, and animators of attractions and destination areas; event tourism strategies should also cover the management of news and negative events.
- A market segment consisting of those people who travel to attend events, or who can be motivated to attend events while away from home.

Although 'MICE' and 'event tourism' cannot be interpreted from literal meanings into 'event' and 'tourism', they truly combine the two different areas. Hall (1992, p. 4) stated 'event tourism is concerned with the roles that festivals and special events can play in destination development and the maximization of an event's attractiveness to tourists'. Getz (1997) also directly indicated that 'event tourism' is formalised as the link between events and tourism. They are two combined elements that can encourage each other. A simple Venn diagram shows this in Figure 2.2.

Consequently 'event tourism' cannot be treated as a fully independent industry because of its cross-industry relativity. Substantially it should be viewed like 'event' as a motivator for tourism and 'tourism' as a supporter or carrier for an event. The two areas are interdependent and also interact. MICE has most of the characteristics that belong to the tourism and event industries. The question is whether MICE is a sustainable industry as 'tourism', or just a transient phase. In order to delve deeper into the MICE industry, it is better to examine the tourism and event strategies of MICE.

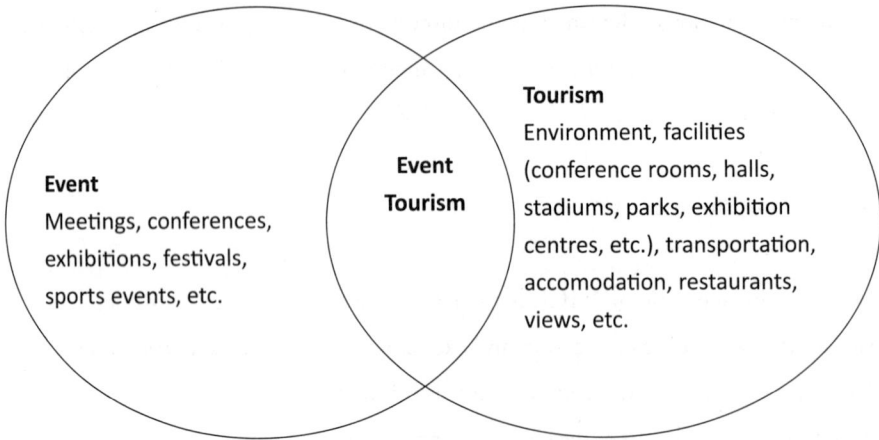

Event
Meetings, conferences,
exhibitions, festivals,
sports events, etc.

Event
Tourism

Tourism
Environment, facilities
(conference rooms, halls,
stadiums, parks, exhibition
centres, etc.), transportation,
accomodation, restaurants,
views, etc.

Figure 2.2   Relationship Between Event and Tourism

Source: Getz. (2007).

2.5 MICE Tourism Development History

Although the terms of 'MICE' and 'event tourism' have been identified comparatively recently, the event industry has a long history. The origins of MICE can be found in ancient Babylonia and Egypt for at that time they hosted many religious festivals, which attracted many people. Similarly early Chinese emperors used religious and other festivals, and state occasions, to reinforce the sovereignty of a given dynasty.

Recent tourism event activities can be traced from small towns and rural areas. In the early 1970s many places suffered from slow development and few economic opportunities, affected by economic restructuring and a farming crisis in the West. According to Wilson, Fesenmaier, Fesenmaier and Vanes (2001), since the 1970s, economic restructuring and the farming crisis caused a severe loss of rural manufacturing plants and many jobs. Walmsley, Dimaranan and McDougall (2000) also thought economic restructuring linked with demographic changes like out-migration and aging caused the loss of social capital in marginalised areas. Sears and Reid (1992) noted that as rural unemployment rates rose above urban levels, real income growth stagnated in rural areas. These changes limited rural areas' economic development, which forced rural communities to find a way to survive. How to generate the economic revitalization of rural areas was consequently eagerly sought, and the potential importance of tourism was duly noted. Edgell and Harbaugh (1993) described this as one of the more popular non-traditional rural development strategies, while tourism also permitted associated entrepreneurship opportunities. Wilson et al. (2001) contended that many rural area planners had realised that rural tourism is less costly and easier to establish than many other rural economic development strategies. Hall, Roberts and Mitchell (2003) described tourism as often being viewed by many rural regions as one of the few opportunities to enhance the local economy. Thus rural tourism started to gradually dominate rural economic development.

However, the usual tourism strategies are not an omnipotent tool for all rural areas or small towns that enables them to overcome their weak, marginal economic position. Lane (1994) mentioned a number of rural factors that can reduce rural areas' tourism economic effectiveness, which included income leakages, volatility, a declining multiplier, low pay, imported labour, the limited number of entrepreneurs in rural areas, and the conservatism of rural investors. Marcouiller (1997) noted other factors that limited tourism developments: dependence on increased public expenditures for promotion that might not be forthcoming, increased local pressures for resultant public services, increased conflict among user groups, and general concerns over societal costs and benefits of public support for tourism development. What is the most 'smart strategy' to stimulate a local economy is examined by many rural communities. Based on these expectations and perceived weaknesses, the development of small events and festivals emerged. Rogerson (2005) noted that, in Western Europe, resort towns were the first to recognise the potential benefits of conference and exhibition tourism and started to develop specialist conference facilities during the inter-war period. By the mid-1960s many rural communities began to produce new annual festivals or street fairs designed for family entertainment and oriented to themes (Janiskee, 1990). Not only was this found in Europe, Janiskee and Drews (1998) also mentioned that in much of the US history, the community-wide celebrations in a typical small town consisted of little more than the ubiquitous Independence Day celebration, which led to the development of other small events, especially in the 1980s.

While primal MICE tourism development was initiated from rural areas, the more dominant development started in urban areas in the 1980s. Getz (1997, p. 2) argued, 'event tourism was a new term in the 1980s, but it has become firmly established as a major component of special interest tourism and a significant ingredient in destinations and place marketing strategies'. Since then many travel agencies, hotels, companies, and other communities have organised and received many different kinds of events in the past decade and some are becoming truly global in their appeal, e.g., Singapore World Gourmet Summit (Cheney & Ryan, 2009).

MICE development did not only progress from rural areas and its small towns but also from urban areas. Historically, event development also started from Europe and expanded to the Asia-Pacific area. MICE tourism's origins could be found in Europe and North America, yet it is the Asia-Pacific region in particular that saw a rapid increase in industry activity from the late 1980s. According to Australian Tourist Commission (ATC, 1997), Australia experienced a 167% increase in the number of international visitors attending conferences or conventions between 1992 and 1996. This rapid development of the MICE industry has exceeded many tourism researchers' expectations. Cooper (1999) had predicted in his landmark study in early 1976 the size of the Australian MICE industry for 1993, whose dollar value estimation of the convention sector (as estimated in 1976 and after correction for inflation) was about 73% of the actual figure. Consequently, it can be easily seen that earlier growth had been much stronger than appeared possible more than two decades earlier. This was not only in Australia. Kim and Sun (2008) mentioned that many Asian governments including China, the Republic of Singapore, the Republic of Korea, and Japan gave substantial support to MICE at the national level because they view it as a highly value-added industry. The MICE industry has developed like 'a raging fire' in the Asian market, and the most pre-eminent increase of MICE development can be found in China.

➡ 2.6 China's MICE Tourism Development

MICE development in China is very recent, appearing in the last decades of the 20th century. According to CNTA (2000) statistics: in 1998 China only ranked 34th in the number of events but, while China's MICE industry is just starting to grow, its development potential cannot be ignored. As Davidson, Hertrich and Schwandner (2004) mentioned, for a rapidly industrialising country like China, the potential for generating

MICE tourism is simply enormous. Wei (2004) mentioned in 2000, that China only held 1.74% of the total 9,433 international conventions hosted around the world and ranked 14th. But in 2014, China hosted over 8,009 events, which occupied a quarter of the total world events (Shen, 2016). CNTA also provided evidence of the increased rate of MICE industry in China with a growth of 20% per year. By 2014 China had more than 2,000 event venues of different sizes, while the number of event enterprises keeps growing. The potential of MICE tourism growth in China is large. According to CNTA (2015), apart from the answer of "others", foreign visitors rank meetings/business as the second most frequent purpose of their visit to China (see Table 2.2).

Table 2.2   Foreign Visitor Arrivals by Purpose, Jan.–Sept. 2015

Total Number of Arrivals /10,000 Persons	Number of Arrivals by Purpose				
	Meetings/ Business	Sightseeing/ Leisure	Visiting Relatives and Friends	Worker and Crew	Others
1899.97	390.90	595.74	59.75	257.04	596.54

Source: CNTA. (2015).

This dramatic increase is not simply an accident. The MICE industry has attracted attention from the Chinese government, and in 2001 the Chinese State Council promulgated a policy 'to actively explore the leisure tourism, MICE tourism, new tourism, and the development of marketable special tourism products to meet the different levels and different consumer interest and requirements'. Not only is there active regulation but also a positive economic environment. Since the 'Golden Holiday' tourism policy was put in place, 'holiday tourism' has become China's rapidly growing MICE tourism booster. Many cities and regions seek to host different events during the long public holidays to attract more tourists. In addition, there is an enthusiasm to host MICE in China supported by many cities, like Guangzhou's annual import and export fair, the Shanghai APEC meeting, the 1999 Kunming Expo, the 2008 Beijing Olympics, the 2010 Shanghai World Expo, and the 2016 G20 Hangzhou Summit.

However, compared with Western countries, and even with China's rapid economic development, China's MICE industry still stands at an early stage. According to Wei

(2004), in 2003 China held more than 2,500 exhibitions, which brought a revenue of 7 billion RMB. However the average production value per convention was 2.8 million RMB. Meanwhile Germany only held nearly 300 exhibitions in that year but generated an average production value of 10 million euros per exhibition. It is obvious that the Chinese production value is far lower than that of Germany. Compared with European countries like Switzerland, which hosts more than 2,000 international conferences every year with its small population, China is currently underperforming. A fashion city like Paris hosts more than 300 international exhibitions every year and is called by many Chinese MICE insiders 'the capital of conferences' (Wei & Qu, 2007). The US is the world's largest MICE hosting country, with a revenue of over a trillion dollars annually. China with its large number of population combined with its varied attractions should possess competitive advantages. However, even though the total number of events is large and growing in China, these events remain limited in size, status, and reputation. What accounts for these deficiencies?

Although the MICE industry has developed dramatically in China, an academic literature is more notable by its absence than presence. During the review of literature, mainly English and many Chinese databases were examined. It should be noted that there is an obvious gap between Western and Chinese MICE research. As noted by Davidson et al. (2004), there had been far less research undertaken on the MICE market for China. The deficiency is obvious. Xu (2002) also provided a similar opinion that MICE research in China was only at an initial stage and most studies were more focused on the descriptive research. Due to its short time of development, there have been limited empirical studies in Chinese MICE research and most remain at the level of simple description or theories of what might be the best. Without this information, it is difficult to identify market opportunities in the current international event market and hard for event operators to manage the event process. There only exists some anecdotal and piecemeal information to help the Chinese MICE tourism business to shape or measure their products to meet the growing demand in the Chinese MICE market. However, based on an urgent need for practical theories and guides, many Chinese tourism researchers like Bao and Dai (2003) have started to pay some attention to the MICE industry. Dai (2005) analysed the 1999 Kunming Expo and provided applicable MICE theories for Chinese MICE market. Liu (2004) and Wang (2004) discussed MICE business sectors like planning, situation, and policies; and Liu (2004) focused on the host destination image. Some researchers have analysed Chinese trade fairs and their state of development (Jin et al., 2010a; Kay, 2005; Yang, 2009), spatial distribution (Jin et al., 2010b; Ju et al., 2006a, 2006b), and the driving forces behind the exhibition industry (Jin et al., 2012). Fu and Zheng (2014) talked about how to better cooperate between MICE and tourism and to build MICE brand is a key factor to enhance the MICE industry development. Wang and Li (2014) also emphasized the important factor to increase regional competitive advantages. Wang and Wang (2015) noted new technology involvement is a trend in the MICE industry, like Internet events through network technology will show the content in the form of a combination of the virtual and the real on the Internet. It can also build a web experience and real-time interaction with other auxiliary functions of exhibition platforms. Although a latecomer, Chinese MICE researchers have undergone an unprecedented catch-up process in terms of MICE industrialisation, technological upgrading, and educational learning. So it can be argued that Chinese MICE research is currently transitioning from an awareness stage to a fast developing stage in research.

Not only is there a lack of academic research in the MICE area, but some limitations have held back its development. During the process of reviewing Chinese literature, it became possible to discern a number of factors that inhibit the MICE development.

◆ Economic Inequalities

China's economic development is obvious to all but this fast development also brings some problems. According to Qian and Wong (2000), China's current huge income gap between the rich and the poor has four divides: first, the income gap between urban and rural areas is widening and the rate of increase in farm incomes has declined and fallen behind urban incomes; second, urban residents in different sectors are experiencing widening gaps especially when laid-off workers' income is low; third, industry income gaps have emerged with some monopoly industries possessing high-income advantage; fourth, a regional income gap with the eastern region being the main beneficiary.

The economic inequality is the source of differences of opinion. Jackson (2006) said significant inequalities in income distribution between inland and coastal regions in China are obvious. Since China started its economic reformation, a dual structure was chosen by the Chinese government, 'let some people and some regions get rich first and gradually achieve common prosperity' was the core of economic policies and the majority of industries were concentrated in the eastern rather than the western region. The reason for this was based on the redistribution of resources between the urban and rural areas; a large number of rural resources were being redirected to the cities to support the industrialisation process. Since the late 1970s and especially the 1980s, the Chinese government dismantled the previous regional economic structure to preferentially encourage and support the development of the eastern coastal zone. Favourable policies were adopted, for example, the opening-up policy, monetary policy, fiscal policy, and resources allocation policy, in terms of support, enabled the eastern region to achieve industrial and business clustering.

Cui (2006) also emphasized that not only has the GDP and financial revenue gap between the eastern and western regions increased, but the same is also true for many other factors such as foreign investment, credit, and bank loans. This imbalance has already aroused attention from many sides. Many Chinese economists have voiced similar opinions about the increasing income gap among residents and different economic development levels between urban and rural areas that exist in China. According to several economic data from Li and Luo (2007), the Gini ratio between urban and rural area was 0.11 : 0.13 before the economy reformation. By 1994 this ratio was up to 0.36 : 0.41 after the commencement of the reform in the late 1970s, which was nearly equivalent to a medium developed country. However, the Chinese Academy of Social Sciences (2008) issued data that showed the income gap between urban and rural residents was as high as 3.22 : 1.

Due to the economic inequalities, many cities in the middle and western areas find it difficult to develop a MICE industry, especially for big international MICE because of a lack of financial support. However, there still remains enthusiasm to host events among different cities, even in small places. In recent years, several international or national trade fairs have failed to take place in such cities, for example in 2004, a sewing equipment fair in Wuxi even failed in the organisational stage. Due to the intense competition among the event tourism market in China, cities are chasing organisations to hold more events, which have caused more financial and social problems. The following are some problems of such events.

◆ Low Recognition

Lack of economic support is not the only reason that has caused low MICE development in China. A lack of recognition is another important reason. China is a fast-developing country, and although its development has attracted worldwide attention, such attraction is mainly focused on a limited number of major cities. Foreigners only recognise cities like Beijing, Shanghai, Guangzhou, etc. The remaining medium and small cities have little reputation from a world view even though they have amazing resources. These cities find it hard to compete with other famous MICE hosting cities, because most are not metropolises with many international visitors. In fact, a large number of MICE in China mainly attract domestic visitors. International MICE companies will not target their events on this limited domestic visitor base. According to Li (2003), although there were more than 4,000 MICE hosted every year in China, only a few provided a good benefit, possessed a brand and image, and few were recognised by UFI.

Many medium and small cities not only have little world recognition but also little fame at the national level. China is a big country, with dozens of provincial-level big cities and thousands of smaller cities. These cities with different geographical features, economic and political status have different reputations, especially for the cities in the northwest and southwest of China, which are mainly recognised as being at a low state of development and are little known even at the national level.

◆ Lack of Professional Management

Along with dramatic MICE development, one of the main issues faced by the Chinese MICE industry is a lack of professional staff because many Chinese MICE experiences and products are being presented to tourism in a less than professional manner. According to *International Business Daily* (2005), although there were many universities and colleges providing event studies in China, only 20% of these graduates had become involved in the event business. What a big loss of the human resources! Event business is a project that needs good management. It is important to have professional staff that understand the event market inside and out, and can give correct and timely leadership during event processes. Being provided or managed by non-MICE industrial people, services have been commoditised for tourists. In MICE developed countries 71.8% of employees had first degree and above educational levels, and more than 23.5% had college education. The formal exhibition manager qualification was college level plus about ten years' work experience. In Chinese MICE industry, there still had not formed a professional system. Zhejiang Asia-Pacific Exhibition Industry Research and Development Centre (2007) reported only 1% of MICE employees had real professional training. There is a scarcity of professional Chinese MICE tourism talents. There is an obvious conflict between MICE development demand and employee supply. The Hong Kong Trade Development Council (HKTDC, 2008) provided a ratio between the numbers of professionals' vacancies and job seekers: Shanghai 10 : 1, Guangzhou 8 : 1, Beijing 8 : 1, which showed a very urgent shortage of professionally qualified employees. The MICE professional education and training has lagged behind the development of the industry.

Due to industry competition and the lack of professional management in the Chinese event market, many cities seek to maximize event benefits by hosting as many events as they can. This trend has caused abnormal competition in the event market. As Wang and Qi (2006) wrote, MICE tourism in China was chaotic and immature, which caused the whole exhibition industry to be less competitive. Wu (2005) also mentioned the same opinion that the lack of related laws and regulations made the Chinese MICE tourism chaotic. Too many similar events have been hosted in neighbouring cities or hosted again in the same place at different times with limited attendance. As Wei and Qu (2007) noted, in Chinese MICE industry we could see a multi-level, multi-channel and confusing situation resulting in excessive exhibitions, and even a 'bubble' phenomenon. Many tourists and delegates do not have high regard for these repeated events and many businesses are intolerant of the repetitive invitations that ask them to attend events and pay registration fees.

Abnormal competition also causes irregular price setting. Zou (2005) noted irregular price setting indicates the same theme and same service, but with different tariffs. Even some national events' prices are set higher than those of international events, but the service and quality levels are much lower. It is imperative to have some formal regulations provided by the government.

There is a proverb of 'more haste, less speed', which means excessively fast development brings not only considerable benefits, but also many mistakes that undermine any gains made.

◆ Excessive Government Involvement

In China, event tourism as an economic stimulant is always treated as a government goal. So in most medium and small cities, events are normally hosted by local governments, and private enterprises only play a coordinating function. As Wei (2007) said, in China most conventions and exhibitions were sponsored and organised by local governments, enterprises or institutions that operated independently without coordination. Thus, the city government controls the whole process of event programming from planning and organising to final practice, which often involves too many administrative activities in the event process. However, a government-controlled event business has its own advantages including providing higher media promotion, this also can be linked with several weaknesses such as limited enterprise initiative. There are deficiencies that limit professional event companies and the development of professional event management. Government intervention always results in a non-market oriented MICE industry, which focuses on the construction of venues rather than management and service. Kim and Sun (2008) stated the growth of MICE industry in the Asian region is evident from the number of events hosted, the construction of large-scale convention and exhibition centres, and the substantial support provided by governments. In China, to host an event is not a simple process but always requires complex approval procedures. China's cautious approval of MICE is always based on its national security concerns and related aspects, but in fact, most current international exhibitions are scientific, commercial, and leisure and have no such risks. In addition, because MICE is a high profit industry, too much government intervention can cause some other problems much more easily. One might conclude that the event business as a commercial process is better led by business operators than municipal government.

◆ Western Style Boom

Given the potentially prosperous event business, many cities are eager for quick success, which has caused a Western style boom. In order to emulate Western centres, many tourism facilities such as hotel conference rooms, restaurants, parks, and business buildings have been built in the Western style, which has led to a loss of unique Asian features. A special feature in *Zhengzhou Evening* (2006) criticised this situation arguing that too much city construction is chasing after a 'Western design' and is willing to pay high prices for such construction in urban planning and project design. In this report, many national experts argued that many cities' architectures were originally of Chinese cultural design but now they try to 'wear' unsuitable 'Western suits'. This situation has caused not only a loss of cultural attraction but also wasteful expenditure. According to the report, there were more than 20 million RMB of public investment in projects in Beijing; foreign designers asked for 11% of the total cost of projects where local designers only required 2%. The argument is that China is an old country, where different cities may have unique history and attractions, and blindly worshiping foreign things will make the cities lose the treasure of unique attractions.

◆ MICE Development Symbol: Convention Venue Building Boom

The most representative and substantive witness of the dramatic MICE tourism development is the convention venue building boom. Oppermann (1996a) noted that many destinations around the world have invested in the construction of convention centres with the dual purposes of improving their image while at the same time generating economic benefits for the community. Convention centres not only host large conventions, but attract delegates to the local vicinity where they spend on accommodation, transportation, food establishments, and also leisure pursuits (Weber & Ladkin, 2003).

According to Weber and Ladkin (2003), in the UK the presence of plentiful convention centres is one of the important factors that assisted the UK to obtain a leading place in the MICE industry. Weber and Ladkin (2003) said this growth of building convention centres was fuelled by the UK government, which aimed to promote economic regeneration in many deprived cities. The convention centres were built in a number of major towns from the early 1980s and had a continued boom into the 1990s. For example, as Rogers (1998) mentioned, the International Convention Centre in Birmingham in 1991, the Cardiff International Arena in 1993, the Edinburgh International Conference Centre in 1995, the Clyde Auditorium at the Scottish Exhibition and Conference Centre in Glasgow in 1997, and the Millennium Conference Centre in London in 1997 provide examples of government-supported initiatives. A similar convention centre building boom also existed in the US. Kim, Morrison and Mills (2003) described the largest convention centres in major cities including Denver's Colorado Convention Center in 1990, Philadelphia's Pennsylvania Convention Center in 1993, and the Atlantic City Convention Center in 1997, and there were also many smaller convention centres that opened in second-tier cities. As Fenich (1995) and Ghitelman (1995) indicated, in the 1990s convention centre expansion replaced other new construction as the main focus of attention in major city development. Carlsen (1999) also argued that the convention market drove a proliferation of meeting facilities in star hotels and a diversification in venues. A similar situation also arose in Asia, according to ICCA (2004), the cities of Singapore, Seoul, Bangkok, Kuala Lumpur, and Hong Kong were the key regional centres of international convention activity in 2003, and each of these destinations had large-scale facilities like Suntec and SingEx Venues in Singapore, COEX in Seoul, IMPACT and Queen Sirikit National Convention Center in Bangkok, and the Hong Kong Convention and Exhibition Centre in Hong Kong.

In China the exhibition venue building boom has also been 'hot'. The statistics from CNTA showed that by 2002, more than 200 convention and exhibition centres had been built in China in order to attract big events. The 2008 Beijing Olympics were hosted in seven different cities, which also brought more demand for suitable facilities. According to Dai (2002), around 1995 there were less than 800,000 square metres of exhibition venue area in China, but as of 2001 the indoor exhibition hall area increased to 5,160,000 square metres. He also listed many examples then under construction or were already built, including: Shanghai New International Expo Centre, Hangzhou International Conference Center, Beijing's new China International Exhibition Center, and Wuhan International Convention & Exhibition Center with a total investment of 930 million RMB, etc.

Many researchers justify the emergence of convention centres as a promoter for MICE tourism development based on economic promotion and benefits. Law (1993) said city event facilities have been built as 'symbols of civic virility'. Lawson (2000) mentioned that new convention centres have often been built due to a government's policy to promote economic regeneration, particularly in deprived areas. Dwyer, Forsyth and Spurr (2005) noted many governments are often prepared to offer generous funding incentives to attract events and to allocate large expenditure to upgrade the facilities needed for the events.

It is argued that the boom in building event centre facilities may have been caused by 'over enthusiastic' event market followers. Commentators such as Law (1993) have worried that there is a considerable over provision of such facilities. Convention centre construction is a large-input project dependent on a city's financial capacity, and Richards and Wilson (2004) argued that the cost of building is perhaps one of the more important aspects of inter-urban competition in recent years. However, after the short-term positive multiplier effects of centre construction, frequent attendance and centre utilisation cannot be guaranteed, thereby creating a potential waste of city resources. Abbey and Link (1994) maintained that, in contrast to permanent tourist attractions, events are temporary, narrowly focused and short-lived. Convention centre occupancy is also not only based on the event timing but also size of the centres. Some centres are more suitable for large events like Olympics, FIFA World Cups, etc. But, for the main part, many existing events are of medium and small sizes that do not need to occupy big convention centres, meanwhile the operating and maintenance costs of such convention centres are high. Safavi (1971), in his early study, said many facilities experienced losses as the building must be let at a low rent in order to attract business because of the competitive nature of the industry, and/or the centres are not used for enough days in a year for the overheads to be covered. That is the reason why Spickard (1996) and Wirtz (2001) suggested in their research that convention centres rarely cover their operating costs and never cover debt service. Fenich (1998) surmised that it is the latter possibility that confirms concerns that convention centres often operate at a loss, as previous research has clearly indicated.

◆ Event Theme Park Building Boom

Due to the varied and mixed event purposes, not only event centres but also many event theme parks have emerged specifically for given cultural and leisure events. For example Kunming Expo Garden was built primarily for the 1999 Kunming Expo, Shenyang World Park was built for the 2006 Shenyang World Horticulture Exposition, and Hangzhou World Leisure Expo Park was also built for the 2006 Hangzhou World Leisure Expo. Each of the theme parks covers a large space after a long period of construction. The event theme park building boom is also not incidental but rose from a search for varied event themes amid strong competition. It was thought that medium- and large-size events need to successfully develop across various platforms, and through cooperation with a park, they can create a new platform for more attractions. Also due to the intense competition, many event planners are struggling to win some advantages over other strong competitors, and thus developing larger and more multi-function parks is one of the competitive strategies employed. For example, Paris Nord Villepinte has decided to extend its exhibition grounds and Kunming Expo Garden is also designing an extension.

Yet amid this building boom there is angst about these event theme parks' future after an initial, specific event. Traditional theme parks are always built for a continuing purpose, e.g., Disney World, sports venues for horse and dog races, and some leisure parks, etc. A specific event theme park is constructed for a specific event, so that after the event or convention is finished the park becomes less attractive to visitors and the number of attendees will fall. The Jiangsu branch of Xinhua News Agency (2007) reported that one of Hangzhou's most famous theme parks, 'Future World', was facing such a challenge and would be diverted to real estate projects. It is not a unique case and event theme parks tend to have a shorter life cycle when compared with other traditional parks. Richtmyer (2005) noted that even the largest and historically most successful centres need to slash rental rates and even give space away to compete. Thus a very important question for planners to think about is how to survive and compete after the event climaxes.

There is always a conflict behind any thriving phenomenon, for many large cities desire a representative event centre or event park that not only improves a city's reputation but becomes an integral means by which to compete with other large cities in the MICE market. However, it is also true that constructing event facilities needs significant financial assets, which means the city needs a strong financial background. City tourism organisers need to understand that a city's financial and environmental carrying capacity is important. It is regrettable that there has been relatively limited research on convention centres (Fenich, 1998), and this limits the examples that organisers can use for reference. In short, the convention centre building wave is a fuel that can incite higher MICE 'flames', or a latent risk that will 'burn' the sponsoring city.

2.7   MICE Market Competition

The Chinese saying that 'there are no waves without wind' means any specific phenomenon that happens must have its own rationale. The boom in convention centre construction has been caused by a growing demand in the MICE market and the desire of urban centres to benefit from this. Due to the dramatic growth and profit potentially brought by event tourism, many cities and regions are very keen to gain an advantage in this market, which in turn intensifies competition. Bramezza (1996) stated that, increasingly, cities and towns adopt the logic of competition in a highly dynamic and complex environment. Listokin (1985) had summarised the reason—the economic reward is great! Richards and Wilson (2004) also stated that due to the increasing integration of the global economy, a growing number of places are drawn into this competitive environment. For example the Sydney Olympics in 2000 not only had provided benefits for two weeks, but were planned to have deep and far-reaching effects for the next several years on the Australian economy, reputation, culture, etc. Event tourism is outperforming the traditional markets and thereby mirroring shifts in tourism development in general. Because the cake is so delicious, everybody wants to share a piece of it and also wants to win the biggest slice. Dwyer and Mistilis (1997) said the market for MICE tourism at both international and domestic levels has shown to be extremely competitive.

Actually the MICE competition can be viewed in two ways: external and internal. The outside competition is fierce for MICE opportunities between countries, while within countries, competition between large cities and small cities is also intense.

◆ Competition Between Countries

Perceived as an important determinant of success in the marketing of tourism, MICE tourism is much sought after by many destinations. The development of the MICE industry is obvious and has appeared as a contributor to economic growth in many countries. Recently, the most competitive MICE countries are mainly located in Europe and America. However, due to the rapid MICE development in the world, cities in other areas are starting to get more attention from this industry. Indeed, as Dwyer and Mistilis (1999) said, the MICE market is growing particularly rapidly in the Asia-Pacific region. The extent of competition among destinations has also been growing rapidly in the Asia-Pacific region. The Commonwealth Department of Tourism (1995) mentioned Japan, Malaysia, and the Republic of Singapore as all having government/national convention-hosting plans to increase the number of international MICE. According to Teerarat (2013), in 2008 Thailand had 821,892 MICE tourists and in 2013 the number of MICE tourists increased to 1,013,502. The Hong Kong Tourism Board also considered the MICE market as a focus and launched 'Image Hong Kong' in 2003 for the sake of more MICE attraction. The pocket-sized state of Singapore owns limited natural resources with a land area of just over 700 square kilometres, but the number of international MICE hosted by this small country is large, and it ranks among the top in Asia and the world as one of the most successful MICE centres. In order to develop greater MICE opportunities for the tourism market, Tokyo has conducted three major construction projects, including Roppongi Hills area, Shinbashi-Shiodome area (Shinbashi business district), and Shinagawa area (Shinagawa business district). In addition, India, Malaysia, and other Asian countries in recent years have also increased efforts to develop the MICE market.

◆ Competition Between Cities

Because of perceived economic benefits derived from the MICE industry (and a need to obtain a rate of return on past investment), inter-city competition continues to become more intense. Many large cities like Sydney and Auckland have gained significant infrastructure development due to hosting events such as the Olympics and the America's Cup. Also, in small cities or towns, and even in some rural areas, as noted by Ryan, Smee and Murphy

(1996), the number of events taking place is also growing. MICE development has caused an uneven and unbalanced competition between large and small cities. Berg and Braun (1999) noted that fundamental changes in the economy, technology, demography, and politics have reshaped the environment for towns and cities in Europe; and these changes have induced competition between towns and cities at regional, national and sometimes international scales. Generally, small cities or towns with little capability or financial support find it hard to compete with larger cities. The gap between larger, better-endowed cities and rural areas and other locations is obvious. Nonetheless, Law (1993, p. 1) stated that 'large cities are arguably the most important type of tourist destination across the world and yet urban areas have been greatly neglected in most academic studies of tourism'.

A large city with its strong financial support and city image maintenance has always tended to have better public services than small places. Mullins (1992) said urban areas, particularly large cities, are especially developed for the production, sale and consumption of goods, and services providing pleasure. Small cities or towns with limited development are perceived unable to compete with larger-population centres because of a lack of tourism products and facilities like transport, accommodation, restaurants, etc., and thus have sought means by which to foster their strengths and circumvent weaknesses by an emphasis on rural peace. Mills (1991) noted that event centres have been built or planned primarily in large cities. Due to the way in which event organisers tend to consider MICE destinations, small cities or towns generally have a low capability to compete with the big cities. Consequently, the tourism planners in many small cities or towns struggle to obtain some advantages and are more likely to develop festivals or shows based on unique cultural or historical attractions.

◈ MICE Competition in China

Although the MICE market in China is thriving and prosperous, competition for the MICE market in different cities that have the capacity to hold events is severe. Major cities in China like Beijing and Shanghai need to compete on a global scale with other large cities, especially in Asia. This provides an opportunity for the remaining cities to seize opportunities for medium-size events like the 2006 Hangzhou World Leisure Expo, 2006

Guangdong International Tourism Culture Festival, etc. Many Chinese cities have seen the potential advantages of event tourism such as high consumer spending and subsequent profits. In recent times, many cities have focused on 'MICE tourism' and, according to their regional characteristics and advantages, have engaged in 'branding their event city'. Xinhua News Agency (2003) noted that due to the popularity of the event industry all over China, municipalities have engaged in building exhibition halls, and many event operators and tourism organisations strive to join international event organisations. Every tourism city that has the capacity wants to share and seize this potential market. The 'event tourism' competition between Chinese cities has aided China's event industry to develop, which provides both experience and further opportunities such as the 2008 Beijing Olympics and 2010 Shanghai World Expo.

Yet the market must have a limit, and exceeding that limit may cause negative impacts, especially in some immature event markets. Some medium and small cities in China are suffering from the consequences of poor financial returns, the high cost of building and promotion, too many convention centres, low space occupancy, and environmental degradation, etc.

2.8 Event Tourism Competitive Capacity

Due to both market competition and a world environment with many natural disasters and political unrest, the demand for conferences has fluctuated as business prefers stable natural and political climates. Hu and Hiemstra (1996) indicated that in a competitive event market environment, associations and their meeting planners seek the best value packages on the market, which can best be done by selecting meeting destinations that fulfil associations' needs and expectations. Go and Govers (1999) also provided a similar opinion, namely as competition in the convention and exhibition industry increases, it becomes more critical for destinations to identify key criteria for success and clients' expectations. Crouch and Ritchie (1998) suggested there is great variation in the structure of the convention site selection process across different associations. To influence the selection choice, three main factors emerge, namely: city's basic service level, image and brand, and destination attractions.

◆ City's Basic Service Level

Lee and Back (2007) identified that city attributes or capacity influence event planners' decision to select a particular destination. City capacity is not a general unique concept; it involves many areas that relate to human life, city development, etc. It is a single integrated comprehensive measure beyond the whole tourism resources of the destination. Johnson and Thomas (1993) said most literature has attempted to define capacity in fairly limited ways: few writers have made serious attempts to embrace all considerations relevant to society as a whole in a unified framework. So, to provide a unique concept of city capacity is problematic, but it is a single integrated comprehensive measure extending beyond the whole tourism resource. Johnson and Thomas (1993) argued that there is an awareness that capacities exist for each of the various inter-related subsystems (economic, social, environmental, and cultural). Murphy (1985) also said the measurement of tourism carrying capacity is difficult and elaborate but the concept may provide valuable insights into residents' perceptions of tourism.

City capacity is the basis for event development. Event development itself is a new 'shining spot' for the tourism industry combining different industries while trading on social elements. As previously noted, the coefficient of event development is 1 : 8; the '1' for the event industry, and the '8' for the transportation, accommodation, food, shopping, entertainment, and travel sectors. Therefore almost every aspect of the life and organisations of cities can be described and incorporated into a city capacity system, which is viewed as a complex process associated with the differing demands of different societies that make an urban population.

Accordingly, decision-making processes and destination images are held by both association meeting planners and potential attendees (Zelinsky, 1994; Oppermann, 1996a; Oppermann & Chon, 1997; Crouch & Ritchie, 1998; Weber, 2001) and incorporate many of the sub-systems of city carrying capacity. The type of tourist resource is deeply implicated in the concept of city carrying capacity because meeting planners are concerned about their main attendees' perceptions, many of whom may be very different in terms of culture, religion, and ethnicity and are likely to seek socio-cultural experiences combined with their event trip (see Table 2.3).

Table 2.3   Elements of Urban Tourism Resources

Primary Elements (Attraction)	
Activity places	Leisure setting
Cultural facilities	Physical characteristics
Sport facilities	Social cultural features
Amusement facilities	
Secondary Elements (Services)	
Hotel and catering facilities	
Shopping facilities	
Market	
Additional Elements (Infrastructure)	
Accessibility and parking facilities	
Tourist facilities information office	
Signposts, guides, maps, and leaflets	

Source: Jansen-Verbeke. (1986).

Schofield (1996) indicated tourism destination products have been conceptualised in a variety of ways including a 'component perspective' where products have been described as bundles of activities, services and benefits, and as physical and service features with symbolic associations. Thus, basic public services can also affect the delegates' satisfaction during their attendance. As mentioned before, event facilities are one important factor considered by meeting planners in their selection decision with reference to the facilities' size, capacity, type, and quality and expertise of management. Event facilities are not simple concepts in this selection process and need to be combined with several hotels and entertainments. Wu and Weber (2005) indicated that as convention centres are non-residential, they require several hotels in close proximity to accommodate convention delegates, in addition to restaurants and shopping facilities. The service quality also has a direct relationship with attendees' satisfaction, which can affect the event planners' next round of place selection. So Wu and Weber (2005) provided an understanding of the importance of specific venue attributes of facilities and services as an imperative for design and construction, and subsequent service provision by convention and exhibition centre owners and management. Furthermore, some main public facilities like medical and transport services, and media promotion are also important factors involved in the city capacity. In short, Wu and Weber (2005) argued that the growth of MICE activity has both been facilitated by and resulted in further significant capital investments in supporting convention infrastructure and in particular in the construction of dedicated convention and exhibition centres.

◆ Image and Brand

The consumer's perception of destination choice is always related with a consumer's degree of recognition of a city 'brand'. Given the emotional power of travel as experience, destinations begin to seek their position as a holistic place brand, and indeed many countries, states and regions are embarking on brand-event initiatives. As Hall (1992) said, events are being viewed as an integral part of tourism development and marketing plans. The importance of city image among the tourism market is obvious from many research studies. According to Pike (2002), from 1973 to 2000, more than 142 articles related to tourism destination image have been published in international tourism journals or presented at conferences. Rod (2003) mentioned every tourist destination in the world has a 'brand image', which puts a destination on the consumer's 'shopping list' and creates an emotional appeal, and seeks to enhance that destination's chances of being chosen over others. Richards and Wilson (2004) said the image of a place is usually very important in attracting visitors and place image research has been particularly prevalent in the tourism studies field. Research shows that appearance is very important and people generally agree on what makes a city look appealing (Grabmeier, 1997). Selby (2004) associated the importance of the image of a city with a high-quality lifestyle, extensive facilities, and a lively ambience as being crucial to attract target market segments. Morgan and Pritchard (1998) even described city image as the 'currency of culture'.

Events and city image complement each other. Getz (1991) said cities have long used mega events such as World Expos and sporting events as a means of revitalising their economies, creating infrastructure and improving their image. Hall (1992) also noted it is apparent that major events can have the effect of shaping an image of the host community or country, leading to its favourable perception as a potential travel destination. This potential has been a reason for events being used as an image-enhancement tool, particularly for large cities (Law, 1993; Holcomb, 1999b; Sassen & Roost, 1999; Judd & Fainstein, 1999; Selby, 2004). To promote a city's image is not a unique process. Kim and Chalip (2003) argued there is a need to evaluate market position dependent on the event's media, sponsorship, and word of mouth, each of which is a function of the event's spectator appeal.

The total branding task is by no means easy, but the rewards are enormous. City branding is a long-term task and one that needs monitoring, updating, and adjusting to suit the changeable market. Cities with an already existing tourism industry may sometimes decide to re-brand their image 'when visitor numbers decline' (Kolb, 2006, p. 19). A decline in visitors can occur when the city is no longer perceived by potential tourists as an attractive destination. Cities should routinely assess how they are branding themselves in a crowded tourism marketplace and adjust their brand if needed.

According to Lombardi (1990), there are two major ways of re-creating a destination image in the minds of visitors after an event has occurred: one is through communication in the mass media; the other is through a real experience. Thus tourists' and event attendees' satisfaction level is one of the important factors that can influence city image building. Gunn (1972) suggested that a traveller's experience proceeds on the basis of seven stages, including an image modification process:

- accumulation of mental images about the vacation experience (first stage);
- modification of those images by further information (second stage);
- decision to take a vacation trip (third stage);
- travel to the destination (fourth stage);
- participation at the destination (fifth stage);
- return (sixth stage); and
- new accumulation of images based on the experience (seventh stage).

Crompton (1979) also indicated that the images of destinations significantly differ between different tourists. He suggested the gap between tourists' ideal and actual perceptions can directly influence the tourists' perceptions of city image. Abbey and Link (1994) suggested satisfied convention attendees may very well turn into repeat visitors and advertise the destination through word of mouth. Also media promotion plays a significant role in the image building process, which paints a true or factual picture of destination to tourists.

The problem of successfully promoting the image of a city that needs to build its own unique attraction is intensified when, due to the global prevalent styles, many cities have built similar attractions. For many metropolises, tourists always have a feeling that 'they are similar' with many skyscrapers, crowded streets, wide roads, and many shopping areas, etc. It is hard for those cities to stand out given their similar urban ambience. Richards and Wilson (2004) underlined that the infrastructure and amenities in many different cities and regions tend to become increasingly similar. Getz and Wicks (1993) suggested the systematic planning development and marketing of MICE as tourist attractions, catalysts and image builders is one possible cause for this. Deery, Jago, Fredline and Dwyer (2005) noted that meetings and events is one niche tourism activity that contributes significantly to GDP as to the branding and awareness of tourist destinations, and that copycat developments tend to occur. However, in the context of travel and tourism, this spectrum becomes limited to that segment of the industry that is unique to a specific geographic location and is limited in duration.

Many Chinese medium and small cities have similar backgrounds and culture, so how to stand out from the crowd is a key question when they are seeking to develop a MICE framework. For example, 'tourism' is a hot topic that is used by many cities, and if one types 'tourism festivals' in search engines the result can show thousands of different kinds of tourism festivals hosted in different cities. Creating a special and attractive city brand in the wider competitive market is important. The 1999 Kunming Expo is an example of success. Kunming Scientific and Technological Bureau (2005) reported that Kunming is one of the first 24 historical and cultural cities of China; the most prominent feature of the city is the stable ecological environment, which gives it the famous nickname of 'spring city'. Kunming Expo is exactly based on the city's major resources with its stable climate, natural resources, multiple ethnicities, and special history. As Kunming Expo Garden Co., Ltd. (2006) mentioned, the 1999 Kunming Expo was originally planned for Beijing, but with the weather and venue difficulties, the site of this horticulture exposition was changed to Kunming. Thus brand image always depends on a resource base, especially for a tourism-based city.

◆ Destination Attractions

What makes a city with its events an exciting place to visit? Carey (1994) defined an event broadly, as encompassing anything attracting an audience by appealing to specific tastes, desires, or needs. Delegates attending any convention or exhibition often look for elements beyond the core of the event to complement their experiences. For Manning (1983, p. 4), celebration is performance: 'it is the dramatic presentation of cultural symbols.' So it is important for cities' tourism organisers to draw upon local cultures to provide special attractions for both tourists and event planners because these can be specific and thereby unique to the area, and so gain attention in the event marketplace.

Not only culture can attract MICE but also culturally-based festivals and events can influence local culture. Robinson, Picard and Long (2004) said tourism in terms of space/place is distinctive, multiple, and many of the physical sites in which tourism happens are not simply 'products' to be consumed. Yeoman et al. (2004) noted the economic phenomena of cultural and cultural-driven festivals and event strategies as global phenomena. There is a close relationship between local culture, festivals, and events. As Robinson et al. (2004) said, there remains a need to address some of the deeper issues of the tourist–festival–culture relationship. Festivals and special events are the 'cultural resources of an area that make possible the successful hosting of visitors' (Uysal, Gahan & Martin, 1993, p. 5). Notzke (2004) provided a similar opinion in an Australian context that the aboriginal tourism experience acquired through attending events has become an important part of aboriginal tourism and is viewed as being a powerful communication tool that is operated by various tourism stakeholders. In short, cultural events possess an ability to impact as inspirational and life-changing experiences for participants.

➡ 2.9   Event Management

Consequently event tourism and MICE management has become an important issue (Peters & Pikkemaat, 2005). Getz (1997) stated whether an event is organised by professionals or volunteers, corporations or non-profit associations, event management remains a weakness of many event businesses. Getz and Frisby (1988), in their early research, had mentioned most community-based events lack sophisticated management. After nearly ten years Getz (1997) still found the same problem, and he thought many events in Ontario, Canada encountered problems with generating resources, both human and financial, and did not package events with other tourist attractions and activities. The basic elements of event management are to find what suits the taste of the consuming public, and what is morally and ethically acceptable to the modern society (Laybourn, 2004).

Event management is one of the core elements that drives event success. Many cities have their obvious limitation of financial support, space, human resources, etc.; so providing good event management can prepare for more efficient and effective implementation of plans. Event management is not an easy concept, as Morris (1994) said, one should manage an event just like a project. So event producers need to adapt and plan carefully to survive in this more competitive environment. Harmonising intra-regional or system competition is one of the important functions that need to be controlled by regional event organisers. As Higham and Ritchie (2002) suggested, event organisers need to understand what types of events exist in their regions, where they exist, and what time of the year they occur so as to minimise intra-regional event competition. As mentioned before, in China, many similar theme events are always hosted in the same or neighbouring cities, so event organisers need to understand the whole regional event market and manage them in a better manner.

Better understanding visitors' needs can better control event success. According to Professional Convention Management Association (PCMA, 2003), recent competition among convention destinations and venues has highlighted a need for better understanding of the convention or conference attendee behaviour, including their decision-making process and their evaluation of the convention experience. Visitors attend MICE for multiple reasons including learning, cultural conditioning, social influence, and various perceptions of potential gain. From the perspective of destination marketing, the goal of cultivating MICE tourism is to attract non-residents with the expectation that their spending will contribute greatly to the local economy while respecting the viewpoints of all stakeholders as well as the sustainability of local resources (Buhalis, 2000). MICE organisers need to understand the characteristics and behaviours of pleasure travellers who attend events during their pleasure trips in terms of trip purpose, information and media used for trip planning, trip characteristics and behaviour, and socio-economic and demographic characteristics (Yoon, Spencer, Holecek & Kim, 2000).

MICE tourism organisers also need to pay attention to the natural environment. As McCabe et al. (2000) described, there is a trend internationally to use environmental-friendly practices within the convention and meeting industry. Environmental problems are not only financial and technical problems, but also a management problem. Better environment and unique heritage are two of the most attractive assets that small cities and rural areas possess. So managing and controlling the environment is an essential means to sustain competitive advantage. In Australia, many cities have realised the importance of environmental management, 'its unique environment, spectacular and diverse range of natural features, wide and unique range of flora and fauna and distinct cultural heritage provide the country with an opportunity to promote and attract MICE visitors who are seeking an event with special environmental focus' (Commonwealth Department of Tourism, 1995, p. 35). Chinese cities' Asian culture and environment are elements that are likely to attract European event tourists, and as far as possible, one must keep this attraction to survive in the international competitive market. Selecting a suitable theme for an event, controlling resource usage, formulating green policies, and limiting the tourist numbers can minimise environmental damage and protect the region's cultural and attraction advantages.

◆ Event-related Price Control

Most studies dealing with MICE have focused on either understanding attendees' behaviour or delineating the direct economic impacts of visitation upon communities in which such events are held. In fact, the price level often has a direct relationship with visitors' destination choice, especially determining the returning to given destinations. As Crouch (1992) said, there is evidence to show that travellers are sensitive to price. MICE profit is more reliant on the attendees' and visitors' payments, so price level is one of the more important factors in attracting delegates. Dwyer, Forsyth and Spurr (2005) emphasized that it is important to pay particular attention to the price, as compared to its competitors, if an industry venue is to continue to grow.

The profit level of an event is one of the critical determinants of how well it performs in the MICE markets. Kim et al. (2002) mentioned that to improve operations, profitability, and the achievement of social objectives, event managers require more accurate information about the gap or congruities that may exist between their perception of the importance of festival offerings and attendees' motivations. The same authors indicated that while price contributions to MICE earnings were positive, in some events, the pursuit of higher profits through higher prices had caused problems. There are two malign pricing setting models in the MICE area: limited pricing and predatory pricing. Price 'cheating', price discrimination, and price monopolisation have emerged in the MICE market, which stunt MICE development (Kim et al., 2002).

◆ Risk Control

Events, especially large ones, always attract large numbers of tourists, which poses problems for risk containment and security. Many kinds of unexpected risks such as epidemic diseases, security incidents, and natural disasters can also lead to fatalities. To be distant from danger and maintain delegate safety are the basic elements in the event planning process. Liu, Longstaff and Pan (2003) also indicated that an investor must also consider the effects of financial security when selecting a dynamic portfolio strategy. Thompson (1999) stated these outcomes have become major planning and security considerations within the destinations that host these events. How to better control risk is one of the most important questions for host cities.

Major disruptions are referred to as shocks, and it is harder to forecast events like financial crisis and terrorist attacks. Rack et al. (2005) also emphasized infectious diseases as of particular importance. These kinds of risks involve a sudden large shock and Table 2.4 below shows a major negative event risks classification based on the work of Li, Li and Zhang (2003).

Table 2.4   Sources and Types of MICE Risks

Classification Standard	Event Risk Type
Characteristics	Natural disaster (natural calamity)
	Contrived crisis (hostility; terrorism; financial crisis; unstable political situation)
Reasons	Political crisis (domestic war; unstable international relationship)
	Financial crisis (domestic or international economic downturn)
	Security crisis (epidemic disease, calamity, terrorist attack)
Affect coverage	International crisis: wholly or partially affect destination
	Domestic crisis: wholly or partially affect destination

Source: Li, Li & Zhang. (2003).

Standeven and DeKnop (1999) mentioned the threat to tourists' safety as the most serious potential negative impact of hosting events. Bentley and Page (2001) argued that crime and safety issues can adversely affect tourism behaviour and experience. Thus pre-event avoidable risks like crime opportunities, traffic congestion, visitor and staff safety, fire stations, poison prevention and treatment stations, advanced communications systems, and other emergency service facilities all need to be seriously considered. To better control event risks, financial support must be considered, which needs government, event and insurance companies' cooperation. Cui (2006) suggested four methods to prevent risks: first, government departments need to strengthen the effective regulatory measures, and build the first security barrier; second, the exhibition venue in the design and construction phases should consider fire, theft and other risk or incident prevention functions; third, the exhibition organisers need to put risk management into the day-to-day operations and management system; fourth, the insurance companies' involvement is required to distribute subsequent protection in a cost-effective manner.

2.10   Involvement

Event process is not an easy task and many sectors are involved and need to cooperate to achieve success. According to Yeoman et al. (2004), the components involved in event management are varied. Event success needs both government and social communities to solve many kinds of problems including financial support, volunteers' motivation, theme selection, and being able to identify market segments and their needs.

◆ Government Involvement

MICE is a rapidly developing industry. Governments have a moral obligation to ensure their decisions to promote appropriate regional economic and tourism development, especially in the Chinese context (Ryan & Gu, 2009). Government in both the regions and specific industries in China has a very strong leading role through state-owned enterprises (SOEs), which can provide interrelated regulations, better logistics, and higher media involvement to better assist MICE development. From this perspective, the government involvement in the MICE market has also increased the effective supply of venues and events, albeit an oversupply of too many 'secondary' events and venues. This is because many government departments have not paid full attention to the general MICE market situation by concentrating on local issues, and many are too enthusiastic about holding exhibitions, and being involved in convention and exhibition construction, often for reasons of personal enhancement or career progression. This has exacerbated industry confusion. Certainly, there is a view that the central government should strengthen its lead, guide and coaching functions, and provide a better comprehensive support system. However, in the Chinese event business, sponsorship development needs a local government's encouragement and management. It is therefore not uncommon for the public sector to be responsible for a large proportion of the special events provided for the community, and the majority of local governments in many countries now have a substantial and varied event program (Thomas & Wood, 2004).

◆ Social Community Involvement

Yet despite the growth in the importance of events and the increasing public sector's role in providing special events (Shone & Parry, 2001), the public service provision of entertainment, culture, and arts remains a non-mandatory requirement (Borrett, 1991). A greater involvement by local communities can reduce the burden of government and provide better experiences for attendees. The more people involved, the more ideas and financial support there may be, which can improve an event's attractiveness. Social communities have shown their importance in the MICE market.

In China, it is common for local governments to control the whole event process. This situation brings pressure on a city's event organisers who have limited financial support and human resources. Gaining support from local societies and local businesses can reduce the risk arising from such limited financial involvement and human resources. Furthermore, the city hosting events always has an interest in economic regeneration, and local business involvement in the events is an opportunity to communicate with other businesses and promote them.

Wilson et al. (2001) argued that event tourism can be developed locally with participation from local government and small business. In larger events, local business support is even more necessary. As Getz (1997) said, whereas private sector involvement in events has always been widespread, particularly through the staging of concerts, consumer shows, and the like, the scope for private entrepreneurial involvement is still rapidly expanding. Local business sponsorship is becoming ubiquitous in modern society and the event market. Even the Miss World competition has more than 30 commercial sponsorships. Event organisers are becoming ever more dependent upon the support of the local and business communities for their success rather than solely upon unique natural or built attractions (Janiskee, 1994; Turco & Kelsey, 1992).

Financial support is an obvious advantage when provided by local sponsors. For example, Sony did not shirk during 2007–2014 from paying 305 million US dollars to become the main sponsor of FIFA competitions. Investment flows from local businesses cannot only reduce financial risks but also improve production mobility. Local business sponsors are expanding their involvement, especially targeting corporations to develop sponsorship and supply to the industry in both the number and diversity of products and services. McCabe et al. (2000) noted that to achieve a successful MICE event, a number of specialists or suppliers in different areas will be called on to manage and coordinate their services. In China, local business sponsorship is accepted by many cities, and according to Ma (2006), the 2008 Beijing Olympic Games sponsorship programme started early in 2000. It included household appliances, dairy products, tourist reception, beer, convenience foods, altogether more than ten categories. Lawson (2000) said the growth in multinational corporations and pan-national agencies and developments in associations represent issues that have fuelled the growth of the MICE industry in particular.

◆ **Resident Involvement**

Watt (1998) mentioned that one important goal of event management is the art of getting other people to do all the work. Lack of a large population is one of the problems that have impeded event tourism progressing in many cities. Thus involving the resident community in the event operation process can reduce the disadvantages of limited human resources and gain local support, thereby, paving the way for better event business development in the future.

Consequently, local event planners really need to understand the residents' attitudes. Many authors (Fredline & Faulkner, 2002a; Getz, 1997; Bowdin et al., 2001) emphasized that local residents are one of the most significant factors in the event process. Andereck and Vogt (2000) stated that before community residents are involved in the development of tourism resources, it is imperative to gain an understanding of residents' opinions regarding development and what a community wishes to achieve. Lindberg and Johnson (1997) noted that most analyses of tourism-related development have found that attitudes are a function of various perceived tourism-related benefits and costs. Gaining support from residents is an important element to make the event successful. Butler (1980) said the large number of visitors and the facilities provided for them can be expected to arouse some opposition and discontent among permanent residents, since at the stagnation stage, the destination capacity levels for many variables will have been reached or exceeded with environmental, social, and economic problems. At this stage, it is then often the local communities (through the rates paid) that have to undertake the necessary reinvestment in facilities or alternatively live with the consequences of a declining tourism asset (Ryan, 2005).

Resident support often equates with sufficient and successful volunteer support. As Getz (1997) described, volunteers are staff that include managers, general workers, and directors who all occupy a special place in event management with no payment received. A number of cities have put successful events out for tender, and more volunteer groups are entering the field. In Western countries, many event processes involve a large and active voluntary input as evidenced by the 2000 Sydney Olympic Games. In China, the voluntary movement is still in the early stages and the basic volunteer groups are students who have passion, time, and energy. Building the base for the recruitment of volunteers while conserving and reserving the volunteer resource is a new strategy for some cities. For example, Ningbo (in Zhejiang Province) had six colleges as the first base for the recruitment of volunteers for the 10th Ningbo International Fashion Festival. Encouraging local volunteers is important, and attracting foreign resident volunteers is more efficient for some international events, especially if they have some experiences. The utilisation of international students and local young people might be a way to achieve this. According to cnnb.com.cn (2006), about 60 international volunteers from Germany, France, Russia, and other countries were recruited in Ningbo volunteer groups. Residents' involvement not only provides human resources support but also better reveals the city's local characteristics.

2.11   MICE Impacts

As a particular form of tourism, MICE tourism has been adopted by tourism planners to promote destinations and their economies. As Getz (1997) mentioned, MICE tourism has become the fastest growing type of tourist attraction and has assumed a key role in international, national, regional, and local tourism marketing strategies. This is based on the strength of MICE's outstanding marketing benefits. As Hall (1992) indicated, events have become an increasingly significant component of destination marketing. That is also the reason why many tourism operators are embracing the MICE market with local regions to establish convention bureaux to better assist in marketing these facilities (Hing, McCabe, Lewis & Leiper, 1998). Getz (2007) appraised the planned event impacts as of increasing importance for destination competitiveness.

Not all events are equal. An event is a combined concept that manifests differences by size, theme, geography, input, etc. Ritchie (1984) identified six types of event impact: economic, tourism/commercial, physical, socio-cultural, psychological, and political. Currently, the majority of research is based on economic orientation with relatively little attention being paid to the important social psychological and physical impacts. As Cooke (1982), Liu and Var (1986), Perdue, Long and Kang (1995) and Ayres (2000) described, tourism development is always justified on the basis of perceived and actual benefits and costs, particularly economic benefits versus social-cultural and environmental costs. Janiskee (2006) agreed with this opinion and said that despite the growing number of MICE throughout the world, they are still managerially unsophisticated because most literature is found by considerations of economic impact and cultural importance, which cannot in themselves provide a totally systematic and sufficient knowledge base for event organisers to plan, produce, and market events.

◆ Social Perspective Impacts

Event impacts are two-faced. Each impact has both positive and negative manifestations. MICE's social positive impact is always obvious because to host an event better, a host city will intensify the main construction and urban infrastructure, develop a large number of new projects and road construction, and enhance city appearance and cleanliness levels. According to statistics for the 1999 Kunming Expo, Kunming accelerated its infrastructure construction by ten years to host the expo. Hosting an event is a perfect opportunity for a city to show and brand its image. A city's brand is always a key factor in the development of MICE; the spread of the city's image, the creation of city activities, etc., all help the destination to shape itself in the world tourism market. As Zhou (2007) said, in the short term, to enhance the image of a beautiful city, raising the visibility of the city is possible just as Sydney created a positive image for Australia's sustainable tourism development as the 'Green Olympics'.

However, as for other industries, rapid growth can become a two-edge sword for MICE as far as environmental issues are concerned. While MICE growth can stimulate the growth of city development with building constructions, a growing road network, increasing numbers of motor vehicles and more tourists, all can result in man-made pollution. Since the Chinese economic reforms, China has experienced increased environmental damage as soil erosion, floods, drought, pollution, earthquakes, and a shrinking biodiversity have emerged as major growing problems in China. Additionally, China has suffered several large natural disasters that were related to, or added to environmental damage such as the floods in southern China in 2007, snowstorms in southern China in 2008, the Wenchuan earthquakes in 2008, large areas of drought in southwestern China in 2010, and an earthquake in Yushu in 2010.

The most sensitive environmental issue is that of air and water pollution. Bingham (1993) found that only 4.5% of municipal waste water in China received treatment by that time. Wen and Tisdell (2001) also mentioned that most large cities in China had air quality of a much lower standard than that set by the World Health Organisation by that year. Hosting MICE may not have an obvious direct relationship with air and water pollution but it still has some influence on, and is influenced by issues of air and water pollution. During the hosting of MICE, many organisations like to set off fireworks for celebration and entertainment, but such action adversely affects city air quality. According to Wang, Zhuang, Xu, and An (2006), the burning of fireworks during the lantern festival in Beijing has caused air pollution. They noted that the burning of fireworks releases many harmful pollutants that are associated with serious human health hazards. Qian (2006) also mentioned that construction materials for event sites are another source for causing pollution. Nowadays many exhibitors prefer more and more specially decorated booths which use building materials, wood products, print ads, carpets, and other items which may release harmful gases. Additionally, during the hosting period, a city needs to receive a potentially large temporary population and the extra flow of people can cause urban issues of traffic congestion, more living wastes, higher volumes of automobile exhaust, and water resource wasting.

Another environmental issue is natural landscape damage. According to 'National Afforestation Condition Report 2014' issued by Office of National Afforestation Committee (2015), the loss of forests in China has been so serious that by 2014 only 21.63% of China's land was covered by forest and woodland. As mentioned before, many cities are willing to build more event-related constructions which leads to further excessive land use. Agriculture land and forests have been used to build MICE venues to high standards that include park areas, hotels, shopping areas, roads, etc. Yang and Zhang (2006) noted that the Chongqing Yongchuan Yuxi Exhibition Center initiated new construction on previously undeveloped areas in 2005, and this building cost 40 million RMB and was used for just five years and went over budget.

An employment opportunity is another important social impact. Some authors think MICE is a positive opportunity for a city to increase its employment by attracting more business to relocate and enhance the local business development. For example, the 2008 'European Capital of Culture' hoped for 4 million visitors and 17,500 jobs. Positive media attention, construction of facilities and infrastructure, and employment increases were identified as the primary beneficial output of the 1996 Summer Olympic Games (Humphreys & Plummer, 1995; Newman, 1999). And also increased hotels, restaurants, entertainment activities enhance the host city's hospitality employment demand. However, others think that, due to MICE, more non-residents come searching for jobs, which causes local resident unemployment rates to rise. Like Zhang and Liang (2008) reported once, the government's importing foreign labour certainly has caused a threat to local job seekers.

◆ Residents' Perceptions on Impacts

As already stated, the main issue of this research is the perceptions of local residents with regard to the Chinese MICE market in Hangzhou. Resident perception is a wide and complex concept because any attempt to assess people's perceptions is not easy. Lindberg and Johnson (1997) noted that most analyses of tourism-related development have found that attitudes are a function of various perceived tourism-related benefits and costs. To state a cliché, humanity is complex and multiple. The need to understand and manage resident expectations and balance both positive and negative perceptions is also of particular importance. Like Easterling (2005) said, residents are key stakeholders in a tourism system; their needs must be identified, considered, and subsequently, satisfied. Bull and Lovell (2007) said in examining residents' perceptions and views about events, it was anticipated that this would also relate to the way in which such promotion was being successful or not.

Due to tourism development, a number of evaluations have been published that report residents' perceptions toward tourism including MICE. Pearce and Stringer (1991) focused variously on biological and physiological processes, cognitive and mental processes, individual differences, inter-individual behaviour, and cross-cultural or between-group behaviours. Fredline and Faulkner (2002b) also defined a social representation theory that events are recognised on the basis of past experiences and prior knowledge serves as the reference point for new encounters. Fredline, Jago and Deery (2003) noted that in the recent decades, substantial work has been conducted examining residents' perceptions of the impacts of tourism, but events are examined to a much lesser extent. LeBlanc, Robinson, Picard & Long (2004) said the growing popularity of travelling to attend festivals and events has prompted researchers to examine this form of tourism. Measuring residents' perceptions is a pluralistic process. Longitudinal studies were also conducted by many researchers. For example, Soutar and McLeod (1989, 1993) studied residents' perceptions of social impacts of the America's Cup Defence over a four-year period. Mihalik and Simonetta (1998, 1999) also did the same thing on the 1996 Atlanta Summer Olympic Games. These researchers focused on the comparison of residents' perceptions before and after given events.

These insights into residents' perceptions have a close relationship with MICE social impacts. Burns and Mules (1986) established a framework to test the social costs related to MICE such as traffic congestion, time lost due to traffic detours, property damage, vehicle thefts, noise and accidents. Sherwood, Jago and Deery (2004) described social benefit as 'psychic income', which represents the 'feel good' impact that local residents feel as a result of the event being staged in their city despite some of the inconveniences. Recently there has been a conscious effort by many local governments to provide social welfare for the residents through MICE. The reason is that whether event impacts are classified as positive or negative is often focused on the evaluations made by local residents. Andereck and Vogt (2000) stated that it is residents who ultimately have a voice in concluding which tourism impacts are acceptable and which are problematic. Residents tend to focus on whether an event enhanced their life quality. The most sensitive life quality standards considered mostly by residents are living costs. Although arguably MICE effects on the daily life quality of residents is often far from obvious and may only exert a subtle influence, residents are still sensitive to some aspects such as price changes, especially in the case of international

MICE. The '2007 China's Regional Financial Operation' report of the People's Bank of China shows that residents and businesses have strong feelings towards change, especially inflation. In 2007 inflation was perceived as reaching 29.9% (when the percentage increase of food was 36%), which was significantly higher than the 2007 CPI increase of 4.8% over 2006. The most direct influence often caused by the MICE industry is on real estate prices. Soutar and McLeod (1989) highlighted the social issues that impact on residents, particularly in regard to housing. Sherwood et al. (2004) were also concerned that the planning and staging of big events such as the Olympic Games always raise issues related to changes such as resident displacement, increased rental and housing prices and forced relocation. Along with the heated real estate market in China, other kinds of real estate transactions have emerged. According to Su and Hu (2007), many cities' residents think some real estate prices have increased because some real estate developers specifically seek to host MICE to increase property values. There may also be other less tangible benefits associated with the staging of MICE that may affect residents' perceptions, like direct or indirect employment opportunities, facility and infrastructure development, entertainment and social opportunities, and pride and self-esteem brought about by being the focus of attention.

MICE sometimes means a general disruption to normal daily routines of residents, so residents are more concerned about MICE events than are the tourists. As Richardson and Long (1991) mentioned, residents' leisure needs and wants must take precedence over development for tourists. However, it is clear that there are invariably some negative impacts associated with an event. Some specific MICE impacts affect the whole of local society with environmental damage, breaks in local residents' normal life patterns, etc. May (1995) noted that there were a range of environmental concerns in regard to the staging of the Winter Olympics in fragile alpine areas such as destruction of vegetation and pollution. Under this type of pressure, local authorities must shoulder the responsibility to prevent environmental damage if they wish to create a long-term sustainable MICE policy.

Thousands of MICE are hosted in different cities in China every year, which cover all types of events. However, those MICE mainly focus on the outside attendees rather than local residents. Local residents are ignored by many MICE organisers, even for some small-sized MICE. Mok and DeFranco (1999) emphasized that very limited research has been reported on the links between cultural values of the Chinese people and their preferences as consumers. Hiller (1995) described MICE as a special kind of tourism as theoretically they represent a separate factor for attending rather than the characteristics of the destination itself. Until very recently, many Chinese residents were only attracted to a few MICE mainly based on aspects of daily lives like cars, real estate, and furniture shows. However, China has a large population and the potential for local resident attendance is large. According to Chongqing governmental statistical analysis released by Chongqing municipal people's government (2007), more than 500,000 Hong Kong urban and rural residents were attracted to the Hong Kong Convention and Exhibition Centre, which provided a positive impact on the city economy. In short, attendees at a MICE may often be local residents, and as incomes and leisure time increase, the range of MICE to attract a local domestic market will increase. Such a trend has implications for local residents, not only as attendees, but for those who may not select to attend a specific show, exhibition, conference, or meeting. It is this reason that motivated the current research, the findings of which may lay a benchmark to which future research may be compared when the trends in the Chinese market for MICE are assessed.

2.12 Chapter Summary

This chapter explained the MICE industry in general and its development in different aspects such as environment, social status, economy, and trade. A synopsis of the current Chinese MICE situation was offered, along with a general framework of the country's MICE development strategy. A brief discussion of Chinese MICE development limits was evaluated, and the country's internal competitiveness in the MICE industry explained. The approach to explaining residents' perceptions of Chinese MICE industry was also discussed.

Chapter Three

Methodology

3.1 Introduction

The previous chapters presented a theoretical groundwork and research background that could be used to define the term MICE and the role of residents' perceptions related to MICE impacts. The previous chapters were based on an extensive review of existing literature but it was found that while residents' perceptions of tourism generally is a well-established theme in the tourism literature, there is little literature specific to MICE, particularly in China. In order to deepen understanding and possibly the definition of the term 'MICE', it is essential that residents' perceptions are analysed. This chapter draws on the previous literature to present the methods used to gather and analyse data in this study.

This chapter, therefore, contains the background to the development of the questionnaire from initial 'utopian' thoughts to practical application. The study undertook a conventional mixed methods pattern of an initial qualitative pilot study followed by a self-completion questionnaire to generate quantitative data. The pilot study's interview questions were designed to obtain a better understanding of residents' perceptions. The results of the pilot study were used as the basis for the items included in the final questionnaire of the main study.

3.2   Research Paradigms

◆ Definitions

Kuhn (1970, p. 175) provided an initial definition of a paradigm as 'the entire constellation of beliefs, values, and techniques which is shared by members of a given community, and it denotes one sort of element in that constellation, the concrete puzzle-solution, employed as models or examples, it can replace explicit rules as a basis for the solution of the remaining puzzle of normal science'. Subsequently many researchers have given their own definitions of 'paradigm'. Morgan (2007) defined a paradigm as the consensual set of beliefs and practices that guides a field. Usher (1996) described a research paradigm as being 'an exemplar or exemplary way of working that functions as a model for what and how to do research, what problems to focus on and work on' (p. 13). Some authors provided an easy access to definitions by explaining paradigms as a 'world view', like Rossman and Rallis's (2003) 'worldviews' and 'shared understandings of reality' as synonyms for paradigms.

As a central methodology in the social sciences, qualitative and quantitative methods have long been associated with different paradigmatic approaches. Bazeley (2004) mentioned different assumptions about the nature of knowledge (ontology), the means of generating it (epistemology), and the methodology. The explicit explanation of a constructionist approach from Denzin and Lincoln (1994, pp. 13-14) 'assumes a relativist ontology (there are multiple realities), a subjectivist epistemology (knower and subject created understandings), and a naturalistic (in the natural world) set of methodological procedures'.

◆ Ontological

Ontology represents a particular view of reality held about the situation in question. There are two main ontologies suggested: either one reality or multiple realities. Guba (1990) argued for an ontological position of accepting no one 'reality out there', but rather an acceptance of multiple interpretations of any given event, with inquiry having the major task of working toward some consensus among the holders of different constructions.

Robert (2000) had a similar opinion that reality consists of an individual's mental constructions of the objects with which they engage in, and that the engagement impacts on the observer and the situation being observed.

◆ Epistemological

Robert (2000) defined 'epistemology' as the relationship assumed to be present between the knower and what is known or being sought to be known. It deals with assumptions about truth and non-truth. Burrell and Morgan (1979) suggested that the relationship could derive from accepting that knowledge can be either viewed as objectively knowable, or in contrast, only subjectively. Guba and Lincoln (1989) supported this suggestion.

Burrell and Morgan (1979) and Guba and Lincoln (1989) agreed that in social inquiry the subjective nature of knowledge produces a subjective relationship between elements of the inquiry, notably between the researcher and the subject of the research and/or respondents.

◆ Methodological

Research methodologies represent complex socio-historical evolutions within the social sciences ranging from reductionism to reflexive sensibilities (Tuchman, 1994). According to Jenning (2001), the methods of data collection would include participant observation, in-depth interviews, case studies, focus groups, and appreciative inquiry. Neuman (1997) said qualitative methods display the construction of social reality and that cultural meaning form part of the interactive processes which also include the researcher.

Although certain methodologies are always associated with one particular research approach or paradigm, Dzurec and Abraham (1993, p. 75) still suggested that 'the objectives, scope, and nature of inquiry are consistent across methods and across paradigms'. A general summary of paradigm and different approaches is shown in Table 3.1.

Table 3.1   Paradigm and Different Approaches

Term	Explanation
Paradigm	Ontology: The reality that the researcher investigates (Asks: What is reality? What is it that we know?)
	Epistemology: The relationship between reality and the researcher (Asks: What constitutes knowledge/science?)
	Methodology: The technique used by the researcher to investigate that reality (Asks: How do we gain knowledge?)
Constructivism	Relativist/Critical relativism: Reality is relative (multiple subjective realities co-exist) Is constructed in people's minds Locally and specifically constructed according to what people believe it to be
	Transactional/Subjectivist: Findings are created
	Primarily qualitative methods
Positivism	Realist/Naive realism/Apprehension: Reality is real Is knowable, the true nature can be discovered Governed by unchangeable natural laws
	Dualist/Objectivist: Findings are true
	Primarily quantitative methods
Post-positivism	Critical realism: Reality is real Imperfectly/Probabilistically Knowable through probabilities Triangulation of source is required to try to know it
	Modified dualist/Objectivist: (subjective knower and objective world) Findings are probably true
	Triangulation of quantitative and qualitative methods
Critical theory	Critical/Historical realist: Virtual reality (multiple realities co-exist) Can be known Shaped by social, economic, ethnic, political, cultural, and gender values, crystallised over time in real and created historic structures
	Transactional/Subjectivist: Findings are mediated by values
	Any with a critical stance. Dialogical/Dialectical

Source: Al-Masroori. (2006).

◆ Constructionist Paradigm

A constructionist paradigm/constructivism builds on 'constructivist' theories based on a fully integrated social perspective asserting that experience is not simply transmitted from destination or activities to a tourist, but actively constructed by the mind of the tourist. Constructionist research methods are qualitative, interpretive, and concerned with meaning.

Most constructionist adherents support the concept of multiple realities such as Jenning (2001), who maintained that the interpretive social science paradigm considers the world as being constituted of such multiple realities. According to their epistemological basis, constructionist researchers focus on the subjective understandings and experiences of individuals or groups and then show how such understandings and experiences are derived from and fed into larger discourses. From the constructionist point of view, the researcher will look at typical phrases, arguments, and stories that can come to the fore.

However, the essence of residents' perceptions is not a simple theory, which can be explained by only one method. The limitations or weaknesses of the constructionist paradigm such as personal bias and a tendency to select material from mass data may impede the researcher from getting 'completed' results. The researcher's opinion may influence the question and material, choosing what may influence the accuracy of the research result. A limited knowledge on the parts of the researcher cannot cover or explain complete meanings presented by tourists. Constructivists are therefore often rightly accused of being idealists with little to say about the material world.

◆ Positivism

Positivism has tended to be the prevailing paradigm in many areas of social science research, especially with the advent of powerful and accessible statistical packages. Mill (1866) described it thus:

Whoever regards all events as parts of a constant order, each one being the invariable consequent of some antecedent conditions, or combination of conditions, accepts fully the positive mode of thought. (p. 15)

All theories in which the ultimate standard of institutions and rules of actions [is] the happiness of mankind, and observation and experience the guides ... are entitled to the name Positive. (p. 69)

Runder (1966) also defined it as a systematically related set of statements, including some law-like generalisations, which are empirically testable. Kenneth and Howe (1988) said positivism is the view that scientific knowledge is the paragon of rationality. Positivism is commonly associated with quantitative methods, which are successfully used in large portions of research.

◆ Post-positivism

This methodological paradigm has the same aim as a positivist framework of 'explanation' does, and it is again important to consider ontological and epistemological concerns. Guba and Lincoln (1994) viewed post-positivism as a variant of the 'received' positivist position, the difference being that a view that truth is complex and may never be fully apprehended, but there remains nonetheless a consensual truth independent of the researcher which therefore may be 'discovered'.

◆ Critical Theory

Critical theory is a view of society and social theory. The aim of critical theory as Guba and Lincoln (1994) stated is the critique and transformation of the social, political, cultural, economic, ethic, and gender structures that constrain and exploit humankind. Hoffman (1987) noted critical theory as a self-understanding and self-reflection that provides a critique of the existing social order, and it points to a capacity for change and for the realisation of human potential.

◆ Applications to Residents' Perceptions

In order to get to the essence of resident experiences, any single paradigm needs the support of others to help researchers obtain a better understanding. For example, researchers doing 1-on-1 interviews may find that respondents provide a large range of information. This information may vary between the respondents that have been interviewed. It is better for researchers to analyse the essence of the interview data and to determine subsequent questions. By using these questions, researchers can obtain useful or meaningful results quickly. In short, a pragmatic perspective may occur where the researcher adopts paradigms as determined by the nature of the research problem rather than defining a problem to fit a specific research approach. Indeed multiple approaches may handle some problems better than taking a single paradigm. In this study, the qualitative method within a constructionist paradigm obtained data about residents' perceptions of MICE impacts in their 'real world' while a quantitative method with a positivist paradigm and a questionnaire-based survey was also used to permit some generalisation.

➡ 3.3 Alternative Research Methods

There are therefore numerous choices of methods for undertaking tourism research. In order to cover the multiple dimensions of perceptions of MICE impacts and differences among sub-groups of gender, age, income, educational background, etc., different research methods were considered. Some often-used methods are shown in Table 3.2.

Human perception is always a complex topic in tourism research. Williams (2001) argued that the tourist experience is a 'moving target' that means many things to many people, a complex, multidimensional, multifaceted human compound, including irreducible biological and cultural components, which arise or emerge in various socio-relational contexts. The experiential essence of the resident experience, in its intangible, un-tradable form is sometimes as transient thought, moving or feeling with emotion. So in order to unearth the deep sense of the tourist experience, to deem it as a feeling is a complex rather than a static and undimensioned thing. For this reason a significant debate exists as to the respective merits of qualitative and quantitative research methods.

Table 3.2   Often-used Research Methods and Analysis Technologies

Method or Technology	Explanation
In-depth interview and random check	Qualitative study
Content analysis	Analyse qualitative data by using quantitative method
Event analysis under society analysis method and theory	Anthropological approach, contextual approaches, critical functionalism, cultural functionalist perspective, Durkheimian approaches, drama to logical perspective, economic functionalist perspective, ethnographic perspective, neo-Marxist approaches, political instrumentalist perspective, phenomenological and structural perspective
Event effect research technology	Extract the true influence of event by using quantitative method, economics method, social impact assessment (SIA). Using systemic and comprehensive method to analyse the correlation existing between the event and benefit relationship among stakeholders
Statistics and sampling research technology	Quantity research method, statistical research method, cluster analysis, multiple discriminate analysis, multidimensional scaling (MDS)
Decision-making research IPA method	Importance–Performance (IP) analysis, IP map analysis
Triangulation study	Verification method by using multiple data sources
Secondary data: use of Internet sources	Searching research articles, find out the event development situation in different countries: low cost, fast, multiple ways (like email, voice mail, etc.) to conduct the data collection

Source: Dai. (2005).

◆ Qualitative Method

As noted above, qualitative research tends to use the constructivist paradigm, yet it can also serve as a post-positivist methodology. In consideration of the diversity of residents' (or tourists') experiences, a tourism researcher may choose this approach to unearth the essence of residents' experiences. Initially, the range of perspectives on emotion can generally be quantified as lying on a continuum between the 'social constructionist' standpoint and that of the positivist position. McIntosh (1998) said, from an experiential view, that tourism may therefore seem 'to defy' empirical research. In particular, through quantification, the subtleties of the nature of tourism as a subjective and personal experience of places and events are possibly lost. While some information acquisition can come from others, it is often only by experiencing the learning in person that valuable knowledge is generated at a personal level. Obtaining the tourist experience is a personal process; the tourists' level of personal development, interests, concerns, personal involvement, and current knowledge directly relate to what they experience. Thus, not everyone will construct the same knowledge even when provided with what appear to be very similar learning experiences. For example, residents may answer a question about the experience of being at the top of the Eiffel Tower, Paris for the first time such as being 'amazed' or 'surprised', but those feelings may have been gotten from the knowledge of reports of past expectation. Residents promised 'experiences' sometimes can achieve this only by staged 'authenticity', which is not a single quality derived from careful attention to historical detail but rather a product of the complex ways in which tourists respond to cultural sites as intellectual and sensual experiences. Just as Ryan (2004) described, experiences may be evaluated against images derived from the Discovery Channel.

In qualitative research, some general research practices such as interviewing, transcription of conversational and other data, data management and analysis (including the use of software programmes), report writing and using research outcomes to influence policy are given up-to-date coverage, consistent with postmodern flavour (Denzin & Lincoln, 1994). So it is also arguably better for the researcher not to behave as 'the expert', but rather take a 'not-knowing' position.

◆ Quantitative Method

Quantitative research is an inquiry into an identified problem, generally based on testing a theory although it can also be exploratory in nature, measuring with numbers, and analyse using statistical techniques. The goal of quantitative methods is to determine whether (a) it is possible to make generalisations and (b) the predictive generalisations of a theory hold true. Babbie (1992) defined quantitative research as the numerical representation and manipulation of observations to describe and explain the phenomena that those observations reflect. Quantitative methods express that public opinion and data can be weighted to better reflect population when the characteristics of the observed population are known. This process represents precision with more reliability and validity. Francisco, Butterfoss and Capwell (2001) made the following observations about quantitative methods:

- Data from large numbers of people lead to a greater breadth of understanding (as opposed to the depth of understanding from qualitative methods).
- Strong inferences are possible, especially when tight experimental control is achieved.
- These approaches are often more systematic than other methods, which makes findings more likely to be replicated.
- But they usually do not include an assessment of the 'meaning' of the data but focus on the strength of relationships between significant variables.

Quantitative research is used to answer a number of questions, which includes issues mentioned by Francisco et al. (2001), namely how many people need to be involved to create a statistically significant difference, how big is the change in behaviour, by how much has the incidence or prevalence of a certain problem changed, and how satisfied people are with a programme, etc. These questions are related to analytical methods with large numbers of respondents. However, Bauer (2000) noted that a quantitative approach representing a purely descriptive study is accordingly considered simple and less interesting than other models of study.

A quantitative method is based on numeric data algorithms generally considered incompatible with qualitative research objectives. Dootson (1995) said quantitative research only results in numerical values amenable to statistical analysis. However 'statistics' is always a hard language to learn, which segments researchers when they cannot measure it, when they cannot express it in numbers, or when their knowledge is meager and unsatisfactory (Merton, Sills & Stigler, 1984). And also there are hypotheses existing in the research process, restricting methods to provable range only under current variables.

◆ Mixed Methods: Triangulation

The exploration of residents' understanding of MICE impacts is fundamental to this research. It is well known that social relationships are often complex and contradictory. Leo Tolstoy wrote in his novel *Resurrection* (1899) 'people are like the river, all the river water is the same... but each has some places narrow, some places wide, some water fast, and some water clear... people as well'. The focus between quantitative and qualitative methods sharpens differences; one is based on the 'number' via survey data and the other on 'words' via interviews respectively. But it is commonly argued, that to obtain more impartial data, it is better to present quantitative and qualitative methods as complementary modes of inquiry. Thus, this study chose to use mixed methods, at least to a minor degree within the time and resources available to collect data combining both qualitative and quantitative methods.

Triangulation is one of the convergent methodologies, which is treated as being synonymous as mixed methods, which are compared with others in Table 3.3.

Table 3.3   Differences Between Qualitative, Quantitative, and Mixed Methods

Research Approach	Knowledge Claim	Strategy of Inquiry	Method
Qualitative	Constructivist and emancipator assumptions	Ethnographic and narrative design	Field observations; open-ended interviewing
Quantitative	Post-positive assumption	Experimental design; survey	Measuring attitudes; rating behaviours
Mixed methods	Pragmatic assumption	Mixed method (triangulation) design	Closed-ended measure; open-ended observation

Source: Creswell. (2003, p. 20).

Many researchers have mentioned the deficiencies and weaknesses that arise from the use of a single research method and have found such an approach as inadequate, especially for some complex and dynamic phenomena such as measuring people's perceptions or attitudes. Based on research difficulties, methodological triangulation is often mentioned as qualitative and quantitative methods should be viewed as complementary rather than as rivals, and they are often utilised by researchers in the research process.

Another rationale for their complementarity is that qualitative methods can provide previously unobserved phenomena, which can avoid wrong hypothetical occurrences found in quantitative methods. Decrop (1999) said the subordinate and exploratory nature of qualitative research is explicitly recognised: qualitative techniques are used to provide information for developing further quantitative research.

Sarantakos (1998) provided four reasons to choose mixed methods in the research:

- to obtain a variety of information on the same issue;
- to use the strengths of each method to overcome the deficiencies of the other;
- to achieve a higher degree of validity and reliability; and
- to overcome the deficiencies of single-method studies.

For example, researchers can conduct a series of qualitative interviews, which can accentuate the key points from respondents' mind. Based on the importance factors derived from the interview process, a more accurate quantitative survey might be developed. On the other hand, if the quantitative process faces problems in a particular aspect of a study, the problems also can be solved by further research through in-depth interviews. It was this approach that formed the current study.

However, to combine two methods is not an easy task. Jick (1979) mentioned that many researchers failed to indicate how this prescribed triangulation is actually performed and accomplished. Morgan (1998) said combining methods is essentially a technical problem and also there are some conflicts among different paradigms under the two methods. He emphasised that most applications of qualitative and quantitative methods rely on very different assumptions about the nature of knowledge; hence, the kinds of information that they produce are often incommensurate. Although there still exits a preference to use mixed methods, it is important to realise that most of the debate of paradigm conflict is not about the practical task of creating research design. Some authors like Creswell (1994) and Guba and Lincoln (1994) have advocated operating with a single paradigm to avoid the difficulties arising from the use of possibly competing paradigms of research. Mitchell (1986) recommended that the research question should be plainly focused, and the strengths and weaknesses of each method appraised so that they supplement one another. The methods should then be chosen according to the purpose of the research and the type of the data. To solve the conflicts between research findings of the quantitative and qualitative methods, Guba and Lincoln (1985) have developed four precise criteria for qualitative inquiry that parallel the quantitative terminology, namely:

- Credibility (internal validity): How truthful are particular findings?
- Transferability (external validity): How applicable are the research findings to another setting or group?
- Dependability (reliability): Are the results consistent and reproducible?
- Comparability (objectivity): How neutral are the findings (in terms of whether they are reflective of the informants and the inquiry, and not a product of the researcher's bias and prejudice)?

3.4 General Research Process

The decision for selecting the mixed methods approach is always difficult, thus it generally is based on the research purpose. Sometimes the mixed methods (triangulation) approach combines interviews, questionnaires, observations, and retrospective projects, and is deemed suit for digging residents' deep perception. A qualitative in-depth interview is always adapted in the first stage, and a following quantitative questionnaire is then developed. Step by step, the general process is undertaken in the data collection procedure as shown in Figure 3.1.

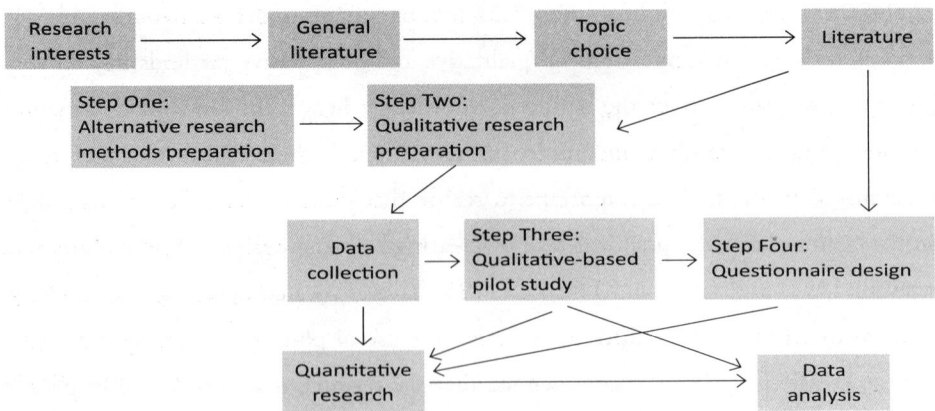

Figure 3.1   Research Process

◆ Step One: Alternative Research Methods Preparation

The first step was to identify potential research methods and problem definition. The question was which method would be the most appropriate for the research problem and how it could be performed. Yin (1994) identified three conditions for determining the appropriate strategy for research: the form/type of research problem and questions to be asked; the extent of control the researcher has over behavioural events; and the degree of focus on contemporary as opposed to historical events. Dependent on the previous study of literature, purposes and goals, advantages and limitations, and location and duration of the research, the mixed methods (triangulation) approach was adapted.

◆ Step Two: Qualitative Research Preparation

A qualitative study was adopted to elicit responses from residents while using a semi-structured questionnaire to prompt conversational data. The questionnaire provided a framework to ensure some commonalities of subject matter across various respondents. One major purpose was to attempt to design sets of interview questions for later use in the quantitative survey. The literature review discussed the basis for compiling attributes that could be used in defining interview questions. Based on the insights provided by the literature, several dimensions such as economic, social, political, city image, and environment impacts were used as themes. Interpersonal conversation is always a flexible activity. However, the literature review revealed a lack of actual resident input about MICE and the impacts, and practical suggestions were often limited to different locations, cultures, and social structures.

◆ Step Three: Qualitative-based Pilot Study—Execute Interviews and Refine Research Problems

This collection process was complex and implied a post-positivistic perspective of a 'truth' independent of the researcher. It became, however, a decontextualised 'truth' for it was separated from the initial series of conversational interplays by a subsequent process of data analysis, but the credibility of the interpretation became understood within another context, that of the wider tourism literature, and of shared recognition of the categories that were formulated and discussed later. Conversation as a research tool implies many nuances. The researcher and respondent are potential equals in the research process; the respondent can control the research agenda as much as the researcher, yet it is the researcher who will offer the interpretive act. Some sensitive topics are avoided unless respondents are particularly interested. Feminist writers have redefined an interview as a dialogue that engages in openness and the sharing of emotion, and as a narrative that can challenge the concepts of scientific positivism (see, e.g., Fontana & Frey, 2000). However, in this instance, the research methodology sought an 'unbalanced conversation' in the sense that the researcher sought responses and adopted a perspective where the researcher's role was to prompt increasing details of response and recall from the respondents (Dall'Alba, 1994; Bowden, 1994).

◆ Step Four: Questionnaire Design

The questionnaire design is a key part of the research, and hence it was important to identify items that measure potentially important variables. The questionnaire was designed initially based on the literature, but was amended in the light of results from the qualitative pilot study.

In general, the pilot samples provided very positive feedback such as identifying topics of interest, comfortable places for interviews, understandable statements, and clear instructions to complete the questionnaire. During the pilot interview, the respondents also raised some useful points related to the event industry, which resulted in the following areas of the questionnaire:

- Event-attending experience affects attitudes to events;
- Media promotion of exposition;
- Benefits from events;
- Government financial investments: Are they worth it? Are there better alternative uses of the money?
- City capability at both domestic and international levels;
- City competitive advantages;

● City changes (positive and negative); and

● Personal life quality changes.

Considering the possible low responses to the questionnaire survey due to the long questionnaire, the use of 'interesting' factors was seen as a key to get respondents' attention. The points stated above were all added to the final questionnaire.

With an increasing reliance on mass involvement in MICE as part of Hangzhou's economic policies, residents' perceptions have become an issue for consideration by the city and MICE promotion authorities. The array of variables identified, the permutations of their influence on residents' perceptions and the range of tourism development situations that might be examined highlight the complexity of social impacts on tourism. Several typical operationalisation variables included the items shown in Table 3.4 with reference to the literature:

Table 3.4 Reference to Related Literature

Questionnaire Factor	Related Literature
City infrastructure: Event facilities like event centres, event parks, etc.; supportive facilities like hotels, shopping places, restaurants; etc.	Oppermann (1996a); Weber & Ladkin (2003); Rogers (1998); Kim, Morrison & Mills (2003); Fenich (1995); Ghitelman (1995); Law (1993); etc.
Social: Entertainment opportunities; maintenance of public facilities like parks and roads around the city; traffic; road quality like highway building, road reconstruction; public services like medical, law, logistics, security; and importance of employment status; etc.	Dwyer, Forsyth & Spurr (2005); Zhou (2007); Glancey (1984); Humphreys & Plummer (1995); Newman (1999); etc.
Political: Government's effort in the event process; policies and regulations; the relationship between government and business; etc.	Ryan & Gu (2009); Thomas & Wood (2004); Wilson, Fesenmaier, Fesenmaier & Vanes (2001); etc.
Event management: Event-related price control	Peters & Pikkemaat (2005); Getz & Frisby (1988); Laybourn (2004); Morris (1994); Yoon, Spencer, Holecek & Kim (2000); etc.

(continued)

Questionnaire Factor	Related Literature
Economic: The whole city economy level; local business opportunities; etc.	Qian & Wong (2000); Jackson (2006); Rogerson (2005); Cui (2006); etc.
Environment: Damage to the natural environment; city pollution levels; etc.	Carey (1994); McCabe, Poole, Weeks & Leiper (2000); etc.
Life quality: The property values and rental costs; the price of goods and services; total living costs; etc.	Pearce & Stringer (1991); Soutar & McLeod (1989, 1993); Sherwood, Jago & Deery (2004); etc.
City brand: City brand image at both national and international levels; city's level of attraction to other cities' people; city's level of attraction to foreign people; etc.	Hall (1992); Rod (2003); Grabmeier (1997); Morgan & Pritchard (1998); Pike (2002); Selby (2004); Law (1993); Holcomb (1997b); Sassen & Roost (1999); etc.
MICE competition: MICE competition at both national and international levels; cities' competition capability; etc.	Dwyer & Mistilis (1997); Bramezza (1996); Richards & Wilson (2004); Berg & Braun (1999); Law (1993); Mills (1991); Mullins (1992); etc.
City competitive capacity: City basic service level	Hu & Hiemstra (1996); Go & Govers (1999); Johnson & Thomas (1993); Murphy (1985); Zelinsky (1994); Oppermann (1996a); Crouch & Ritchie (1998); Weber (2001); etc.

The issue was how to operationalise the above list of variables. So the principles of the questionnaire and research direction are illustrated in Figure 3.2.

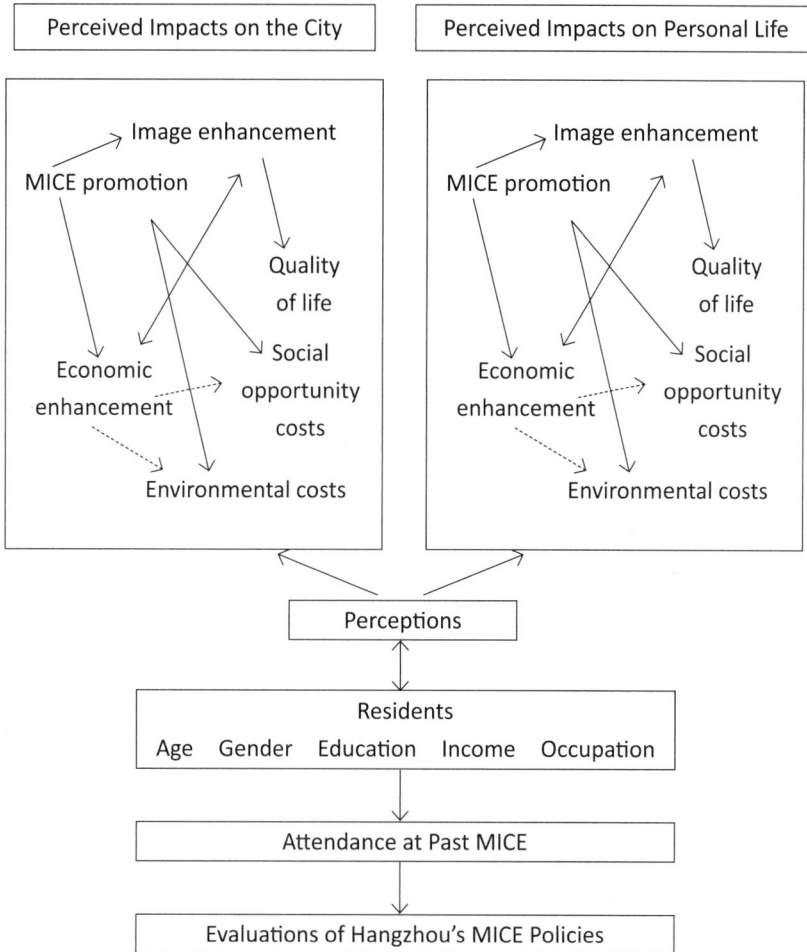

| Perceived Impacts on the City | Perceived Impacts on Personal Life |

Image enhancement

MICE promotion

Quality of life

Economic enhancement

Social opportunity costs

Environmental costs

Image enhancement

MICE promotion

Quality of life

Economic enhancement

Social opportunity costs

Environmental costs

Perceptions

Residents

Age   Gender   Education   Income   Occupation

Attendance at Past MICE

Evaluations of Hangzhou's MICE Policies

Figure 3.2   Framework for Research Design

Figure 3.2 shows that the 'residents' are characterised by socio-demographic variables such as age, gender, education, income, and occupation. The residents have two sets of perceptions about Hangzhou and the city's MICE policies—the first relates to the impacts of these on the city in which they reside, and the second relates to how these impact on their personal daily life. The policies are designed to enhance the image of the city and its economic development—a process that is mutual and complementary. Image enhancement also creates assets that improve the quality of life for both residents and visitors through enhancing, conserving, and restoring attractions such as the West Lake and the development of restaurants, cafes, and retail and entertainment facilities.

But the MICE promotion comes at a cost. First, money spent on MICE promotion and asset development has a special opportunity cost—it is not being spent on social projects such as further development of education or combating crime. Second, the development of MICE and the growing number of visitors have impacts on the natural, urban, and social environment in terms of traffic congestion, air pollution, increasing property price, and social disruption. Of course, in the longer run, it is hoped that subsequent economic enhancement will generate the resources that will permit these problems to be addressed— hence, in some form of 'trickle-down' economic theory, the dotted lines in Figure 3.2 indicate a relationship between economic enhancement and these costs.

It seems legitimate to distinguish between a perception of impacts of MICE on the city and impacts of those policies on the residents themselves—but in assessing the impacts of the MICE policies on the individual it seems legitimate to assume that the same pattern of considerations will be used for both city and 'self' evaluations. However, while saying that the same variables come into play, this does not imply that the same weightings will occur. For example, the residents may attach more importance to the quality of life factors when thinking of themselves than when considering from the city perspective.

It also needs to be recognised that the categories of variables identified in Figure 3.2 do not possess fixed boundaries. For example, while increasing property prices and rents might be perceived as social costs, they also impact on the quality of life.

Finally, Figure 3.2 also inserts one more variable before residents come to an assessment of the MICE policies—and that is their personal history in attending MICE. Attendance of MICE is in part dependent on their own socio-demographics and life stage, and hence these variables may also be directly related to an evaluation of MICE. This last observation thus leads to the following testable propositions:

Proposition One
Socio-demographic variables have impact on residents' perceptions of MICE at the city and personal levels, and on evaluations of Hangzhou's MICE policies.

It is to be noted that the term 'proposition' is used rather than 'hypothesis'. The latter term implies quantifiable relationships are thought to exist for testing. The literature review reveals a deficiency generally about residents' perceptions of MICE and very specifically almost nothing about the Chinese situation, so at this stage it is proposed that a relationship exists, but no specific hypothesis of quantifiable relationships exists to be tested.

Proposition Two

There will be differences between residents' perceptions of the impacts of MICE policies when they are asked to consider (a) impacts on Hangzhou generally, and (b) impacts on personal daily life.

Proposition Three

There will be differences in perceptions that can be caught in psychometric measurements that will enable different clusters to be discerned, whereby some will be supportive of MICE policies and others less so, such differences being determined by the evaluations of social and environmental costs as against economic gains. In short, there is an inherent tension between the economic, social, and environmental aspects within the current state of Hangzhou as a fast-developing city in a fast-developing nation.

Proposition Four

A history of past attendance at MICE will be a variable that shapes support for MICE development and evaluations of the MICE policies.

◆ Step Five: Data Collection (Quantitative Survey)

The data collection focused on local Hangzhou residents and other people who had lived in Hangzhou for more than five years. The participants were also selected to represent a varied range of ages, household incomes, and education levels. The surveys were completed using a convenience sampling technique. This involved speaking to participants in gardens, offices, shops, and other public areas. Many social networks provided considerable support during the research such as residential committees, hotels, companies and even some hospitals. Data were mainly collected through three ways: respondents each filled in a self-completion questionnaire that was handed to them; the researcher asked respondents the questions according to the questionnaire and the responses were written down by the researcher; and some respondents filled the questionnaire together with some discussion. The data were entered initially into Microsoft Excel with the Chinese open questions translated into English. SPSS 16.0 was used for the main analysis as will be described in the following chapters. The original textual data were analysed using content analysis method aided by CatPac.

3.5 Chapter Summary

This chapter identified methodology used in this book. This research was mainly in the positivist tradition, and used a triangulation (mixed) research method. This chapter justified the use of the mixed methods as the most appropriate for this study.

Chapter Four

Pilot Study: Qualitative Research Analysis

▶ 4.1 Introduction

This chapter provides a detailed description of the findings from the qualitative research based on interviews with 40 residents of Hangzhou, China. The analysis was conducted by an initial reading of the text followed by a subsequent use of the software package 'CatPac'. This package is based upon artificial neural network analysis and identifies patterns between words based on their location in the text. Like many other such packages, it is useful in enforcing a disciplined approach on the researcher since the process requires 'data cleaning' as the researcher creates a series of files that accounts for differences in the use of tenses, of singular or plural form, of active or passive voice, and of synonyms and antonyms. As the process proceeds, categories within the text are formed and links between the text become clearer. The software also produces dendrograms at any stage of the research, and in addition the associated package 'Thought View' produces diagrammatic representations of the links of concepts. For the purposes of this chapter, simplified versions of the diagrams are used based on elicited categories formed from the text. The usefulness of this latter package is that in addition to simply identifying thematic categories, it provides evidence of the patterns of links between the categories.

The influence factors are divided into four constructions: 1) motivation; 2) media involvement; 3) MICE impacts; 4) MICE competition between cities.

➡ 4.2 Motivation

The interview was started by a question that asked respondents if they had attended MICE events and shows, and if so, they were asked to specify the type. Just over half of the sample (*n*=26) indicated that they had, while the most common reason for not going was not a lack of interest but a lack of time, or a perceived lack of an interesting event to attend. Thus two respondents replied simply, 'No, no time', while another stated, 'No, no time and no interesting shows'. Of those that had gone to an event or a show, three categories emerged, these being (a) a 'frequent attendee' of MICE, perhaps because of occupation or business, (b) a more 'selective attendee' who went solely out of a specific interest, but who had seemingly been to a number of events, conferences or shows, and (c) the 'occasional attendee'. The subject area of shows and events mentioned ranged from academic conferences, car shows, agricultural shows, home and housing shows, beauty events, to exhibitions in museums of arts and crafts. Car shows were the most commonly mentioned as trade-related shows.

Many tourism researchers have recognised that tourists' motivation is rarely a single factor (see, e.g., Crompton & McKay, 1997), and can include social, learning, cultural reasons, amusement, etc. MICE attendees' motivations are not equally simple. In order to continue promoting MICE, it is important for MICE organisers and tourism marketing people to understand the multiple and complex dimensions used by attendees. Noticeably, motivations may not be similar between local residents and visiting attendees. Popular MICE selection is directly triggered by attendees' desire to meet a need. Getz (1991) suggested the basic needs met by MICE can be classified as physical, interpersonal, social, and personal.

From this study, 'selective attendees' selected events based on their interests and personal life factors. The popularity of car shows was caused by the enthusiasm for car ownership. In the past, a vehicle was viewed as a luxurious item, owned only by officials or rich people. However, along with economic development, many Chinese people not only have more money but also a higher desire to own vehicles. That is also the reason many international car manufacturers have invested in factories in China or cooperated with

Chinese local manufacturers, which has lowered car prices to the level that people can afford. Additionally the Chinese government is encouraging people to purchase more cars to stimulate the domestic vehicle market. Consequently Chinese private car ownership has reached many milestones. According to statistics (Dong, 2003), from 2000 to 2002, cars owned by Chinese people numbered 16,089,100 in 2000, 18,020,400 in 2001, and 20,531,700 in 2002. Thus the average annual growth rate for 2001 and 2002 was 12% and 13.94%. The growth of demand for private cars has accelerated further recently, meaning China became the world's second largest car market only behind USA in 2003. Xinhua News Agency (2006) provided a convincing evidence of development of car ownership in China: in the five years before 2006 the average annual growth rate of China's auto consumption was 24.2%, which was much higher than the global average annual vehicle growth rate of 4.4%, and in 2005 the number of China's domestic cars sold reached 5,700,000. Thus the MICE/car shows and associated attendance have a direct relationship with people's desire and needs and help people's decision-making processes in purchasing. Thus, while attendance at MICE is an individual behaviour, it is influenced by the external socio-economic context. A similar situation also occurred in the real estate market, and various real estate shows were hosted in many cities and even in some small towns. According to China Exhibition (2007), previously Beijing only hosted real estate shows twice a year, but in 2006 this number increased to 13 and in 2007 from March to May, Beijing hosted six different real estate shows in total. Nearly all other cities have a similar situation and thus the media call it 'all-buyers phenomenon'.

As mentioned previously, MICE is not a single business, but is combined with many business elements like accommodations, restaurants, entertainments, etc. Within the academic literature there exists at least one conundrum. On the one hand, a common motivation for the development of an event portfolio is the further development of tourism whereby delegates attracted to a conference, festival, trade show or similar event not only engage in expenditure associated with that event, but also may prolong stays in order to visit other attractions and therefore increase the number of tourists visiting attractions otherwise not related to the trade show, conference, etc. However, on the other hand, some research into festivals and sporting events (see, e.g., Ryan & Saleh, 1993; Ryan & Lockyer, 2001) has indicated that in the majority of cases, those going to an event are primarily motivated by a wish to attend that specific event, and there is little visitation to other attractions. Consequently one might expect to find that the present sample would exhibit the same intended behaviours. Generally, this was found not to be the case. Of the 40 respondents, only five said that they would not find time to travel to other attractions in the region of the event. Of the remaining 35, the majority indicated that they would definitely make such visits, or normally did so, while just five indicated that they would usually do so dependent upon time and money available. Thus one respondent stated:

> Yes, I will spend a little time on it, but it depends on the schedule. If the event is in the city where I live, I will not spend time to make such visits. If the event is in another city, I will travel around because I have already paid the transportation fees.

Indicative of the majority opinion were the two respondents who stated:

> Definitely I will do that because otherwise the opportunity (to travel) is hard to come by.
> Yes, I will also do some travel because I do not always have time to go travelling. During the event time one can both do the work and travel, which is good.

Why do people prefer a trip far away but combined with a MICE opportunity rather than a trip close to home? That is a case commonly noted within the Chinese situation. A possible reason for this behaviour is that people may value an opportunity to travel far from home more than the close trip. Thus, to make full use of the transportation fees and the time spent on travel is considered worthwhile if a trip is to a previously unvisited location.

4.3 Media Involvement

The next question specifically sought to know about whether residents were always aware of Hangzhou's events, and if so, what the source of their information was. All respondents knew about the West Lake Expo, and nearly all stated that they received their information through TV and newspapers. The media with their public communication functions and wide coverage are always treated as an important element in event management. What the impact of the media is, in part, a consequence of their capacity to attract both delegates and local attendees. MICE is a business activity that needs image enhancement and promotion to increase its attractiveness and this has a very close relationship with media. Once image and financial planning have been determined, a MICE organiser needs to promote and introduce the event to the potential attendees to get them to the event. The majority of respondents noted the following:

Yes, the government has promoted some events very well through TV and newspapers.

Yes, of course I know some Hangzhou events. Normally from TV, newspapers, etc.

The result shows the major media used by residents by the time of the pilot study were newspapers, TV, and radio, which reflects the major existing media types in China in spite of the growing use of the Internet and apps like WeChat. Zhang (2005) mentioned that by 2002 there were 357 TV stations existing in different cities in total and that in 2005 the average number of TV channels received by a Chinese family was 20. Not only TV but also newspapers and radio occupy an important position in the media. Newspapers, as one of the main types of media, are always involved in the MICE industry. Table 4.1 below shows the involvement level of the three main Hangzhou newspapers during the 2005 West Lake Expo.

Table 4.1　Reports of West Lake Expo by Hangzhou's Main Newspapers During Oct. 16–31, 2005

Name of the Newspaper	Number of Reports
City Express	108
Qianjiang Evening News	109
Hangzhou Daily	172

Source: Zhu. (2006).

There is an observation about the total role of media involvement. Why don't people regard the Internet and WeChat as the main sources of information? During the interview, only a few respondents mentioned new technological media like news websites or WeChat news. Both of these have a large number of users. China Internet Network Information

Center (CNNIC) (2008) reported that by the end of June 2008, the number of Internet users in China reached 253 million, substantially more than that of the US for the first time. Additionally, according to the figures from China International Trade Promotion Committee (2007), Internet promotion is widely used by business attendees. By the time of the pilot study, Chinese MICE organisers still preferred strong traditional media like the print versions of *People's Daily*, or *Economic Daily News* more than other new technological or professional media to attract more attendees. Chinese MICE organisers still had some reliance on the large number of their customers using these traditional media and regard the latter as having a strong influence on people. It is true that traditional media have strictly local and regional appeals. Nonetheless, due to Internet developments, more and more people like to gather information from websites, especially the young generations. Many professional attendees such as business delegates also like using the Internet as one of their main promotion methods. In short, MICE promoters need to mix promotional efforts between media on the basis of the type of events, and the nature of sponsors and delegates. Figure 4.1 shows the effective promotion methods for MICE events as chosen by 160 domestic business attendees.

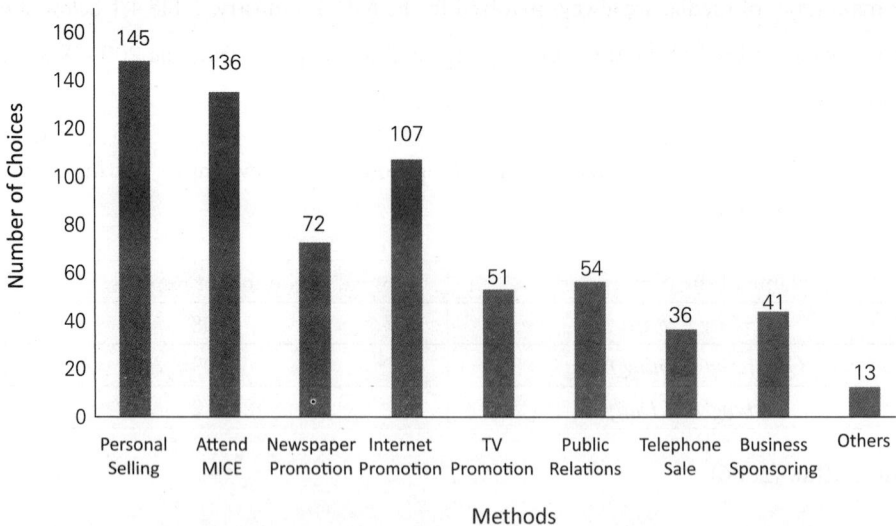

Figure 4.1   **Effective Promotion Methods for MICE Events Chosen by Chinese Domestic Business Attendees**

Source: China International Trade Promotion Committee. (2007).

The reason for restricted new media acceptance by local residents is varied. Not only is it because MICE organisers paid more attention to the traditional media but also people still remained more attracted to TV. Although many websites provided online videos, due to the problems in network speed, picture definition, and unprofessional report, Internet penetration was still low in the MICE context. And the Internet also had many other negative aspects such as doubtful stories or fake data, meaning many people remained suspicious of the Information they got from the web at this stage of Internet development in China. Mobile apps like WeChat were primarily treated as a communication tool rather than a source of information by the time of research.

During the process of completing this book, new technology has been changing the society dramatically especially with the popularization of Internet and smart phones. The new apps such as WeChat have explored new promotion platforms providing not only the information but also the concept of event-based visualisation that combines event-based methodology and visualisation technology. People can get tons of MICE information through Internet and smart phones, and marketers can target their customers much more easily and accurately. MICE industry using modern communication networks is systematically better reported than by other traditional promotion methods. These changes have enhanced MICE industry's development. Thus this is not surprising given the new recognition by MICE industry of the possibilities of new technologies, and the differences brought about by new technologies will be examined in future research.

4.4   MICE Impacts

Taking into account the location of the research, and the previously cited literature, it was expected that residents would be supportive of MICE on the general ground that economic improvement would be generated for the city. However, a reconsideration may be required due to the context of this study and the controversies referred to earlier about free entry to the West Lake, while past evidence also suggests that residents are more cautious about claiming social and environmental benefits, and can reconsider economic gains on the ground as to whether the costs, both financial and others, are too high. Additionally, it was thought possible to prompt respondents to assess to what degree they gain from the effects created by MICE tourism, and eventually obtain an overall assessment based upon an evaluation of these factors filtered through personal value systems. Figure 4.2 indicates these anticipated response sets.

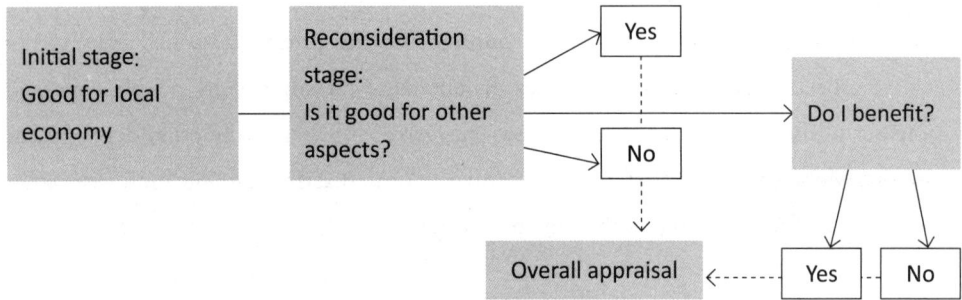

Figure 4.2　Anticipated Sets of Responses

However, how can one really allocate or estimate returns from such events when, as noted, some of the returns are psychological rather than material? In terms of negative impacts, half of the respondents immediately mentioned the worsening traffic. Also, many mentioned a gradual degradation in the environment, and most of these respondents (who also identified worsening traffic) were at pains to mention this additional degradation was an additional and not solely traffic related observation.

Figure 4.3 attempts to summarise the resultant perceptual map derived from the software. The boxes illustrate the responses while the arrows indicate links between the dimensions that comprise attitudes toward perceived negative impacts of this form of tourism. The first observation is the degree of disconnectedness that exists—the components lie united in that they create a negative impact on Hangzhou—but the articulation of their inter-relatedness was not well formed in the responses given.

As axiological and cognitive development occurs over time, any evaluation of MICE by residents might become increasingly well informed. It does appear that Hangzhou residents are reaching a point where claims of city economic development via events seems to have become an inane slogan for local people. Opinions among residents have started to cluster around issues of daily life improvements and others. Transportation in urban areas is highly complex because of the modes involved, the multitude of origins and destinations, and the

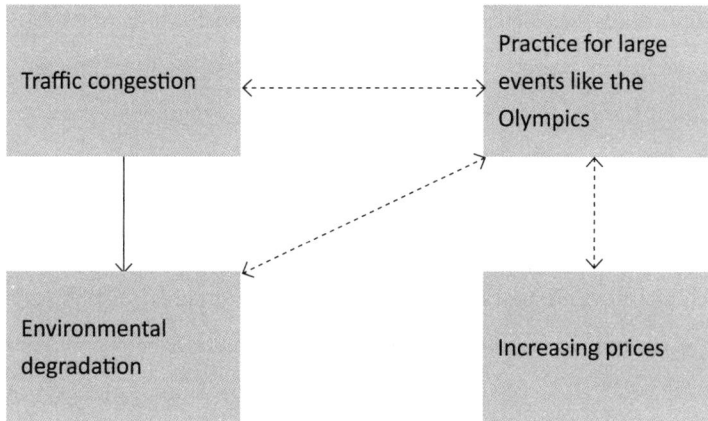

Figure 4.3   Dimensions of Perceived Negative Impacts

amount and variety of traffic. For example, the increasing number of private cars causes traffic congestion, especially during some special periods such as major MICE events. The role of transportation becomes very important during the MICE hosting period, not only attendees need to transport their products but also many visitors need to drive to the destination. More cars and people on the road increase traffic congestion, and residents may easily have inimical emotions. Not only that, before some mega events, the government often needs to improve the city's infrastructure like repairing roads, building new highways and railways, installing new pipes and new road lights, and renovating buildings. These changes worsen the situation of a city's traffic, which often causes inconvenience to the local residents' daily life. It is true that the government has improved a city's transportation through building more roads, but it may not be able to solve the problem completely. If currently there is competition between growing cars and insufficient roads, it is impossible for the latter to win. Currently many cities have become bogged in this situation, even in Beijing which has developed six loop lines, traffic congestion still keeps getting worse.

Traffic congestion adds to environmental degradation, and increasing car numbers aggravate environmental pollution, especially urban air pollution. During the development of cities, due to economic progress, the city infrastructure continues to improve. However, the traffic issue is always a scar for a city's MICE development. During events, the transportation departments always choose to limit the traffic flow to solve the traffic problem, which causes the inconvenience to residents. Such kinds of problems are more obvious in some urban centres, especially in big cities like Beijing. Not only traffic but slow speed, loose standards on emissions, and a higher number of cars are three main factors that lead to the worsening of air pollution. And also roads, car parks, and other transportation infrastructure cause pressure on land resources. Like Ling, Wang and Liu (2001) noted, the rapid development of urban economy brought a series of environmental problems such as urban air pollution, coal pollution, and chemical pollution of tail gas, which have caused more than 500 cities not meeting the national environmental standards. Not only that, in order to successfully host MICE, many organisers and governments have, as noted earlier, been too optimistic about construction projects like convention centres, theme parks, and other public facilities. Many plough fields and mountains have been appropriated and green lands replaced by concrete. It has caused many negative impacts on the environment like damaging vegetation, undermining the stability of the terrain, destroying the water and land systems, and eroding the ecological environment. According to Hao, Li, Tan, Zhang and Zhang (2015), by the time of their study, land use intensity was high in China and land structure was also irrational. They also emphasized that in most Chinese cities, industry sites used about 30% of city land, much higher than in Western countries (generally not more than 15%); urban pollution was quite serious, 50% of the urban underground water was subjected to different levels of pollution, and the ecological environment had been greatly damaged. In many large cities, residents have suffered from major disasters that are linked with environmental degradation like flooding, turbid flow, landslide, and land collapse. Also there are other issues linked with overcrowding and the over-use of leisure and recreational facilities, which are perceived separately from the traffic congestion problem alone.

Given that respondents could identify negative impacts, the responses to the question 'Is it worthwhile for the government to spend money on these events?' nonetheless overwhelmingly produced a positive response where nearly two-thirds of the respondents stated that it was worthwhile, with two specifically stating 'of course it is worthwhile'. The reasons given for this positive response were the economic benefits, the development of future tourism, and the strengthening of the city's image. Of the remaining one-third of the respondents, a third approved the expenditure, but with varying concerns, while only about one-sixth of the respondents expressed criticism of such expenditure, arguing that the costs involved exceeded the benefits gained. Typical comments of this last category were:

> I heard that the expenditure was too much and caused an imbalance between the input and return. Currently, the situation is in deficit. The problem is that the government should learn from this experience. (It should) try to attract more social groups to be involved in this and use smaller investors, which can bring the most economic benefits.

> It is not worth (the expenditure), the government has put lots of money into promotion and marketing but it did not attract enough foreign tourists and attendees.

Even though most MICE investors and organisers are governmental organisations, residents still care about the investment input and output. Although most residents have no idea about the real benefits or data from MICE, there was a wide recognition that Hangzhou is a 'tourism city' and thus needs to develop its tourism further to sustain its image and advantages.

The perception that the impact for Hangzhou to host large events is not heavily linked to some other aspects, while the increasing prices related to housing is a major concern of the residents. A fifth of the respondents mentioned the rising costs of living, of which property was the most immediately identified. The real estate price was a hot topic as noted below:

> The cost of living has increased. As Hangzhou is a tourism city, the cost of living here has increased to a really high standard, some prices like house prices even go beyond those in Shanghai and Beijing.

> Hangzhou as a tourism city presents a very high real estate price in China.

These comments are substantiated by other evidence as shown in Table 4.2 which shows 10 large cities' average real estate prices and average personal income in 2005.

Table 4.2   10 Large Cities' Average Real Estate Price and Average Personal Income in 2005

Average real estate price ranking	City	Average price (RMB/sqm)	Average personal income ranking
1	Wenzhou	9,278	2
2	Shanghai	8,627	4
3	Hangzhou	7,210	7
4	Beijing	6,232	6
5	Shenzhen	6,037	1
6	Ningbo	5,900	5
7	Guangzhou	5,660	3
8	Xiamen	5,156	9
9	Nanjing	4,960	11
10	Tianjin	4,760	12

Source: Embassy of the People's Republic of China in the United States of America. (2005).

These average prices do not fully represent urban city centre's real estate prices, for the average prices in Table 4.2 are influenced by surrounding countryside prices. According to China News Service (2011), Hangzhou's urban real estate price was around 20,000 RMB per square metre and it was still growing specifically for the education zones. These prices are not equitable and balanced when compared with the income levels of local people. People are afraid of high real estate price increases, and some residents worry that MICE hosting may increase the price due to the higher construction standards that inflate construction costs. This statement may overestimate the impact generated by MICE, but there is definitely a perceived link between the real estate price and MICE. According to the FFW Topic (2008), in September 2000, before Xiamen International Conference and Exhibition Center was built and put into use, that area's residential real estate price was only 2,800 RMB per square metre; but the centre's construction set off a construction boom around that area and increased the average price to nearly 20,000 RMB per square metre. Similarly, in Hangzhou, the Leisure Expo increased the real estate price around the Leisure Expo Park and some other related areas.

The research then began to assess how events can impact upon people, and at first the question was at a general rather than personal level. Thus people were asked how hosting an event impacted on Hangzhou. Nearly all respondents recognised economic benefits that could contribute to the city, and the dimensions of these responses were threefold and interlinked. The categories are as follows, and representative quotes are provided as being illustrative of the content of the dimensions.

1) Of general economic benefit to the city.

Events are good for a city's tourism development and can also bring many economic opportunities.

2) Of benefit to the tourism industry, which in turn benefits the city.

The main purpose of holding events is to attract more tourists, so this benefit should be achieved. Large events always contain many different kinds of small shows; many of them are related to business. Many foreign companies were attracted to attend these events so the economic opportunities are obvious.

3) Of benefit to specific attributes of the city.

Events can attract many foreign businesses, so it is good for a city's economy and development.

When asked what the actual benefits to the city were, a relatively long list of advantages was produced including not only economic benefits, but infrastructure development, better branding and knowledge of the city, knowledge of foreigners, development of overseas business and personal links, environmental improvement through tree and flower planting and garden enhancement, cultural development through care of heritage buildings and the development of recreational facilities. Additionally, many residents felt able to point to specific examples of such improvements, while some referred to the more fashionable appearance of the city and a feeling that the city was more lively as evidenced by more neon lights and signs. However, five residents were unsure in terms of either not being able to identify specific improvements, or being unsure about how much of the improvement could be attributed to tourism and the MICE industry. It is hard for residents to predict long-term effects, and their answers were more based on guesses or expectations rather than specific knowledge.

Residents were then asked to what extent they had been influenced directly by these changes. Of the 40 respondents, 26 answered that there had been some impact. The remaining 14 noted the changes tended to be psychological rather than physical, in terms of feeling the pride in the city and its achievements, having some improvement in their leisure lifestyles through using some of the facilities that had been developed for various events such as new gardens, new roads etc., or through being introduced to new foods. None of the respondents had been involved in any direct way through community action with these events, and indeed there was some doubt expressed as to what degree these events had involved local communities. As already noted, respondents were able to point to economic and other benefits at a city level; but little direct involvement or impact on personal lives seems to have been perceived as was resulted from MICE or similar events.

4.5 MICE Competition Between Cities

The question then turned toward residents' perceptions of Hangzhou as a destination in itself, its capabilities of hosting such major events and its competitive positioning. First, all the respondents agreed that Hangzhou had the capacity to host large events given its fast development of economy, infrastructure, and convention buildings. Thus one respondent noted:

> Hangzhou definitely has the capability. In the last ten years Hangzhou's economy has dramatically developed, so the economy is one of the strong foundations. Secondly, Hangzhou municipal government has the daring and resolution (to do this). Finally, the leisure and tourism environment is good.

In terms of competitive positioning, almost all the respondents commented that the competition was very strong, but that Hangzhou possessed significant advantages that permitted it to compete. Common opinions are illustrated by quoting two respondents as below:

There are many strong competitors in other places like Kunming, Guangzhou, etc., but Hangzhou has it own special advantages.

There should be many competitors. Because holding events can make a city very famous in China, many cities are trying this method. However, Hangzhou's capability is also strong.

One of the reasons for these positive views is the natural features of Hangzhou and its reputation, at least within China, for being a beautiful city with lakes and gardens. Other advantages lie in the city possessing an appropriate infrastructure, experience in hosting such events and access to a large population—including that of Shanghai. Hangzhou's MICE competitive advantages are varied and include location and related economic advantages, government support, basic MICE service, Shanghai exhibition links, and successful stories. Local residents have very high confidence and pride in their city. These high levels of satisfaction shown by local Hangzhou residents are not a surprise. Many statistics show that Hangzhou residents have higher satisfaction levels of city life than other cities' residents. Lian (2006) indicated in the *China City Life Quality Report* that Hangzhou's city life quality was ranked third among 287 cities in China. Not only that, there were other researches that showed Hangzhou reached the highest score of national well-being or resident confidence.

Nowadays many cities have attached high attention to the development of the MICE industry, with an unprecedented number of policies showing support. Hangzhou's MICE industry is facing increasingly fierce competition from other cities. Domestically, Beijing, Shanghai, Guangzhou, and Shenzhen with comprehensive advantages of MICE are among the top tier. In the second tier, Wuhan, Chongqing, Nanjing, Chengdu, Qingdao, etc., have put forward their new development goals, with many exhibition areas and centres rapidly put in place. Even in Zhejiang Province, Hangzhou is still facing the competition pressure from Ningbo, which has proposed to build itself into an 'international exhibition centre'. In recent years, Ningbo's exhibition facilities, level of service management, and policy support are at the forefront of the province. Additionally, Yiwu's small commodity market with its specialised international influence has been on the rise, while holding various trade fairs and other events. So there is still a gap for Hangzhou to fill up in its MICE development environment, large-scale exhibition facilities, and a leading city brand for hosting MICE.

Respondents were then asked to consider potential visitors to MICE-type events and to assess what would attract them to Hangzhou. The answers fell into two main categories, and Figure 4.4 represents a simplified perceptual diagram. The two categories were (a) content and interest of the event itself to a potential visitor and (b) the nature of Hangzhou as a host city. Figure 4.4 indicates that the two main dimensions had little direct interaction—they stood as two separate perceptual dimensions with little interaction between them. However, the second dimension—the nature of Hangzhou as a host city had three sub-themes, namely the number of tourist attractions that were often based on natural features, the fame and culture, and the beautiful scenery.

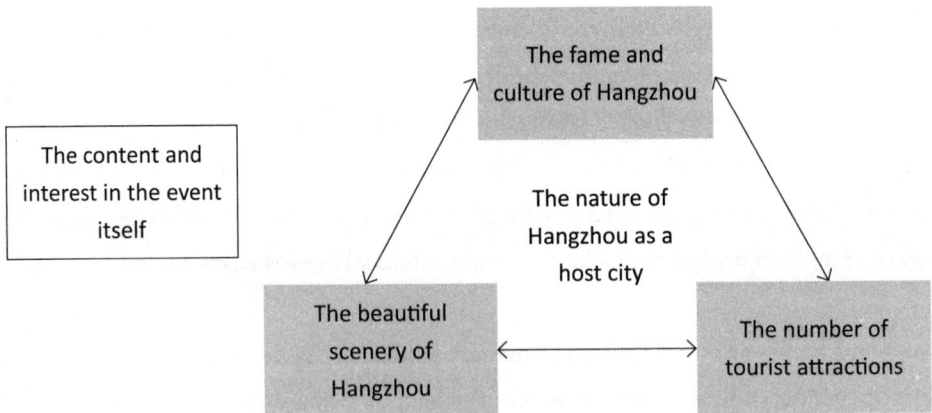

Figure 4.4   Perceptual Diagram of What Attracts Visitors to Hangzhou

4.6 Chapter Summary

The results indicate that economic benefits were immediately identified as being associated with events. The data also indicate, at least in part, the basis of these perceptions. First, there was a very high awareness based upon media usage, and media reports which not only referred to the content of the events, but also would estimate the anticipated economic gain. Second, evidence of economic benefits was observed and included the development of lakes, improvement in roads and the development of Hangzhou in surrounding areas. The signs of economic development were obvious. As was predicted though, while economic growth occupied a salient awareness of the respondents, one can question the degree to which it becomes a determinant of attitudes when the nature of the questions changes. Degradation of the environment was equally obvious in many parts of Zhejiang Province, and air and water quality had been negatively impacted by industrialisation (Swanson, Kuhn & Xu, 2001). A significant reason for this has been the failure to implement legislative safeguards and the under-resourcing of environmental agencies (Swanson et al., 2001). A tension thus arose in answers between perceived economic growth that can, at least in part, be attributable to developing tourism and specifically to events on the one hand, and a perception that these impacts bring about congestion, environmental degradation, and little immediate direct benefit. For the moment though, the evaluations are being filtered through perceptions of pride in the development of the city and the increased international attention that such events bring. Much of this can be explained by reference to the policies enacted prior to the opening of the Chinese economy to the outside world, policies that meant a city of the size of Hangzhou would have been generally unrecognised in the wider world. Thus to some extent, attitudes are explicable by reference to an evolutionary process of establishing a self-belief and city identity for Hangzhou as not only a major Chinese city, but also a major international city capable of managing, establishing, and exploiting events.

Chapter Five

Sample Characteristics and Overall Results

⮕ 5.1 Introduction

Consequently, the aim of this chapter is to undertake a general description of the results including the nature of the sample and the overall results. The demographic characteristics were measured by age, gender, employment, education, place of residency, commonly used transportation, and income level. The correlations among different demographics were also examined and explained considering the possible interactions between them in subsequent analyses. Finally, the overall results of three scales are provided—an assessment of the impact of MICE events on the city generally, on the respondent's daily life, and on the importance of events including the role of MICE in developing Hangzhou's general image.

⮕ 5.2 Data Collection

Since the major investigation focus of this study is local residents, the research units chosen were four of the eight major residential districts in Hangzhou, and the specific survey places were selected using convenience sampling and were usually business centres, shopping centres, parks, cafés, libraries, etc. The participants were selected by age, gender, education level, and employment status during the questionnaire selection stage. Thereby a quota sampling was undertaken loosely to ensure a mix of respondents to ensure sufficient sub-sample sizes based on gender, age, education, income, etc. As noted, participants were usually interviewed in a certain leisure environment such as a park, café or teahouse where people feel comfortable and are willing to answer questions. When the survey was conducted in some busy places like an office or shopping centre, the survey time chosen was during the lunch time when participants had more free time to talk.

5.3 Demographics of Survey Respondents

There were 405 valid surveys completed in Hangzhou. The fourth part of the questionnaire was designed to deal with those questions relating to the demographics of the survey respondents and was measured by gender, age, place of residence, commonly used transportation, monthly salary, education level, and employment status. The results are presented in Table 5.1. (The number under each variable indicates the number of respondents that answered a certain question, while the number under frequency is the total number of valid surveys.)

Table 5.1 Demographics of Survey Respondents

Variable	Category	Frequency (n=405)	Valid Percentage
Gender (n=402)	Male	182	44.9%
	Female	220	54.3%
Age (n=405)	18 and under	15	3.7%
	19–25	124	30.6%
	26–30	105	25.9%
	31–35	74	18.3%
	36–40	39	9.6%
	41–45	21	5.2%
	46–50	8	2.0%
	51–55	8	2.0%
	56–60	6	1.5%
	61–65	4	1.0%
	66 and above	1	0.2%
Place of residence (n=399)	Centre of the city	117	28.9%
	A little distant from the centre of the city	203	50.1%
	On the city periphery	62	15.3%
	Outside the city	17	4.2%

(continued)

Variable	Category	Frequency (*n*=405)	Valid Percentage
Commonly used transportation (*n*=404)	Private car	81	20.0%
	Public bus	160	39.5%
	Bicycle	115	28.4%
	On foot	32	7.9%
	Taxi	5	1.2%
	Company car	9	2.2%
	Others	2	0.5%
Monthly salary (*n*=404)	1,000 RMB and less	96	23.7%
	1,001–3,000 RMB	189	46.7%
	3,001–5,000 RMB	80	19.8%
	5,001–7,000 RMB	24	5.9%
	7,001–10,000 RMB	4	1.0%
	More than 10,000 RMB	11	2.7%
Education level (*n*=404)	Primary school	9	2.2%
	Middle shool and high school	41	10.1%
	Associate degree	139	34.3%
	Bachelor's degree	187	46.2%
	Master's degree	12	3.0%
	Doctor's degree	16	4.0%
Employment status (*n*=404)	Employed	293	72.3%
	Unemployed	7	1.7%
	Retired	14	3.5%
	Student	76	18.8%
	Engaged in part-time work	11	2.7%
	Engaged in home duties	3	0.7%

The respondents were divided between males (44.9%) and females (54.3%), and it was found that during the survey females were more willing to participate, perhaps because of socio-cultural factors such as a greater willingness to help or a wish to conform to requests for information that might be seen as 'official'.

Age groups have been recorded under 11 segments; the result showed that 30.6% of the respondents were 19–25 years old, followed by those aged 26–30, accounting for 25.9% of the sample while respondents aged 31–35 represented 18.3%; these three age groups were the major age groups and indicate the majority of respondents were young people aged 19–35. For the middle-aged respondents, those aged 36–40 accounted for 9.6% and those aged 41–45 accounted for 5.2% of the respondents. However, a substantial difference exists in the proportion of people aged 46–50 (2.0%), 51–55 (2.0%), 56–60 (1.5%), 61–65 (1.0%) and 66 and above (0.2%), which indicates these age groups were under-represented in the survey. Yet the survey is not as un-representative as many other similar surveys (Ryan & Gu, 2009) and reflects ease of access to people. The greater willingness of younger generations to answer is because they are (a) better educated, (b) more used to surveys, and (c) have less fear of expressing personal opinions when compared to older generations with different experiences of life (Ryan & Gu, 2009).

The places of respondents' residency indicate that the majority of respondents lived a little distant from the city centre (50.1%), followed by those living in the centre of the city (28.9%). Respondents who lived on the city periphery accounted for 15.3% of the total.

The questionnaire was also designed to ask about the most common transportation method used by the respondents. The results showed the most favoured transport was the public bus with 39.5%; the second favoured transport was the bicycle with 28.4%. The private car was also popular and was chosen by 20.0% of the respondents, which to some extent reflects the 'car boom' in China as explained in Chapter Four.

The respondents' monthly income indicates that 46.7% of the respondents had a monthly income between 1,001 and 3,000 RMB. This figure is consistent with Hangzhou's employment average monthly salary of 1,965 RMB (Sohu News, 2007). The next two income groups had similar numbers. Respondents with a monthly income of 1,000 RMB and less were 23.7% of the sample, followed by those with an income between 3,001 and 5,000 RMB (19.8%). However, the higher income level groups were under-represented in this survey; for example, those with an income of 7,001 to 10,000 RMB (1.0%) and more than 10,000 RMB (2.7%) together accounted for less than 4% of the sample.

Respondents were asked to provide information about level of their education. The results indicate that 46.2% of respondents had Bachelor's degrees and the second largest group was respondents with associate degrees (34.3%). The higher educated group of people was poorly represented, with only 3.0% of the respondents having master's degrees and 4.0% of the respondents having Doctor's degrees. In addition there were 2.2% of the respondents who had not completed middle school. With the implementation of the nine-year compulsory education in China, most Chinese citizens have at least middle school education, especially in the urban areas where more people have at least finished high school. Most of the respondents without completing middle school came from poor cities or rural areas.

As part of the survey, the respondents were asked to indicate their employment status, which was categorised as employed, unemployed, retired, student, engaged in part-time work, and engaged in home duties. In terms of respondents' employment status, it was found that the majority of respondents were employed (72.3%) and only 1.7% respondents were unemployed. Students formed 18.8% of the sample and 3.5% of the respondents were retired. There was data conflict for the part-time work respondents, which may have contained some with student status. 'Engaged in home duties' was the least common employment status chosen by respondents and accounted for only 0.7% of the sample.

In order to understand the details of respondents' employment status, the questionnaire included an open-ended question "What is your occupation?" to clarify the respondents' current occupation. Not surprisingly, respondents' answers were varied and covered different occupations in multiple areas. Based on a general analysis through SPSS frequencies, the categories have been summarised from the original answers. As shown in Table 5.2, various occupations were discernable in the research (only 347 respondents answered this question).

Table 5.2   Respondents' Occupations

Category	Frequency	Valid Percentage
Accountant	12	3.0%
Civil servant	16	4.0%
Residential area service	10	2.5%
Doctor	7	1.7%

(continued)

Category	Frequency	Valid Percentage
Engineer	10	2.5%
Hospitality service	36	8.9%
Worker	33	8.1%
Marketing	3	0.7%
Media	15	3.7%
Office employee	39	9.6%
Part-time worker	8	2.0%
Police staff	2	0.5%
Retired	9	2.2%
Sales	10	2.5%
Scientist	4	1.0%
Security guard	4	1.0%
Self-employed	14	3.5%
Student	76	18.8%
Teacher	22	5.4%
Technician	6	1.5%
Tourist guide	4	1.0%
Unemployed	7	1.7%

According to the results, 'student' was the most common occupation identified by respondents (18.8%), which could be a result of the locations selected. Although students were the largest group, it still occupies a low percentage of the total sample so there was little to influence the overall result. The next popular occupation was 'office employee' at 9.6%, followed by 'hospitality service' (8.9%) and 'worker' (8.1%). As mentioned before, the survey areas contained a large number of educational institutions so the 'teacher' respondents occupied 5.4% followed by 'civil servant' with 4.0%. Respondents who were self-employed accounted for 3.5%.

However, there were some inconsistencies in the representativeness of the sample in terms of personal occupation. Some responses such as 'office employee' and 'worker' may be overlapping, and some retired people may have also written down 'self-employed' if they were engaged in some kind of work after retirement.

5.4 Correlation Between Demographics

Cross tabulation (SPSS 16.0) was used to find relationships between different demographic variables. The reason for undertaking this analysis was based on the premise that in multiple regression, age, gender, and income might be seen as potentially significant determinant variables that influence overall attitudes. However, regression assumes the determining variables are independent, but a moment's thought shows that older respondents may have higher incomes than younger respondents simply because of career progression and hence issues of multicollinearity might arise. In short, these tests were undertaken to assess whether such issues might arise. Indeed, some significant relationships were found to be between monthly salary and education level, employment status, transportation choice, and age.

5.5 Correlation of Monthly Salary, Education Level, Employment Status, Transportation Choices, and Age

Monthly salary is always a sensitive demographic item in a questionnaire survey. It had correlations with many other variables. Tables 5.3 shows the close relationship between monthly salary and education level. The direct relationship between them was significant ($p < 0.01$). For example, 4 of the total 9 respondents who had not completed middle school earned 1,000 RMB and less for a month. On the other hand, 4 of the 12 respondents with Master's degrees had earned 5,001–7,000 RMB per month. In China, higher education levels are often considered as a direct pathway to higher incomes, but it is not absolute. At the post-graduate level, respondents with a higher education background had no advantage in monthly income in this case. For the respondents who had doctor's degrees, there was a gap between monthly incomes of 3,001–5,000 (10 of 16 respondents) and 5,001–7,000 (4 of 16 respondents).

With reference to the monthly income level, 1,001–5,000 RMB is the most common. The largest groups who earned 1,001–3,000 RMB monthly were respondents with associate degrees (98 respondents) and Bachelor's degrees (69 respondents). Half of the respondents with monthly earnings of 3,001–5,000 RMB had undergraduate qualifications (40 respondents).

Table 5.3   Correlation Between Monthly Salary and Education Level

Unit: Number of respondents

Education Level	Monthly Salary/RMB						Total
	1,000 and less	1,001 –3,000	3,001 –5,000	5,001 –7,000	7,001 –10,000	More than 10,000	
Primary school	4	1	2	1	1	0	9
Middle school and high school	17	17	6	0	0	1	41
Associate degree	14	98	18	7	0	2	139
Bachelor's degree	61	69	40	8	2	7	187
Master's degree	0	2	4	4	1	1	12
Doctor's degree	0	2	10	4	0	0	16
Total	96	189	80	24	4	11	404

The correlation between monthly salary and employment status was examined and reported in Table 5.4. For the higher monthly salary level of 7,001–10,000 RMB, all 4 respondents were employed. Interestingly of those in the monthly salary level of 5,001–7,000 RMB, 1 respondent was classified as a 'student', while most of 'students' responded 1,000 RMB and less. In addition 3 respondents earned less than 1,000 RMB monthly after retirement.

Table 5.4   Correlation Between Monthly Salary and Employment Status

Unit: Number of respondents

Employment Status	Monthly Salary/RMB						Total
	1,000 and less	1,001 –3,000	3,001 –5,000	5,001 –7,000	7,001 –10,000	More than 10,000	
Employed	21	160	75	23	4	10	293
Unemployed	5	2	0	0	0	0	7
Retired	3	10	1	0	0	0	14
Student	65	9	1	1	0	0	76
Engaged in part-time work	2	6	3	0	0	0	11
Self-employed	0	2	0	0	0	1	3
Total	96	189	80	24	4	11	404

Table 5.5 shows there was also a correlation between monthly salary and daily transportation choice of the respondents. The results showed that the higher the income, the more expensive form of transport was used. The respondents who earned 1,000 and less mostly preferred 'public bus' (41 respondents) and 'bicycle' (40 respondents) as their daily transportation. At the monthly salary level of 1,001–3,000 RMB there were still a large number of respondents who chose 'public bus' (86 respondents) and 'bicycle' (53 respondents) as their common daily transportation. At the monthly salary level of 3,001– 5,000 RMB the situation had changed. The most popular choice of daily transportation was 'private car' (33 respondents) instead of 'public bus' (25 respondents) and 'bicycle' (18 respondents). Although the latter two forms of cheaper transport still had many users at this income level, the percentage was smaller when compared with the first two income categories. However, at the salary levels of 5,001–7,000 RMB and 7,001–10,000 RMB, respondents preferred to choose a private car as their daily transportation with 17 respondents and 2 of 4 respondents respectively. The interesting point was that respondents earning a salary of 5,001–10,000 RMB monthly largely ignored the 'company car', 'on foot', and 'taxi'. However, in recent years more and more higher income people are starting to care about healthy lifestyles and the numbers of people who choose to ride bicycles or walk to work are on the rise.

Table 5.5 Correlation Between Monthly Salary and Daily Transportation

Unit: Number of respondents

What main transport do you use daily?	Monthly Salary/RMB						Total
	1,000 and less	1,001– 3,000	3,001– 5,000	5,001– 7,000	7,001– 10,000	More than 10,000	
Private car	5	19	33	17	2	5	81
Public bus	41	86	25	4	1	3	160
Bicycle	40	53	18	2	1	1	115
On foot	9	21	2	0	0	0	32
Taxi	1	4	0	0	0	0	5
Company car	0	6	2	1	0	0	9
Others	0	0	0	0	0	2	2
Total	96	189	80	24	4	11	404

Table 5.6 illustrates the relationship between level of education and age. Cross tabulation (SPSS 16.0) was also used to examine their relationship.

Table 5.6   Correlation Between Level of Education and Age

Unit: Number of respondents

Age	Level of Education						Total
	Primary school	Middle school and high school	Associate degree	Bachelor's degree	Master's degree	Doctor's degree	
18 and under	2	10	2	1	0	0	15
19–25	1	2	27	93	1	0	124
26–30	0	10	42	47	5	1	105
31–35	1	2	38	21	5	7	74
36–40	0	6	10	18	1	4	39
41–45	0	1	10	6	0	4	21
46–50	1	3	4	0	0	0	8
51–55	2	2	4	0	0	0	8
56–60	2	2	1	1	0	0	6
61–65	0	4	0	0	0	0	4
66 and above	0	0	1	0	0	0	1
Total	9	42	139	187	12	16	405

The results from Table 5.6 showed that respondents who had associate degrees were mostly young people of 26–30 years (42 of 139 respondents) and 31–35 years (38 of 139 respondents). The older groups of respondents between 46 and 60 were influenced by the political factors, which significantly impacted this generation's education at that time. Respondents who had middle school and high school qualifications were mostly found in the 26–30 age group (10 of 42 respondents) and 18 and under (10 of 42 respondents) age group. Receiving education takes time, and respondents who had higher education tended to be older.

➡ 5.6   MICE Attendance Experience

Respondents were also asked about their previous MICE attendance experience. Of the sample, approximately 68.15% had previously attended a MICE in the past five years, while 31.85% had not.

In order to determine respondents' attendance behaviours, an open-ended question to elicit the reason that they did not attend those events was set to clarify the reasons why respondents did not attend MICE. The answers were varied but based on a general analysis through SPSS Frequencies; the reasons were broken down into seven categories. The most common reason for not attending an event is 'No time' (n=31), followed by 'no opportunity' (n=14). This confirms the qualitative pilot study as 'no time' was the most common reason inhibiting respondents' attendance. What is noteworthy is that few respondents stated that 'no interest' was a major reason, but it might be observed that if interest is high, then people will find time to attend, and that the category of 'no time' may be little more than an excuse for 'not of high enough priority'.

Respondents were also asked to provide main reasons for their MICE attendance. It was a multinomial question that contained 10 choices of provided reasons. Table 5.7 indicates that the most popular reason was 'it is interesting' (39.8%), followed by 'leisure purposes' (33.0%). Respondents who attended MICE for 'work related' and 'study' reasons accounted for 27.2% and 27.0% of the sample respectively. The reason 'shopping' was chosen by 24.9% of respondents, followed by 'to acquire new knowledge' (22.2%), 'accompanying friends' (21.2%), and 'family related' (20.2%). However, there were only 12.3% of respondents who attended MICE as part of their wider travel arrangements.

Table 5.7   Main Reasons for Previous Attendance

Main Reason	Percentage	Main Reason	Percentage
Work related	27.2%	Accompanying friends	21.2%
Business related	16.9%	To acquire new knowledge	22.2%
Study	27.0%	Shopping	24.9%
Leisure purposes	33.0%	Travel related	12.3%
Family related	20.2%	Others	0.3%
It is interesting	39.8%		

That 'shopping' as a popular reason for attending MICE was chosen by 24.9% of the respondents may be because many MICE held in China are part of a business promotion and many people prefer to attend these kinds of MICE for better direct factory wholesale prices.

Respondents attending previous MICE may not only have different reasons but also have different demographic profiles. Table 5.8 summarises the different gender distribution among respondents regarding their previous MICE attendance experience in the five years before the survey. No statistically significant difference based on gender was found.

Table 5.8   Previous Attendance and Gender

Have you attended any events in the last 5 years?	Gender	
	Male	Female
Yes	66.5%	69.1%
No	33.5%	30.9%

The researcher also asked about the residents' support for further development of MICE, and 91.6% replied affirmatively for supporting the hosting of other big events. Only 8.4% did not agree with such future plans.

5.7   Descriptive Analysis of Measurement Scales

The major part of the questionnaire contained 40 items related to the large events hosted in Hangzhou and their impacts on both the city and individuals with each question carrying a scale of: 1=Has gotten really bad/Things are now very bad; 2=Has gotten significantly worse; 3=Has gotten quite a bit worse; 4=Has gotten a little worse; 5=Has neither improved nor gotten worse/No change; 6=Has improved just a little; 7=Has improved quite a bit; 8=Has improved considerably/significantly/quite a lot; 9=Has improved vastly; 0=Have no opinion/Don't know/Not applicable. Table 5.9 illustrates the different descriptive statistics (Mean/M, Std. Deviation/Standard Deviation/SD) for event impacts upon the city of Hangzhou—in other words, respondents were asked how they thought the events impacted on the city itself, not themselves personally. Respondents were asked about items to measure the economic, socio-cultural, environmental, and political impacts of large events.

Table 5.9   Respondents' Perceptions of MICE Impacts on the City

Item	Mean	Std. Deviation
Number of tourists	7.31	1.72
Pride in and satisfaction with the city	7.03	1.72
Level of local government's interest in events	7.00	1.79
City's image in China	6.97	1.84
City's competitive position compared to similar cities	6.84	1.71
Level of promotion and media involvement	6.84	1.64
City's level of attraction to people from other cities in China	6.80	1.80
City's level of attraction to foreign people	6.78	1.89
Government involvement in the event business	6.77	1.73
Success of the events	6.72	1.69
City's image in the world	6.71	1.90
City's economy as a whole	6.66	1.71
Entertainment opportunities	6.61	1.77
Providing suitable plans for the city's event tourism development	6.59	1.96
Event facilities (event centres, event parks, etc.)	6.57	1.80
Suitability of policies and regulations related to tourism	6.53	1.77
Suitability of policies and regulations related to events	6.53	1.80
Government promotion to business participants	6.53	1.73
Related facilities (hotels, restaurants, shopping places, etc.)	6.49	1.67
Tourism's relationship with local businesses	6.46	1.66
Local business opportunities	6.44	1.82
Efforts to stimulate local business involvement in events	6.39	1.86
Control of the city's event economy and business	6.35	1.82
Business cooperation level (both domestic and international)	6.30	1.95
Relationship between government and local businesses	6.20	2.05
Maintenance of public facilities like parks and roads	6.13	2.04
Event risk control level	6.09	2.00
Quality of road infrastructure (highways, etc.)	6.05	1.87
Relationship between government and local residents	6.04	1.85
Public services (medical, law, logistics, security, etc.)	6.03	1.84
Employment rate and opportunities	5.94	1.94
Price of goods and services	5.74	1.83
Unemployment rate	5.61	2.15

(continued)

Item	Mean	Std. Deviation
Total living costs	5.61	1.76
City's safety level and crime rate	5.46	2.25
Price levels and management of prices for events	5.29	2.09
City's pollution level	5.01	1.94
Damage to the natural environment	4.94	1.93
Traffic congestion in the city	4.68	2.04
Property values and rental costs	4.59	2.15

Based on a descriptive analysis, the mean score of each item shows that from a city perspective, respondents tended to strongly agree that large events increased tourist number for the city's tourism industry (M=7.31, SD=1.72). Respondents also agreed that due to the large events hosted in Hangzhou, residents' pride in and satisfaction with the city had increased (M=7.03, SD=1.72). The third highest score was that the local government's interest in MICE had increased because of large events (M=7.00, SD=1.79). The next two items indicate that respondents thought Hangzhou's image in China and competitive position compared to other similar cities had improved (M=6.97, SD=1.84; M=6.84, SD=1.71).

In contrast, the results also indicate some differences in respondents' perceptions. Respondents thought the management of MICE tickets and entry prices and the city's pollution level had only marginally improved as a result (M=5.29, SD=2.09; M=5.01, SD=1.94). Damage to the natural environment was another issue that caught respondents' concern (M=4.94, SD=1.93). The most negative impacts created by large events were traffic congestion in the city (M=4.68, SD=2.04) and an increase in property values and rental costs (M=4.59, SD=2.15).

Table 5.10 uses the same items but this time it records respondents' perceptions of the impacts of the large events from a personal perspective, that is, how the events had impacted their daily lives.

Table 5.10 Respondents' Perceptions of Personal Impacts from MICE

Item	Mean	Std. Deviation
Level of promotion and media involvement	6.89	4.97
Number of tourists	6.78	1.82

(continued)

Item	Mean	Std. Deviation
Level of local government's interest in events	6.70	4.45
Pride in and satisfaction with the city	6.61	1.75
Government involvement in the event business	6.51	1.71
City's level of attraction to people from other cities in China	6.50	1.74
City's economy as a whole	6.48	2.95
City's image in China	6.46	1.93
City's competitive position compared to similar cities	6.43	1.72
City's image in the world	6.39	1.87
City's level of attraction to foreign people	6.39	1.85
Success of the events	6.38	1.77
Providing suitable plans for the city's event tourism development	6.24	2.01
Suitability of policies and regulations related to events	6.21	1.85
Suitability of policies and regulations related to tourism	6.14	1.81
Control of the city's event economy and business	6.12	1.72
Efforts to stimulate local business involvement in events	6.11	1.90
Entertainment opportunities	6.10	1.65
Government promotion to business participants	6.06	1.83
Relationship between government and the local businesses	5.96	1.99
Local business opportunities	5.94	1.91
Relationship between government and local residents	5.93	1.75
Event risk control level	5.88	1.80
Related facilities (hotels, restaurants, shopping places, etc.)	5.87	1.63
Maintenance of public facilities like parks and roads	5.85	1.82
Tourism's relationship with local businesses	5.85	1.74
Public services (medical, law, logistics, security, etc.)	5.76	1.84
Quality of road infrastructure (highways, etc.)	5.73	1.67
Business cooperation level (both domestic and international)	5.73	2.04
Event facilities (event centres, event parks, etc.)	5.63	1.81
Employment rate and opportunities	5.60	2.00
Unemployment rate	5.40	2.11
Price of goods and services	5.25	1.60
City's safety level and crime rate	5.22	2.13
Price levels and management of prices for events	5.22	2.01

(continued)

Item	Mean	Std. Deviation
Total living costs	5.11	1.76
Damage to the natural environment	4.91	1.83
City's pollution level	4.86	1.79
Traffic congestion in the city	4.46	1.97
Property values and rental costs	4.02	1.85

The above results indicate that respondents from their own perspectives tended to strongly agree that they saw that level of promotion and media involvement during the MICE had increased (M=6.89, SD=4.97). They also agreed that they were aware of the extra tourists that events had attracted (M=6.78, SD=1.82). They certainly had more pride in and satisfaction with the city and government involvement in the event business (M=6.61, SD=1.75; M=6.51, SD=1.71).

At the other end of the scale, the issues of most concern were the total living costs (M=5.11, SD=1.76), the damage to the natural environment (M=4.91, SD=1.83), the city's pollution level (M=4.86, SD=1.79), traffic congestion (M=4.46, SD=1.97), and rising property values and rental costs (M=4.02, SD=1.85).

When looking at both the top and bottom five issues from the city and personal perspectives, it can be seen that there were some similarities. These two perspectives share some issues in both positive and negative sides: 'number of tourists', 'level of local government's interest in events', 'pride in and satisfaction with the city'; and 'damage to the natural environment', 'traffic congestion', 'property values and rental costs'. In short, respondents drew the same main conclusion when considering the impacts on their own lives, and those on the city more generally. However, with reference to differences between the mean scores on the scales, the great majority were statistically significant at p<0.05; therefore implying that respondents were able to draw distinctions between the two scales.

The third section of the questionnaire asks the respondents their level of agreement with a few statements (see Table 5.11). The respondents were asked to circle a number from a 10-point scale (1=Very strongly disagree; 2=Strongly disagree; 3=Moderately disagree;

4=Slightly disagree; 5=Neither agree nor disagree; 6=Slightly agree; 7=Moderately agree; 8=Strongly agree; 9=Very strongly agree; 0=No opinion/Not applicable).

Table 5.11 Agreement or Disagreement Statements

Statement	Mean	Std. Deviation
An event that relates to the people's lives is more interesting and valuable	6.77	1.70
An event should fit the city's culture and history	6.74	1.66
I think the government should use the money for education and medical care	6.72	1.72
Hosting big events can entertain local residents and give them the opportunity to attend major international events	6.62	1.70
Hosting big events is a good way to know about cultures of other countries	6.58	1.71
I believe hosting big events will directly give Hangzhou's tourism and hospitality industry a positive impact	6.58	1.54
The price of the entrance ticket is the most important factor for attending an event	6.52	1.64
Because of hosting big events, the property values and rental costs will increase	6.50	1.99
I would love to have an opportunity to be involved in the event process	6.46	1.60
Hosting big events can increase recognition of the city in the world	6.43	1.60
Hosting big events can always have long-term benefits for city development	6.35	1.68
Because of hosting big events, life in Hangzhou will be more interesting	6.33	1.84
I think distance to the event venue is the most important factor that inhibits me from attending an event	6.31	1.76
Hosting big events can quickly stimulate local business development	6.24	1.54
Because Hangzhou is hosting big events, I like living here	6.22	1.80
I will also consider some important events in other cities	6.20	1.90
Hosting big events can quickly stimulate the city's economic development	6.15	1.58

(continued)

Statement	Mean	Std. Deviation
I think the government is spending too much money hosting events	6.05	1.87
Hosting big events is the best way to show to the world the city's capabilities	6.00	1.63
Because of hosting big events, poorer people can no longer afford living in the urban area	5.57	2.14
Building event theme parks is worthwhile	5.56	2.12
I believe my personal economic status will be better	5.46	3.96

A number of respondents thought the government should use the money for the education system rather than hosting MICE (M=6.72, SD=1.72). Many respondents also expressed concerns that they thought the government has spent too much money on hosting MICE and ignored many other important issues related to residents' lives such as education and medical care. Respondents also agreed that hosting big events can entertain local residents (M=6.62, SD=1.70). Some issues like 'I think distance to the event venue is the most important factor that inhibits me from attending an event' did not get a high mean score (M=6.31, SD=1.76) but it got lots of attention during the interview. The bottom five issues on the ranking were 'I think the government is spending too much money hosting events' (M=6.05, SD=1.87); 'Hosting big events is the best way to show to the world the city's capabilities' (M=6.00, SD=1.63); 'Because of hosting big events, poorer people can no longer afford living in the urban area' (M=5.57, SD=2.14); 'Building event theme parks is worthwhile' (M=5.56, SD=2.12); and 'I believe my personal economic status will be better' (M=5.46, SD=3.96). It should be noted that from the results for most of the issues, there is not a large difference in the means according to the standard deviation.

➡ 5.8　The Role of Socio-demographic Variables

It might be argued that socio-demographic variables such as age, gender, income, etc. might influence people's attitudes toward MICE policies. In addition, other data such as past attendance or non-attendance might also influence responses to the questions. Consequently, analysis of variance (ANOVA) was undertaken to assess these factors—the purpose was to assess to what degree they may help in identifying possible market segments with residents and those clusters that may be more critical to the MICE policies of the Hangzhou government.

◆ Gender

T-tests revealed that gender was not a discriminatory variable except for one item where more males (6.41) felt the MICE policies brought different departments of the government closer than females (6.0) did at $p<0.01$.

◆ Age

Age was not a discriminatory variable for the items related to the impacts of events on the city and personal lives. However, there were statistically significant differences between MICE policies and alternative possible expenditures of money. For example those aged 45 and under were considerably more concerned about the impacts on increasing property prices and rents ($p<0.001$) compared to those over 45, and a similar pattern exists with reference to thoughts that the money could be better spent on improving education and medical care. Those aged 30 and under were much more interested in attending events ($p<0.001$), while those aged between 26 and 30 scored significantly higher on the item that events should match people's interests, possibly reflecting a life stage centred around establishing family and career.

◆ Income

Table 5.12 summarises those items for which income was found to be a discriminatory variable. Two general observations may be made about the table. First, the number of items is comparatively small, indicating that for the greater part income was not a discriminatory variable here. Second, there is a tendency for higher income groups to express slightly lower levels of agreement with the items, and this generally carried through the whole table, albeit, as just noted, not at statistically significant levels.

Table 5.12   Respondents' Perspectives of MICE Impacts by Monthly Salary (Mean
Score and *F* Value)

Perception Item	Monthly Salary/RMB						*F* value
	1,000 and less	1,001 –3,000	3,001 –5,000	5,001 –7,000	7,001 –10,000	More than 10,000	
City Perspectives							
City's economy as a whole	6.69	6.83	6.44	7.08	6.00	4.50	2.39*
Pride in and satisfaction with the city	4.24	4.16	6.65	7.50	5.75	5.50	2.86*
Providing suitable plans for the city's event tourism development	6.56	6.76	6.36	6.88	4.00	5.50	2.32*
City's level of attraction to foreign people	6.93	6.86	6.78	6.46	5.00	4.25	2.56*
Personal Perspectives							
Related facilities (hotels, restaurants, shopping places, etc.)	6.15	5.90	5.43	6.33	5.00	6.00	2.44*
Public services (medical, law, logistics, security, etc.)	6.17	5.75	5.48	5.75	4.25	4.00	2.61*
Number of tourists	7.13	6.86	6.41	6.75	5.25	5.00	2.82*
Pride in and satisfaction with the city	6.97	6.63	6.33	6.96	5.00	5.50	2.52*
Assessment of Statements on Policies							
Hosting big events can increase recognition of the city in the world	5.91	6.60	6.75	6.58	6,50	6.50	3.54**
Hosting big events can always have long-term benefits for the city	6.30	6.70	6.47	6.00	5.00	5.00	2.64*

Note: *p*<0.05; **p*<0.01.

◆ Education

When applying ANOVA to the variables of level of education and the perceptions of Hangzhou's MICE, as shown in Table 5.13, it implies there was comparatively little relationship in the ways in which the education variables influenced perceptions of the MICE hosted by the city. It can also be noted that the trends within the scores are not uniform. For example, while the more educated appeared to be more cynical of the success of the MICE events, they also tended to feel that MICE will increase house prices and rents. On the other hand, they tended to express less agreement with the notion that MICE will increase traffic congestion.

Table 5.13　Respondents' Perspectives of MICE Impacts by Education Level (Mean Score and F Value)

Perception Item	Education Level						F value
	Primary school	Middle school and high school	Associate degree	Bachelor's degree	Master's degree	Doctor's degree	
City Perspectives							
Event facilities (event centres, event parks, etc.)	6.67	6.86	6.81	6.45	5.25	6.00	2.54*
Maintenance of public facilities like parks and roads	6.56	6.93	6.42	5.73	6.08	6.06	3.51**
Traffic congestion in the city	4.89	4.93	5.04	4.48	3.25	4.25	2.79*
Personal Perspectives							
Property values and rental costs	3.95	3.98	4.19	4.33	3.25	4.25	2.89*
Success of the events	6.43	6.53	6.26	6.17	5.00	4.50	2.39*

(continued)

Perception Item	Education Level						F value
	Primary school	Middle school and high school	Associate degree	Bachelor's degree	Master's degree	Doctor's degree	
Level of local government's interest in events	6.53	6.75	6.30	9.46	4.75	6.00	5.08**
Assessment of Statements on Policies							
Because of big events, the property values and rental costs will increase	5.22	5.80	6.38	6.99	6.83	6.53	4.89***
Because of hosting big events, life in Hangzhou will be more interesting	6.50	6.20	6.39	6.72	6.16	6.19	3.12**

Note: *$p<0.05$; **$p<0.01$; *** $p<0.001$.

◆ **Employment**

Employment status emerged as a significant variable and F values were at statistically significant levels for about half of the items. The unemployed tended to score lower on the scales than the employed, while those who were retired tended to give the highest scores of all. Those who were in part-time work tended to score mid-way between the fully employed and the unemployed. The self-employed tended to show the greatest variation in their scores, being seemingly more selective over items, and seemed to be particularly sensitive to issues of increasing prices and costs. Students also showed a high variance in their pattern of scores—being the highest to be aware of the increasing numbers of events and the second lowest in items concerning MICE creating employment opportunities.

◆ Past History of MICE Attendance

A history of past attendance at events proved to be a statistically significant discriminatory variable for a number of items as shown in Table 5.14. Generally those who had attended events tended to be more supportive of MICE having positive impacts than those who did not. Table 5.14 relates to evaluations at the city level, while Table 5.15 relates to the personal impacts. The two tables tend to mirror each other, but one factor of interest is that those who have attended past MICE considered not only aspects such as ticket pricing situations have improved, but also the improvements in wider social and environmental factors. This would lend support to the city's policies that MICE can generate benefits that go beyond simply economic aspects and thereby enhance the overall quality of life in the city as perceived by residents.

Table 5.14   Differences in Perceptions at City Level Based on Past MICE Attendance

Perception Item	Have you attended any events in the last 5 years?	Number of Respondents	Mean	Std. Deviation	T-Test
Event facilities (event centres, event parks, etc.)	Yes	274	6.8321	1.69925	3.73***
	No	128	6.1563	1.67161	
Related facilities (hotels, restaurants, shopping places, etc.)	Yes	272	6.7132	1.42154	2.31*
	No	126	6.3571	1.45032	
Entertainment opportunities	Yes	272	6.8640	1.49534	2.36*
	No	125	6.4800	1.52717	
Quality of road infrastructure (highways, etc.)	Yes	269	6.3309	1.65894	2.36*
	No	126	5.9206	1.49988	
Public services (medical, law, logistics, security, etc.)	Yes	266	6.4173	1.45457	3.06**
	No	124	5.9435	1.35132	
City's pollution level	Yes	272	5.2831	1.88723	2.72**
	No	125	4.7520	1.62469	
City's safety level and crime rate	Yes	259	5.9923	1.75206	2.37**
	No	119	5.5294	1.79842	

(continued)

Perception Item	Have you attended any events in the last 5 years?	Number of Respondents	Mean	Std. Deviation	T-Test
Property values and rental costs	Yes	262	4.9466	2.04663	2.38**
	No	127	4.4409	1.78020	
Price of goods and services	Yes	275	6.0109	1.79717	3.91***
	No	127	5.2835	1.58814	
Tourism's relationship with local businesses	Yes	272	6.7463	1.45219	3.74***
	No	127	6.1654	1.42408	
Price levels and management of prices for events	Yes	265	5.7094	1.82639	3.39***
	No	125	5.0400	1.80233	
Event risk control level	Yes	264	6.5606	1.53913	3.71***
	No	123	5.9350	1.55627	

Note: *$p<0.05$; **$p<0.01$; ***$p<0.001$.

Table 5.15   Differences in Perceptions at Personal Level Based on Past MICE Attendance

Perception Item	Have you attended any events in the last 5 years?	Number of Respondents	Mean	Std. Deviation	T-Test
Traffic congestion in the city	Yes	275	4.6582	1.96118	2.34**
	No	126	4.1746	1.82463	
Quality of road infrastructure (highways, etc.)	Yes	274	5.9161	1.59793	2.50**
	No	127	5.4961	1.49536	
Damage to the natural environment	Yes	270	5.1556	1.71313	2.05*
	No	125	4.7840	1.56877	
City's pollution level	Yes	273	5.1392	1.73704	3.45***
	No	125	4.5200	1.47342	
City's safety level and crime rate	Yes	262	5.7786	1.66915	3.67***
	No	118	5.0932	1.71961	
Property values and rental costs	Yes	266	4.2895	1.76412	2.44*
	No	127	3.8346	1.64154	

(continued)

Perception Item	Have you attended any events in the last 5 years?	Number of Respondents	Mean	Std. Deviation	T-Test
Price of goods and services	Yes	273	5.4286	1.57748	2.35*
	No	128	5.0469	1.36814	
Total living costs	Yes	271	5.3063	1.69266	2.04*
	No	128	4.9453	1.56391	
Tourism's relationship with local businesses	Yes	271	6.1328	1.51440	2.75**
	No	124	5.6935	1.37443	
Price levels and management of prices for events	Yes	268	5.5858	1.81445	3.56***
	No	126	4.8889	1.79877	
Event risk control level	Yes	267	6.2322	1.44784	3.11**
	No	125	5.7440	1.45305	

Note: $*p<0.05$; $**p<0.01$; $***p<0.001$.

Another facet of this analysis is that the variable of past attendance did emerge as possibly important in generating perceptions, and thus this needs to be borne in mind in further analysis.

➡ 5.9 Chapter Summary

The overall scores show the agreement that MICE policies benefit the city in terms of its image and general economic benefits, albeit at costs to the environment including at least some traffic congestion in that the score for this item was still above the mid-point of the scale. Residents also produced results related to perceived personal gains from the policies, with the great majority of scores being 5 or 6 on a 0–9 scale. There were, though, some criticisms of the policies, and among sub-groups, there were concerns expressed as to whether some of the money spent on MICE might be better allocated to, for example, an improvement of educational policies.

Overall it can be concluded that while some concerns exist, generally respondents supported the direction of the MICE policies and saw the city benefitting not only economically but also in terms of gaining national and international recognition. Given this, it can be argued that the next steps are to further assess the reliability of the data, to assess whether more clearly specific clusters of respondents can be identified, and then finally to assess whether causal relationships might be found within the data set. Consequently the next chapter will examine the reliability of the data by using various measures of reliability and by the use of factor analysis to assess whether latent (unobserved) summary variables can be identified.

Chapter Six

Data Reliability and Exploratory Factor Analysis

6.1 Introduction

The previous chapter described the mean scores and variance, and in addition undertook *t*-tests and ANOVA in an initial examination of the role played by socio-demographics and other nominal variables. The data analysis revealed some differences existed, and thus it is worth exploring these in more detail, and that the data are reliable. The purpose of this chapter is to examine the reliability of the scales, and examine prior to further analysing the data in terms of identifying possible clusters and undertaking any form of regression analysis. A key test beyond the descriptive analysis performed earlier was to ascertain the reliability of the data, and as far as possible, the validity of the data set. Factor analysis is valuable in this respect that associated with it are a number of tests that help assess the reliability of the data, while the identification of factors that represent the underlying dimensions behind the items used to create a scale of measurement is an indicative, albeit not necessarily conclusive, test of the validity of the measures being used. In order to understand residents' perceptions more deeply, three different areas of importance of events for the city, impacts of events on personal lives, and importance of event assessments were analysed separately.

The next stage is to determine the number of respondents that might be used in the analysis. If the default settings in SPSS are used, then the analysis will be undertaken using those respondents who have answered all the questions of the scales. An alternative is to engage in a simple form of data fusion whereby those respondents who missed one item are allocated the mean score for that item. To do this, it is necessary to check the pattern of responses and the use of the missing option. For this sample, of the 405 respondents, at least 390 responded to an item, while the pattern of missing responses appeared to be random. Thus the option of allocating a mean score was used to retain all 405 respondents in the factor analysis. A second check is to examine the correlation matrix for patterns of association, while the third method of checking is to examine the communality scores provided by SPSS. The communality score is the degree of variance within an item that is 'explained' by the discerned factors.

6.2   Factor Analysis

One means of ascertaining if the data possess an internal logic is to undertake factor analysis. This technique has been available for several decades. For example Darlington, Weinberg and Walberg (1973) described the purpose of factor analysis as being the discovery of simple patterns of relationships among the variables. In particular, it seeks to discover if the observed variables can be explained largely or entirely in terms of a much smaller number of variables called factors. There are two main types of factor analysis (Hair, Anderson, Tatham and Black, 1992):

- Principal component analysis (PCA): this method provides a unique solution, so that the original data can be reconstructed from the results. It looks at the total variance among the variables, so the solution generated will include as many factors as there are many variables, although it is unlikely that they will all meet the criteria for retention. There is only one method for completing a principal component analysis.

- Common factor analysis, also called principal factor analysis (PFA): this is what people generally mean when they say 'factor analysis'. This family of techniques uses an estimate of common variance among the original variables to generate the factor solution. Because of this, the number of factors will always be less than the number of original variables. So, choosing the number of factors to keep for further analysis is more problematic using common factor analysis than in principal component analysis.

Figure 6.1 illustrates the basic principle where five measures can be divided into two latent variables of factors not directly measured in the initial data set.

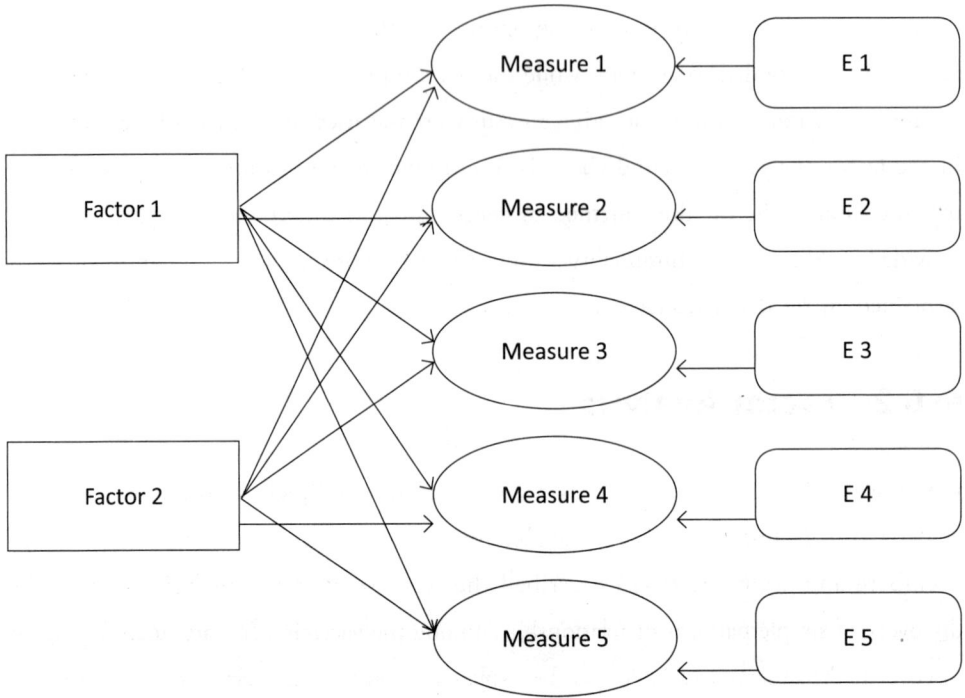

Figure 6.1   The Common Factor Analysis Model

The major reasons for conducting factor analysis are: to determine patterns of relationships, parsimony or data reduction, structure of a domain, classification or description of empirical typology, scaling for rating, hypothesis testing, and data transformation, mapping phenomenological terrains or theory building (Rummel, 1970). What has made both exploratory factor analysis (EFA) and confirmatory factor analysis (CFA) more popular in recent decades has been the appearance of powerful software packages such as SPSS, Statistica, Stata and AMOS.

6.3   Factor Analysis for the Scale—Impacts of Events on the City

The following results for this scale will be first described, and second some points about the conclusion will be noted. The measurement for city perspectives comprises 40 items. All items were into the PCA analysis process utilising the oblimin procedure. The six factors 'explain' 61.97% of the total variance and might be described as follows (details shown in Table 6.1):

Factor 1, labelled 'Government event management and local economy stimulation', relates to government involvement and its policies related to urban revitalisation and economic gain. This factor accounted for 39.65% of the total variance and included 18 items. These items include governmental function in business and media participation in the event business, direct government involvement in event development, city's economic development, and tourism relation with other businesses. The highest four loading items were all related to 'event tourism'.

Factor 2 relates those items that represented costs and negative impacts linked to MICE and this factor accounted for 7.70% of the total variance and was labelled 'living quality'.

Factor 3 accounted for 4.71% of variance and relates to city infrastructure and was labelled 'city infrastructure'.

Table 6.1   Factor Analysis for Impacts on the City

Perception Item	Factor					
	1	2	3	4	5	6
Government promotion to business participants	0.797	0.257	−0.425	0.518	0.225	−0.088
Government involvement in the events business	0.781	0.087	−0.421	0.530	0.290	−0.055
Levels of promotion and media involvement	0.769	0.105	−0.406	0.485	0.215	−0.100
Control of the city's event economy and business	0.755	0.239	−0.527	0.495	0.213	0.012
Local business opportunities	0.741	0.243	−0.467	0.553	0.501	−0.115
City's economy as a whole	0.713	0.212	−0.392	0.533	0.407	−0.157
Success of the events	0.708	0.108	−0.444	0.628	0.398	0.190
Pride in and satisfaction with the city	0.698	0.126	−0.472	0.620	0.321	−0.157

(continued)

Perception Item	Factor					
	1	2	3	4	5	6
Event risk control level	**0.666**	0.461	−0.529	0.546	0.323	0.058
Level of local government's interest in events	**0.663**	−0.076	−0.343	0.468	0.380	0.084
Efforts to stimulate local business involvement in events	**0.655**	0.318	−0.242	0.455	0.502	0.298
Suitability of policies and regulations related to tourism	**0.654**	0.134	−0.465	0.589	0.495	0.200
Relationship between government and local businesses	**0.650**	0.310	−0.213	0.430	0.473	0.202
Business cooperation level (both domestic and international)	**0.633**	0.260	−0.485	0.557	0.498	−0.338
Tourism's relationship with local businesses	**0.615**	0.321	−0.523	0.545	0.557	−0.350
Providing suitable plans for the city's event tourism development	**0.609**	0.031	−0.456	0.544	0.401	0.156
Relationship between government and local residents	**0.586**	0.474	−0.383	0.446	0.416	0.236
Suitability of policies and regulations related to events	**0.538**	0.128	−0.341	0.493	0.469	0.486
City's pollution level	0.128	**0.813**	−0.245	0.191	0.352	0.056
Damage to the natural environment	0.143	**0.778**	−0.212	0.190	0.309	0.089
Traffic congestion in the city	0.195	**0.721**	−0.403	0.277	0.247	0.069
Property values and rental costs	0.204	**0.637**	−0.291	0.194	0.158	−0.172
Total living costs	0.474	**0.630**	−0.421	0.426	0.532	−0.250
Price levels and management of prices for events	0.500	**0.598**	−0.353	0.439	0.201	0.097
Related facilities (hotels, restaurants, shopping places, etc.)	0.429	0.225	**−0.833**	0.471	0.363	−0.027
Entertainment opportunities	0.436	0.188	**−0.827**	0.384	0.391	−0.186
Event facilities (event centres, event parks, etc.)	0.420	0.257	**−0.820**	0.401	0.339	−0.132
Maintenance of public facilities like parks and roads	0.339	0.239	**−0.782**	0.328	0.249	−0.060

(continued)

Perception Item	Factor					
	1	2	3	4	5	6
Public services (medical, law, logistics, security, etc.)	0.313	0.356	**−0.685**	0.440	0.541	0.057
Quality of road infrastructure (highways, etc.)	0.307	0.357	**−0.641**	0.347	0.274	0.154
City's level of attraction to people from other cities in China	0.533	0.123	−0.353	**0.865**	0.249	−0.063
City's level of attraction to foreign people	0.437	0.176	−0.381	**0.855**	0.185	0.099
City's image in the world	0.429	0.193	−0.333	**0.831**	0.286	0.163
City's competitive position compared to similar cities	0.481	0.184	−0.431	**0.814**	0.268	−0.086
City's image in China	0.523	0.199	−0.295	**0.792**	0.358	0.037
Number of tourists	0.455	−0.102	−0.414	**0.471**	0.315	−0.154
Unemployment rate	0.220	0.229	−0.328	0.289	**0.781**	0.078
Employment rate and opportunities	0.424	0.267	−0.396	0.369	**0.733**	−0.041
City's safety level and crime rate	0.285	0.389	−0.446	0.242	**0.675**	0.046
Price of goods and services	0.488	0.551	−0.419	0.439	**0.553**	−0.274
Eigenvalue	16.25	3.16	1.93	1.62	1.33	1.11
Contribution to Variance	39.65	7.70	4.71	3.95	3.25	2.71
Alpha Coefficient	0.94	0.84	0.84	0.90	0.75	NA

Extraction Method: Principal Component Analysis.

Rotation Method: Oblimin with Kaiser Normalization.

Factor 4 relates to improvements in the city's image and competitive position while Factor 5 clearly relates to employment and crime. This left Factor 6 that eventuated from the criterion that the number of factors is determined by the number possessing an eigenvalue that is greater than one. Examination had shown that five factors was a 'usable' option, and thus Table 6.2 retains the sixth factor simply for completing the record. However it is evident that it fails to meet the criterion of weightings being above 0.4. In total, the five factors account for 59.26% of the total variance. While this figure is 'acceptable', it is below the usual required minimum of 60%.

However, oblimin rotation was specifically selected because SPSS specifically provides a correlation matrix for the factors, which is shown in Table 6.2. From this it can be seen that Factor 1 does correlate 'highly' with factors 3 and 4 (−0.430 and 0.593 respectively).

Table 6.2   Component Correlation Matrix

Component	Factor					
	1	2	3	4	5	6
1	1.000	0.182	−0.430	0.593	0.372	−0.001
2	0.182	1.000	−0.270	0.202	0.264	0.021
3	−0.430	−0.270	1.000	−0.450	−0.355	0.071
4	0.593	0.202	−0.450	1.000	0.352	0.028
5	0.372	0.264	−0.355	0.352	1.000	0.050
6	−0.001	0.021	0.071	0.028	0.050	1.000

Extraction Method: Principal Component Analysis.
Rotation Method: Oblimin with Kaiser Normalization.

However, linkages between economic development, entertainment, infrastructure, image, and competitiveness are arguably linked even though all are distinct.

➡ 6.4   Factor Analysis for the Scale—Impacts of Events on Personal Lives

The full statistics for this analysis are shown in Table 6.3, the reason for this being that they complemented Table 6.2 although not wholly replicating it. Again, by using oblimin rotation, six factors were found:

1) Items relating to the management of events

Factors included levels of promotion and media involvement, success of the events, suitability of policies and regulations related to tourism, event risk control level, etc.

2) Potential negative impacts on the environment, traffic, and prices

Some items involved included city pollution level, total living costs, increasing property values and rental costs, price levels and management of prices for events, damage to the natural environment, traffic congestion, etc.

3) Infrastructure aspects such as roads, facilities, restaurants, etc.

This factor is more about the city's basic infrastructure like the entertainment facilities, related facilities such as hotels, restaurants, shopping places, high ways, etc.

4) The city's image and attractiveness to visitors

Items related to the level of city's attraction to both international and domestic tourists, city's image in China and the world, city's competitive position, etc.

5) The regulatory framework

This factor is more concerned about the relationship between government and local businesses, and future plans for event tourism development.

6) Employment and security

The last factor shows more items under employment issue and safety areas like safety level, crime rate, number of tourists, and public services including logistics and security.

In total, these six factors 'explained' 60.40% of the variance. The data also again show the correlation matrix and coefficients exceeded 0.4 for factors 1, 3, and 4.

Table 6.3   Factor Analysis for Impacts on Personal Lives

Perception Item	Factor					
	1	2	3	4	5	6
Level of promotion and media involvement	0.729	0.218	0.079	0.117	0.171	0.055
Government promotion to business participants	0.714	0.222	0.130	0.153	0.227	−0.008
Government involvement in the event business	0.691	0.292	0.083	0.072	0.184	0.196
Control of the city's event economy and business	0.668	0.157	0.173	0.252	0.283	0.026
Local business opportunities	0.617	0.229	0.224	0.266	0.134	0.281

(continued)

Perception Item	Factor					
	1	2	3	4	5	6
Business cooperation level (both domestic and international)	**0.596**	0.182	0.334	0.232	−0.009	0.336
Pride in and satisfaction with the city	**0.587**	0.385	0.096	0.239	0.061	0.111
Success of the events	**0.548**	0.322	0.059	0.156	0.453	0.177
Tourism's relationship with local businesses	**0.531**	0.170	0.453	0.224	−0.004	0.305
Level of local government's interest in events	**0.512**	0.388	−0.135	0.082	0.263	0.237
Suitability of policies and regulations related to tourism	**0.499**	0.221	0.048	0.192	0.455	0.242
City's economy as a whole	**0.499**	0.355	0.173	0.126	0.194	0.282
Event risk control level	**0.428**	0.224	0.382	0.188	0.308	−0.053
City's level of attraction to foreign people	0.250	**0.804**	0.171	0.157	0.108	0.082
City's level of attraction to people from other cities in China	0.343	**0.792**	0.130	0.110	0.109	0.128
City's image in the world	0.195	**0.750**	0.142	0.150	0.222	0.102
City's competitive position compared to similar cities	0.316	**0.748**	0.162	0.221	0.136	0.128
City's image in China	0.220	**0.743**	0.103	0.052	0.205	0.178
City's pollution level	−0.066	0.038	**0.752**	0.105	0.156	0.278
Total living costs	0.298	0.168	**0.712**	0.168	−0.008	0.049
Damage to the natural environment	−0.088	0.084	**0.693**	0.155	0.276	0.236
Traffic congestion	0.051	0.079	**0.634**	0.298	0.185	0.117
Property values and rental costs	0.103	0.086	**0.624**	−0.109	−0.303	0.063
Price of goods and services	0.361	0.056	**0.621**	0.209	0.036	0.134
Price levels and management of prices for events	0.219	0.230	**0.614**	0.042	0.323	0.006
Event facilities (event centres, event parks, etc.)	0.224	0.209	0.162	**0.778**	0.077	0.156
Entertainment opportunities	0.282	0.061	0.102	**0.754**	0.021	0.171
Related facilities (hotels, restaurants, shopping places, etc.)	0.169	0.237	0.145	**0.746**	0.192	0.151
Maintenance of public facilities	0.190	0.097	0.206	**0.740**	0.106	0.190

(continued)

Perception Item	Factor					
	1	2	3	4	5	6
Quality of road infrastructure (highways, etc.)	0.081	0.244	0.265	**0.435**	0.179	0.350
Efforts to stimulate local business involvement in events	0.386	0.269	0.206	0.044	**0.605**	0.141
Suitability of policies and regulations related to events	0.362	0.242	0.035	0.150	**0.597**	0.242
Relationship between government and local residents	0.263	0.272	0.386	0.191	**0.551**	−0.015
Relationship between government and local businesses	0.436	0.148	0.290	0.087	**0.547**	0.122
Providing suitable plans for the city's event tourism development	0.318	0.401	−0.076	0.244	**0.449**	0.329
Unemployment rate	0.119	0.125	0.287	0.228	0.263	**0.637**
Employment rate and opportunities	0.184	0.144	0.313	0.196	0.160	**0.632**
Numbers of tourists	0.299	0.306	−0.050	0.223	−0.049	**0.524**
City's safety level and crime rate	0.187	0.042	0.416	0.173	0.038	**0.511**
Public services (medical, law, logistics, security, etc.)	0.113	0.171	0.374	0.398	0.178	**0.500**
Eigenvalue	16.54	3.32	1.96	1.59	1.34	1.11
Contribution to Variance	40.35	8.09	4.79	3.89	3.27	2.71
Alpha Coefficient	0.94	0.92	0.84	0.78	0.85	0.80

Extraction Method: Principal Component Analysis.

Rotation Method: Varimax with Kaiser Normalization.

➡ 6.5 Factor Analysis for the Scale—Importance of Events Based on Statement Assessments

This scale comprises items from which five factors emerged. These are shown in Table 6.4, again using oblimin rotation. In total the five factors 'explain' 60% of the variance. After the table is summarised, the emergent factors might be:

1) A somewhat difficult factor to interpret but one that offers discrimination based on

convenience for residents in terms of prices and distance while also offering contact with a wider world

This factor is more about the event itself, issues like the price of the entrance ticket, distance to the event location, choosing suitable events for the city, etc.

2) Social criticisms of MICE in terms of identifying alternative demands for governmental expenditure such as education and social policies

Some financial issues were involved in this factor category like government had spent too much money on events, because by hosting events, property and rental prices were increased, poorer people could not afford the increasing living costs, and government should put more money on education system rather than hosting events.

3) Stimulation of the local economy and gaining recognition of the city

This factor category involves many positive attitudes like hosting events can stimulate city's economy and tourism industry, increase recognition of the city in the world, stimulate the local business development, and benefit city development.

4) Personal interest and involvement with MICE subject matter

For this factor category, respondents showed high passion involved in MICE like considering to attend more MICE in other cities, willing to attend international events and get involved in the event process, etc.

5) The value of the events for the quality of life

Issues involved in this factor category are more related to personal life like personal economic status will be better, preference to live in the city, life getting more interesting, and increased pride level of the city.

Table 6.4 Importance of Events Based on Statement Assessments

Statement	Factor				
	1	2	3	4	5
The price of the entrance ticket is the most important factor for attending an event	0.797	0.286	0.189	0.242	−0.101

(continued)

Statement	Factor				
	1	2	3	4	5
I think distance to the event venue is the most important factor that inhibits me from attending an event	**0.754**	0.273	0.202	0.250	−0.354
Hosting big events can entertain local residents and give them the opportunity to attend major international events	**0.638**	0.119	0.519	0.583	−0.259
An event should fit the city's culture and history	**0.579**	0.303	0.459	0.494	−0.089
Hosting big events is a good way to know about cultures of other countries	**0.571**	0.163	0.558	0.518	−0.313
I think the government is spending too much money hosting events	0.267	**0.782**	0.108	0.253	−0.147
Because of hosting big events, the property values and rental costs will increase	0.191	**0.768**	0.271	0.341	−0.074
Because of hosting big events, poorer people can no longer afford living in the urban area	0.084	**0.738**	0.138	0.200	−0.379
I think the government should use the money for education and medical care	0.286	**0.681**	0.125	0.180	0.093
Hosting big events can quickly stimulate the city's economic development	0.224	0.203	**0.817**	0.288	−0.413
I believe hosting big events will directly give Hangzhou's tourism and hospitality industry a positive impact	0.322	0.143	**0.780**	0.360	−0.243
Hosting big events can increase recognition of the city in the world	0.269	0.088	**0.760**	0.220	0.025
Hosting big events can quickly stimulate local business development	0.079	0.240	**0.758**	0.285	−0.357
Hosting big events is the best way to show to the world the city's capabilities	0.187	0.088	**0.741**	0.252	−0.374
Hosting big events can always have long-term benefits for city development	0.344	0.110	**0.709**	0.427	−0.498
An event that relates to the people's lives is more interesting and valuable	0.396	0.257	0.327	**0.791**	−0.181
I will consider some important events in other cities	0.346	0.344	0.257	**0.727**	−0.318
I would love to have an opportunity to be involved in the event process	0.410	0.253	0.478	**0.627**	−0.268

(continued)

Statement	Factor				
	1	2	3	4	5
I believe my personal economic status will be better	0.294	0.207	0.377	0.236	−0.783
Building event theme parks is worthwhile	0.144	0.130	0.379	0.501	−0.659
Because Hangzhou is hosting big events, I like living here	0.429	0.185	0.459	0.308	−0.638
Because of hosting big events, life in Hangzhou will be more interesting	0.435	0.212	0.481	0.401	−0.539
Eigenvalues	8.17	2.23	1.53	1.25	1.22
Contribution to Variance	34.06	9.29	6.35	5.21	5.06

Extraction Method: Principal Component Analysis.

Rotation Method: Oblimin with Kaiser Normalization.

6.6 Chapter Summary

This chapter has shown that the data sets possess high reliability and good sampling adequacy as measured by tests such as the alpha coefficients. Additionally, intuitively appealing factors emerged from an exploratory factor analysis.

However, before seeking to establish causal relationships using various forms of discriminatory analysis, there is first a need to examine the ways in which the attitudinal and socio-demographic and nominal data interact. One way to do this is to undertake a cluster analysis that seeks to assess the degree to which separate groupings of respondents can be identified within the data sets. This forms the subject matter of the next chapter.

Chapter Seven

Cluster Analysis

➡ 7.1 Introduction

As stated before, one of the purposes of the project was to assess the degree to which residents might be divided by psychometric measures and also to what extent did behavioural and socio-demographic factors impact upon such clusters. Chapter Five revealed that some socio-demographics such as gender had very little impact, whereas others like occupation did have a role to play while the behavioural attendance of past visitation was a statistically significant variable in a number of instances.

This chapter presents the results of a series of analyses, being primarily a k-means sort of clusters based upon perceptions of the impacts of MICE on the city and personal daily life, and an analysis of the degree of common membership that existed. The next stage is a simple ANOVA as to cluster membership and evaluation of MICE policies. After that a two-step cluster is reported that introduces the variables of income, education, occupation, and past MICE attendance behaviour to see if clusters become better defined. The processes were thus to:

- cluster based on perceptions of impacts on the city;
- find the characteristics of the clusters;
- cluster membership and event evaluation; and
- combine nominal data with psychometric data.

There are different forms of cluster analysis, and hierarchical and standard two-step were assessed, but as is very common, such an analysis simply sorted respondents into two clusters, the first scoring higher than the second. Consequently, k-means was used, but this entails a series of value judgments on the part of the researcher who defines the numbers of required clusters and who then assesses the 'validity' of the outcome based on the numbers that comprise a cluster and the pattern of the scores. Decisions also have to be made about the extent to which outliers might be influencing cluster membership. It has already been noted that missing data existed but was infrequent and random, and thus to retain the full sample, the item mean score was allocated to the missing value.

7.2 Clusters Based on Perceptions of MICE Impacts on the City

Of the alternatives examined, a five-cluster solution based on k-means seemed to offer a better interpretation. However, of these clusters, two had very small numbers of respondents, and thus these were deleted from the analysis, leaving three clusters, which basically comprised a high, medium, and low score across the items. The full result is shown in Table 7.1. In one sense this finding is not particularly enlightening, for the three clusters are more or less equally divided across the sample. Hence what are of more interest are the characteristics of the sub-samples. The first step is to compare them with clusters derived from the personal perspectives scale.

Table 7.1   Clusters Derived from MICE Impacts on the City

Perception Item	K-Means		
	1	2	3
Event facilities (event centres, event parks, etc.)	7.91	6.00	6.56
Related facilities (hotels, restaurants, shopping places, etc.)	7.63	5.00	6.66
Entertainment opportunities	7.74	6.67	6.80
Maintenance of public facilities like parks and roads	7.42	6.67	6.47
Traffic congestion in the city	6.15	3.67	4.36
Quality of road infrastructure (highways, etc.)	7.33	3.67	5.97
Public services (medical, law, logistics, security, etc.)	7.27	5.67	6.34
Damage to the natural environment	6.19	6.00	4.82

(continued)

Perception Item	K-Means		
	1	2	3
City's pollution level	6.16	6.00	4.86
Employment rate and opportunities	7.11	5.00	6.30
Unemployment rate	6.84	5.33	6.08
City's safety level and crime rate	6.95	5.67	5.76
Number of tourists	8.09	6.33	7.32
Property values and rental costs	5.94	8.67	4.32
Price of goods and services	7.19	6.33	5.55
Total living costs	7.02	5.67	5.50
Tourism's relationship with local businesses	7.65	6.67	6.66
Business cooperation level (both domestic and international)	7.56	5.33	6.80
Local business opportunities	7.73	5.00	6.73
City's economy as a whole	7.78	6.67	6.90
Pride in and satisfaction with the city	8.06	5.33	7.42
Government involvement in the event business	7.86	3.00	7.00
Level of promotion and media involvement	7.89	4.67	6.95
Control of the city's event economy and business	7.57	3.33	6.67
Government promotion to business participants	7.78	5.00	6.59
Price levels and management of prices for events	6.89	3.67	5.26
Event risk control level	7.71	5.67	6.27
Success of the events	7.79	3.00	6.99
Suitability of policies and regulations related to tourism	7.70	2.00	6.75
Suitability of policies and regulations related to events	7.63	3.67	6.73
Relationship between government and local businesses	7.55	6.67	6.60
Efforts to stimulate local business involvement in events	7.75	4.67	6.49
The relationship between government and local residents	7.50	6.33	6.09
Level of local government's interest in events	8.02	3.33	7.07
Providing suitable plans for the city's event tourism development	7.69	4.33	7.01
City's image in China	8.02	4.67	7.32
City's image in the world	7.85	4.00	7.01
City's level of attraction to people from other cities in China	7.88	2.67	7.10
City's level of attraction to foreign people	7.87	1.33	7.07
City's competitive position compared to similar cities	7.81	3.00	7.21
Numbers in the cluster	135	106	149

In Table 7.2, four clusters emerged of unequal numbers. The largest was the third cluster with 144 respondents in total. The main focus for this group is the image of the city with items such as 'City's image in China' scoring 7.27. The second largest group (Cluster 4 in the table, 102 respondents) appears to shadow Cluster 3 but is less concerned with event entry prices and management as well as the city image due to MICE. Cluster 1 comprised 79 respondents who scored the highest of the four groups, however most of the high-score factors are mainly related to city elements like 'Event facilities', 'Public services', 'Government involvement in the event business', 'City's economy as a whole', etc. The only one factor with low score in Cluster 1 was 'Property values and rental costs', scoring 5.05 and this factor was also the only factor with low scores in all four clusters. While Cluster 2 comprised only 67 respondents and mainly scored around 5, 'Maintenance of public facilities' was the highest score at 5.91.

Table 7.2   Clusters Derived from Personal Perspectives on MICE Impacts

Perception Item	K-Means			
	1	2	3	4
Event facilities (event centres, event parks, etc.)	7.43	5.17	5.79	5.19
Related facilities (hotels, restaurants, shopping places, etc.)	7.42	5.47	6.03	5.52
Entertainment opportunities	7.69	5.83	6.08	5.71
Maintenance of public facilities	7.52	5.91	5.96	5.47
Traffic congestion in the city	6.77	4.55	4.13	3.44
Quality of road infrastructure (highways, etc.)	7.28	5.39	5.81	5.09
Public services (medical, law, logistics, security, etc.)	7.59	5.74	6.09	5.04
Damage to the natural environment	6.78	5.09	4.86	4.03
City's pollution level	6.44	5.33	4.82	3.79
Employment rate and opportunities	7.47	5.43	6.01	4.83
Unemployment rate	7.21	5.29	6.08	4.86
City's safety level and crime rate	7.14	5.27	5.69	4.52
Number of tourists	7.87	5.69	7.13	6.86
Property values and rental costs	5.05	4.62	4.00	3.45
Price of goods and services	7.01	5.00	5.16	4.60
Total living costs	6.99	4.90	5.14	4.27
Tourism's relationship with local businesses	7.51	5.35	6.27	5.27

(continued)

Perception Item	K-Means			
	1	2	3	4
Business cooperation level (both domestic and international)	7.53	5.42	6.36	5.36
Local business opportunities	7.66	5.43	6.50	5.63
City's economy as a whole	7.63	5.42	6.86	6.03
Pride in and satisfaction with the city	7.87	5.63	7.25	6.41
Government involvement in the event business	7.89	5.34	7.09	6.27
Level of promotion and media involvement	7.78	5.47	7.16	6.30
Control of the city's event economy and business	7.58	5.32	6.70	5.65
Government promotion to business participants	7.47	5.13	6.67	5.76
Price levels and management of prices for events	7.12	4.95	5.61	4.19
Event risk control level	7.49	5.67	6.37	5.16
Success of the events	7.74	5.24	7.20	5.94
Suitability of policies and regulations related to tourism	7.67	5.09	6.66	6.00
Suitability of policies and regulations related to events	7.65	5.31	6.87	5.95
Relationship between government and the local businesses	7.60	5.47	6.63	5.60
Efforts to stimulate local business involvement in events	7.68	5.25	6.78	5.76
Relationship between government and local residents	7.57	5.31	6.32	5.34
Level of local government's interest in events	7.59	4.97	7.26	6.87
Providing suitable plans for the city's event tourism development	7.47	5.18	7.04	6.26
City's image in China	7.56	5.38	7.27	6.43
City's image in the world	7.74	5.58	7.10	6.05
City's level of attraction to people from other cities in China	7.83	5.26	7.14	6.26
City's level of attraction to foreign people	7.74	5.31	7.11	6.14
City's competitive position compared to similar cities	7.79	5.37	7.09	6.13
Numbers in the cluster	79	67	144	102

The next stage is to assess the degree of 'cross over' between the two sets of clusters. According to the theoretical structure proposed in Chapter Three, there should be some degree of separation between the two sets of clusters. The first method of testing was a simple cross tabulation between the two. This produced Table 7.3.

Table 7.3 Cross Tabulation Between Clusters Based on City and Personal Perspectives

Item			Cluster (City)			Total
			1	2	3	
Cluster (Personal)	1	Count	70	8	1	79
		Expected Count	27.3	30.3	21.4	79.0
		Residual	42.7	−22.3	−20.4	
	2	Count	15	27	21	63
		Expected Count	21.8	24.2	17.0	63.0
		Residual	−6.8	2.8	4.0	
	3	Count	41	94	9	144
		Expected Count	49.7	55.3	39.0	144.0
		Residual	−8.7	38.7	−30.0	
	4	Count	8	20	74	102
		Expected Count	35.2	39.2	27.6	102.0
		Residual	−27.2	−19.2	46.4	
Total		Count	134	149	105	388
		Expected Count	134.0	149.0	105.0	388.0

This shows that the two high-scoring clusters (city and personal) of Cluster 1 heavily overlap, which raises an issue as to whether the 70 respondents responsible for this were truly MICE enthusiasts or were simply used to score high. On the other hand the distribution of 'personal perspectives'low scorers are not heavily concentrated in the low-scoring city perspectives cluster, thus indicating that the scales were being used to measure differences, thereby suggesting that the 70 high scorers are indeed unconditional MICE supporters. Assessing the residuals indicates a differential pattern across the matrix, which is however 'mixed'. The distribution is statistically significant as measured by Cramer's V (a test of distribution for nominal data) where $p<0.001$ but the Spearman correlation is 0.58 ($p<0.001$).

➡ 7.3 Characteristics of the Clusters

The next stage is to assess the composition of the clusters. As in Chapter Five, gender factor was not a differentiating variable. In turn, age, education, income, occupation, and past attendance at MICE were assessed. Using Cramer's V and Spearman's correlation, no statistically significant relationships were found between cluster membership and these variables other than in the case of occupation, where the statistical significance was 'spurious' due to the large number of data containing a frequency of less than 5. It could only be concluded that the psychometric measures were independent of the socio-demographic variables.

That left the variable of past attendance at a MICE event to be examined. In the case of the city perspective scale, it did prove statistically significant with Cramer's $V=0.185$, $p=0.001$. Cluster 1 (high scorers) was over-represented in those that had attended an event and under-represented among those that had not attended an event, while Cluster 3 (low scorers) showed an inverse relationship. For the personal perspective scale, Cramer's $V=0.147$, $p=0.037$. Again the highest scorers were over-represented among those who had attended a past event, while Cluster 4 (who scored generally high but not on issues related to event management) was under-represented among those who had attended, and over-represented among those who had not attended. Therefore they form an interesting cluster in that they perceive that they have benefitted from MICE but are not directly impacted by attending any other past MICE.

➡ 7.4 Combining Nominal Data with Psychometric Data

Given that socio-demographics generally had no statistical relationship with attitudes, and past attendance was significant in some but not all measures, it was thought that it might be of interest to see if adding the attendance data to the psychometric data might improve the clustering. The means by which this was done is through the use of two-step cluster analysis. Table 7.4 and Table 7.5 present a summary of findings with reference to cluster numbers of city perspectives and attendance at a MICE event, and the first impression is that the inclusion of this variable does impact cluster membership.

Table 7.4 Differences in Evaluations Between Those Who Have and Have Not Attended MICE

Statement	Have you attended any events in the last 5 years?	Number of Respondents	Mean	Std. Deviation	T-Test
Hosting big events can increase recognition of the city in the world	Yes	274	6.6241	1.45793	2.87**
	No	128	6.1641	1.57629	
Hosting big events is the best way to show to the world the city's capabilities	Yes	276	6.1304	1.58780	2.27*
	No	129	5.7364	1.69797	
Hosting big events can quickly stimulate the city's economic development	Yes	275	6.3345	1.47141	2.05*
	No	126	5.9444	1.39889	
Hosting big events can always have long-term benefits for city development	Yes	273	6.5897	1.39860	2.12*
	No	123	6.2683	1.37943	
Because of hosting big events, the property values and rental costs will increase	Yes	271	6.7269	1.68192	2.07*
	No	128	6.3203	2.11457	
An event should fit the city's culture and history	Yes	272	6.9816	1.38642	2.02*
	No	125	6.6560	1.30819	

Note: *$p<0.05$; **$p<0.01$; ***$p<0.001$.

Table 7.5 A Two-step Cluster Analysis of City Perspectives

Cluster	Yes (MICE attendance during the last 5 years)		No (No MICE attendance during the last 5 years)	
	Frequency	Percent	Frequency	Percent
1	11	5.4%	4	4.7%
2	11	5.4%	22	25.6%
3	51	25.0%	12	14.0%
4	65	31.9%	26	30.2%
5	66	32.4%	22	25.6%
Combined	204	100.0%	86	100.0%

However, the two-step cluster analysis is working on a smaller sample than that previously used, as it only involves that part of the sample that answered all the questions and does not permit missing data. Replicating those conditions with the psychometric variables only resulted in a different set of numbers in the clusters, with one cluster possessing 102 members and another with over 100. It could be concluded that past attendance at a MICE was potentially a significant variable in the analysis.

7.5 Chapter Summary

Given this, two observations might be made. First, it seemed that past attendance at a MICE was necessary to use this as a determining variable in trying to measure possible evaluations of MICE. The second is to question whether it is a first order determinant, or whether it is a second order or proxy variable in that the question arises, what is it that determines attendance? The next chapter therefore uses multiple regression to begin to answer these questions.

Chapter Eight

Examining Causal Relationships

⟹ 8.1 Introduction

The previous chapters have described the overall results and indicated that the scales for city and personal perspectives can be reduced to a smaller number of factors, and that the sample can be divided into clusters based on the same scales. In terms of the proposition, what has not been shown is whether any causal linkages exist between these factors and evaluations of MICE and Hangzhou's policies. In terms of subsequent analysis, one can identify four potential items that can serve as proxies for the policies, namely:

- Hosting big events can quickly stimulate the city's economic development (Stimcity);
- Hosting big events can always have long-term benefits for city development (Citydev);
- Hosting big events can increase recognition of the city in the world (Image);
- I think the government is spending too much money on hosting events (Critical).

The first three items refer to economic progress and wider development that include infrastructure and entertainment facilities and city image, while the fourth covers the critical concern expressed by respondents in a general manner.

Then label the factors from the two scales, City Perspectives and Personal Perspectives as Cityfac1...Cityfac5 and Persfac1...Persfac6 respectively.

The model suggests that:

Stimcity = f(Cityfac1...Cityfac5, Persfac1...Persfac6).

Citydev = f(Cityfac1...Cityfac5, Persfac1...Persfac6).

Image = f(Cityfac1...Cityfac5, Persfac1...Persfac6).

Critical = f(Cityfac1...Cityfac5, Persfac1...Persfac6).

For purposes of assessing a simple linear regression, the mean aggregated factor scores can be used at the first stage in the analysis. The second stage of the analysis can use stepwise multiple regression, introducing all the separate items to better identify the individual items that decide the determined variables of Stimcity, Citydev, Image, and Critical. A third stage would be to introduce nominal data, particularly given that past attendance appears to be a determinant variable. For this, multinomial logistic regression was used given that data such as past attendance, age, income, employment, etc. are nominal or categorical data.

Given the nature of the items used, there is a high probability of multicollinearity. For example, one can expect high correlations between the different items that relate to, say, the city image. Indeed, if there was an absence of correlation, it would not be possible to create factors, which might be described as items possessing high correlation. This is therefore tested by the tolerance (for scores between 0 and 1) and variance inflation factor (for scores between 1 and less than 10). Additionally one can look for the Durbin–Watson statistic, for which an ideal figure is 2, meaning that there is a lack of positive or negative autocorrelation between the residuals. SPSS also produced a chart of residuals, where the desired outcome is one where the residuals follow a 45-degree line, implying a good fit between expected and observed data. For purposes of reporting the data, given that all determining scales use the same measure, unadjusted coefficients of determination (R^2) and beta coefficients (β) are reported.

Consequently, the next sections of this chapter take each of the above four determined variables in turn to assess what might be the determined variables.

8.2 Determining the Evaluation of MICE on Hangzhou's Economic Development

The first step is to evaluate:

Stimcity = f (Cityfac1...Cityfac5, Persfac1...Persfac6).

The results for the first analysis are shown in Table 8.1. The coefficient of determination (R^2) equals 0.19, that is, 19% of the variance in the evaluation of MICE on Hangzhou's economic development is due to the factors listed. Given that the determinants are factor mean aggregate scores, multicollinearity is not an issue here.

Table 8.1   Determining the Evaluation of MICE Impacts on Hangzhou's Economic Development

Model Factor	Unstandardized Coefficient		T	Sig.
	β	Std. Error		
Constant	1.772	0.545	3.251	0.001
Cityfac1	0.302	0.120	2.516	0.012
Cityfac2	−0.033	0.096	−0.348	0.728
Cityfac3	0.254	0.091	2.792	0.005
Cityfac4	0.080	0.105	0.759	0.448
Cityfac5	−0.002	0.089	−0.021	0.983
Persfac1	0.057	0.127	0.448	0.654
Persfac2	0.255	0.117	2.181	0.030
Persfac3	−0.092	0.090	−1.026	0.305
Persfac4	−0.215	0.115	−1.868	0.062
Persfac5	0.036	0.092	0.397	0.692
Persfac6	0.075	0.101	0.744	0.457

Dependent variable: Hosting big events can quickly stimulate the city's economic development.

The main determinants as measured by beta coefficient scores are Cityfac1, Cityfac3, Persfac2, and negatively Persfac4. These are measures of:

City Perspectives

Cityfac1: Factor 1, labelled 'Government event management and local economy stimulation', relates to government involvement and its policies related to urban revitalisation and economic gains.

Cityfac3: Factor 3, related to city infrastructure.

Personal Perspectives

Persfac2: Potential negative impacts on the environment, traffic, and prices.

Persfac: The city's image and attractiveness to visitors (but note $p=0.06$).

It thus appears that the evaluation of MICE impacts on the city are primarily governed through evaluations of government event management, changes to the city's infrastructure, and negative ways in which respondents are affected by changes to the environment, traffic and prices, and benefits derived from a change in the city's image. Figure 8.1 presents a plot of the residuals and this indicates a good fit exists between the expected and observed data.

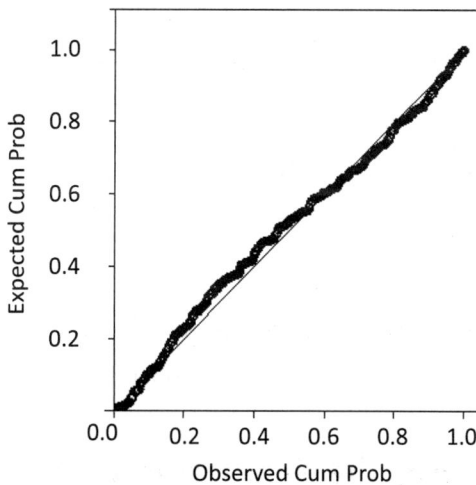

Figure 8.1   Residual Analysis

Normal P-P Plot of Regression Standardized Residual.

Dependent Variable: Hosting big events can quickly stimulate the city's economic development.

The next stage in the analysis was to identify individual items that had predictive significance using the stepwise function in SPSS. Using this technique, the coefficient of determination started at 0.12 but doubled to 0.25 with seven items accounting for this. Table 8.2 summarises the data, and lists the seven items. The Durbin–Watson statistics is 1.95, and tolerance and VIF data are within the required guidelines. Generally the two sets of analyses are congruent with each other.

Table 8.2   Determining the Evaluation of MICE Impacts on Hangzhou's Economic Development (Individual Items)

Model Factor	Unstandardized Coefficient		T	Sig.
	β	Std. Error		
Constant	2.907	0.406	7.153	0.000
Event facilities (event centres, event parks, etc.)	0.200	0.046	4.373	0.000
Relationship between government and local residents	0.192	0.049	3.955	0.000
Tourism's relationship with local businesses	0.134	0.055	2.458	0.014
City's pollution level	0.095	0.042	2.278	0.023
City's image in China	−0.150	0.047	−3.218	0.001
Local business opportunities	0.190	0.058	3.306	0.001
Entertainment opportunities	−0.122	0.052	−2.351	0.019

Attempting to improve the data fit by adding nominal data did not produce any improvement: indeed the Cox and Snell Pseudo Coefficient fell to zero and a classification table showed that less than half of the respondents were allocated to a 'correct category'. This indicates that the psychometric measures are telling and independent of the nominal data.

8.3   Determining the Evaluation of MICE Impacts on Long-term City Development

The evaluation is now of:

Citydev = f (Cityfac1...Cityfac5, Persfac1...Persfac6)

and Table 8.3 summarises the results. In this case R^2=0.22. Again there was no issue of multicollinearity.

As above, the main city factors are government event management and local economy stimulation (β=0.18) and city infrastructure (β=0.21), but this time Cityfac4 (which is related to improvements in the city's image and competitive position) also has a role (β=0.17). However, only the second and third of these factors are statistically significant. Persfac 4—the city's image and attractiveness to visitors is the main personal impact factor (β=–0.27, p=0.011). Again an examination of the residuals provides a good fit.

Table 8.3   Determining the Evaluation of MICE Impacts on Long-term City Development

Model Factor	Unstandardized Coefficient		T	Sig.
	β	Std. Error		
Constant	1.770	0.511	3.463	0.001
Cityfac1	0.183	0.113	1.626	0.105
Cityfac2	0.016	0.090	0.176	0.860
Cityfac3	0.214	0.085	2.507	0.013
Cityfac4	0.174	0.098	1.772	0.077
Cityfac5	0.089	0.084	1.068	0.286
Persfac1	0.145	0.119	1.216	0.225
Persfac2	0.121	0.110	1.100	0.272
Persfac3	–0.145	0.084	–1.719	0.086
Persfac4	–0.276	0.108	–2.551	0.011
Persfac5	0.094	0.086	1.098	0.273
Persfac6	0.128	0.094	1.361	0.174

Dependent Variable: Hosting big events can have long-term benefits for city development.

Examining the individual items as shown in Table 8.4 found again seven items 'explaining' 31% of the variance in the determined variable, with the Durbin–Watson statistic being 1.97. It is notable that the first three items alone accounted for 25% of the variance, and from that perspective it might be said that these three variables hold the key to long-term development of MICE and city development in Hangzhou.

Running a multinominal logistic regression achieved a classification fit of 71%, but it also showed that of the socio-economic variables only employment status was statistically significant. However, the overall fit of the model can only be described as poor and the Cox and Snell Pseudo Coefficient was again zero. Possibly the main finding from this analysis was that past attendance at MICE was not statistically significant.

Table 8.4 Determining the Evaluation of MICE Impacts on Long-term City Development (Individual Items)

Model Factor	Unstandardized Coefficient		T	Sig.
	β	Std. Error		
Constant	2.341	0.384	6.100	0.000
Success of the events	0.218	0.051	4.295	0.000
Relationship between government and local residents	0.162	0.045	3.640	0.000
Tourism's relationship with local businesses	0.191	0.047	4.061	0.000
City's image in China	−0.116	0.049	−2.347	0.019
Public services (medical, law, logistics, security, etc.)	0.166	0.049	3.405	0.001
City's economy as a whole	0.161	0.051	3.138	0.002
City's competitive position compared to similar cities	−0.131	0.056	−2.320	0.021

8.4 Determining the Evaluation of MICE Impacts on the City Image in the World

In this case, the coefficient of determination equals 0.17, the relationship is significant, free from multicollinearity and Table 8.5 shows the beta coefficient. As might be expected, the main determinants are related to government event management and economic development (β=0.41), city infrastructure (β=0.35), costs and negative impacts of MICE (β=−0.24), personal impacts of employment, safety, and security (β=−0.34), and personal impacts of negative environmental, traffic, and price effects (β=0.30).

Table 8.5   Determining the Evaluation of MICE Impacts on the City Image in the World

Model Factor	Unstandardized Coefficient		T	Sig.	Collinearity Statistics	
	β	Std. Error			β	Std. Error
Constant	2.879	0.572	5.033	0.000		
Cityfac1	0.409	0.126	3.246	0.001	0.360	2.778
Cityfac2	−0.241	0.100	−2.409	0.016	0.299	3.345
Cityfac3	0.354	0.095	3.713	0.000	0.422	2.368
Cityfac4	−0.013	0.110	−0.117	0.907	0.348	2.870
Cityfac5	0.065	0.094	0.692	0.489	0.404	2.474
Persfac1	−0.154	0.134	−1.150	0.251	0.263	3.807
Persfac2	0.305	0.123	2.486	0.013	0.244	4.100
Persfac3	−0.046	0.094	−0.491	0.624	0.369	2.707
Persfac4	0.129	0.121	1.070	0.285	0.258	3.880
Persfac5	0.074	0.096	0.774	0.440	0.374	2.673
Persfac6	−0.345	0.106	−3.271	0.001	0.361	2.772

Dependent Variable: Hosting big events can increase recognition of the city in the world.

Yet again single items were examined and seven items were found to 'explain' 21% of the variance, but of this, three items 'explained' 18% of variance. The Durbin–Watson statistic was 1.77. Tolerance and VIF statistics were again of a required nature.

All the items were statistically significant at $p<0.026$ and fit well with the analysis in Section 8.3, indicating a link between long-term city development and image of Hangzhou. On this occasion, however, the multi-nominal logistic regression was successful with a Cox and Snell Pseudo Coefficient as high as 0.97. Of the categorical data only levels of education and past attendance at a MICE event were shown as significant at $p<0.001$. The other determining items from the personal perspectives where $p<0.001$ related to MICE have a personal impact on individuals and business, implying that within the sample there were some respondents who had business interests related to the MICE industry. Of the city perspectives, the key items were impacts on city traffic and congestion, impacts on the city economy, government promotion of business interests, and the success of the events.

Taken as a whole what seems to drive perceptions of whether Hangzhou is able to generate a global recognition and image is not so much as to government involvement in marketing per se, but whether the city is able to generate actual business from the MICE policy, build better city facilities and have better traffic flow, and create MICE that are perceived as successful—of which possibly a key criterion of success is not simply visitor numbers but the spending and profitability that stem from MICE. However, there are things worthy of notice to the findings. One is that while the model does display good classification fit, there is a significant issue of empty cells and while the forecast model does allocate zero sums to these cells, the overall validity of the model remains to be tested. This issue is taken up in Section 8.6.

➡ 8.5 Determining the Evaluation of Whether Too Much Money Is Spent on MICE

In this case, the coefficient of determination is much lower at 0.077 and the main factor operating as a determinant is the personal perception factor of employment, safety, and security. The item analysis also indicates a weak pattern of relationships with nine items emerging where $p<0.025$, but these 'explained' 17% of the variance. It can be concluded that determinants of whether money is being wasted on a MICE policy are much more diffuse, but they are of an expected nature. For record, the nine items were labelled 'City's safety level and crime rate', 'Unemployment rate', 'Quality of road infrastructure (highways, etc.)', 'Government promotion to business participants', 'City's pollution level', 'Event facilities (personal perspectives)', 'Event facilities (city perspectives)', and 'Related facilities (city perspectives)'. One reason for the diffuse nature of the number of variables and relationships is because on the whole, the sample was supportive of Hangzhou's policies.

The final stage was to again run a multi-nominal logistic regression. As in Section 8.4, this was found to generate a positive Cox and Snell score, again of 0.97. It had previously been noted that the 'solution' was diffuse, and this is clearly indicated in the Likelihood Ratio tests, and a summary of this is shown in Table 8.6. From the items listed, the concerns do not appear to be about economic policies as much as a sense of public well-being in a MICE policy that attracts visitors, involves local businesses, and at a personal level produces a safe and entertaining city that is affordable. While this interpretation has a *prima facie* logic, again it should be noted that the equation is not wholly rigorous due to a large number of empty cells for the reasons to be discussed in the next section.

Table 8.6   Likelihood Ratio Tests for 'Too Much Money Spent on MICE'

Effect	Model Fitting Criteria	Likelihood Ratio Tests		
	-2 Log Likelihood of Reduced Model	Chi-Square	Df	Sig.
Intercept	0.029(a)	0.000	0	
Personal Perspectives				
Entertainment opportunities	357.976(b)	357.947	8	0.000
Public services affecting self	338.434(c)	338.405	8	0.000
City crime and public safety	72.675(b)	72.646	8	0.000
Pride in and satisfaction with city	239.961(b)	239.932	8	0.000
Price of goods and services	807.240(c)	807.211	8	0.000
Appropriate tourism policies	271.527(c)	271.498	8	0.000
Improved quality of life	500.396(b)	500.367	8	0.000
City Perspectives				
Local and international business cooperation	366.205(b)	366.176	8	0.000
Stimulating local business	240.947(b)	240.918	8	0.000
Level of local government's interests in events	233.411(b)	233.382	8	0.000
City's image in China	26.741(b)	26.712	8	0.001
Attractiveness of city to people of other places in china	218.439(b)	218.410	8	0.000
Attractiveness of city to foreign people	87.585(b)	87.556	8	0.000
Monthly salary	453.658(c)	453.629	40	0.000
Level of education	212.130(b)	212.101	40	0.000
Past events attended	147.303(b)	147.274	8	0.000

➡ 8.6   Path Analysis

Thus far the regression analyses have shown that the factors possess some predictive ability and that of the categorical data, the general socio-demographics have limited value as determining variables, only employment status, education, and particularly past attendance have some statistical significance at varying times. It was also noted in Section 8.4 that issues occurred within the multi-nominal logistic regression. Essentially this was an issue of empty cells occurring in the data—a problem that was due to the number of cells created by the large numbers of variables when compared to the size of the sample. Although a sample of over 400 is generally regarded as sufficient, there are problems occurring in this technique, as each item has multiple cells associated with it due to the scale used, and with some sub-sample groups, for example age groups, being small in number, there were insufficient numbers of respondents to fill all the cells.

Another issue is a need to assess the interplay between the different factors and variables. In a sense, the analysis is only partial due to assumptions of independence between different variables. One way to further assess the model is to assume degrees of inter-dependence. In theory, one way of undertaking this is to utilise structural equation modeling or confirmatory factor analysis. This is a technique that is subject to high degrees of manipulation (Mazanec, 2009; Ryan, 2009) to a degree where it is legitimate to argue that researchers may have over-manipulated data to obtain high goodness of fit indices, but have failed to note that parsimonious approaches may be better and the real issue is that a model has not been supported. Of more practical concern in this thesis is that it can be argued that EFA and CFA should not be performed on the same data set. Klein (2004) noted that one seeks to explore relationships and thus the latter should be tested on a second set of data. For this reason, this study reverted to a path analysis that tests for causal relationships within linear relationships. For this, the software package AMOS was used. The first relationship analysed was to take the four evaluative criteria from Section 8.1, namely:

- Hosting big events can quickly stimulate the city's economic development (Stimcity);
- Hosting big events can always have long-term benefits for city development (Citydev);
- Hosting big events can increase recognition of the city in the world (Image);
- I think the government is spending too much money on hosting events (Critical).

Then we argued that they created the latent (unobserved) variable 'Evaluation of MICE policy' and measured the relationships between the four and the dependent, latent variable. The results are shown in Table 8.7.

Table 8.7   Maximum Likelihood Estimates

(a)

Regression Weight	Estimate	S.E.	p
Image ← Evaluation	1.000		
Stimcity ← Evaluation	1.488	0.177	***
Citydev ← Evaluation	1.048	0.113	***
Critical ← Evaluation	0.335	0.103	0.001

(b)

Intercept	Estimate	S.E.	p
Image	6.479	0.075	***
Stimcity	6.213	0.073	***
Citydev	6.482	0.070	***
Critical	6.248	0.077	***

(c)

Variance	Estimate	S.E.	p
Evaluation	0.732	0.139	***
Error—Image	1.544	0.131	***
Error—Stimcity	0.497	0.162	0.002
Error—Citydev	1.145	0.114	***
Error—Critical	2.268	0.164	***

Note: ***$p<0.001$.

From these it can be seen that all results are statistically significant at $p<0.002$ or less, but that the 'Critical' has the lowest regression weight, the highest variance and hence the highest error rate in explaining the lowest proportion of variance in the determined variable 'Evaluation'. The next section of results tests the fit of the model. The literature on path analysis and SEM (Structural Equation Modeling) provides a wide range of fit measures, and these can be seen in Klein (2004). The most common, but prone to error index is the CFI (Comparative Fit Index), which was 0.989. Many researchers favour the RMSEA (Root Mean Square Error of Approximation), which was 0.062. RMSEA is often used because it eliminates the size of the sample as affecting results. While many authorities state the

RMSEA should be below 0.05, and a minority will accept values of less than 0.1. In this case, the former is preferred as a criterion, and the issue can be seen that it is the variable 'Critical' that reduces the goodness of fit.

For accepting this, it is possible to progress to the fuller path diagram that was established as Figure 3.2 in Chapter Three.

To utilise this diagram in full for a path analysis would create a difficult and overly complex set of relationships, and in any case, models used in theory building are often required to be parsimonious. Given that the results from Chapter Six on factor analysis, the regression analyses above and understandings derived from Chapter Seven on cluster analysis enable two simpler alternatives to be constructed. This is illustrated in Figure 8.2.

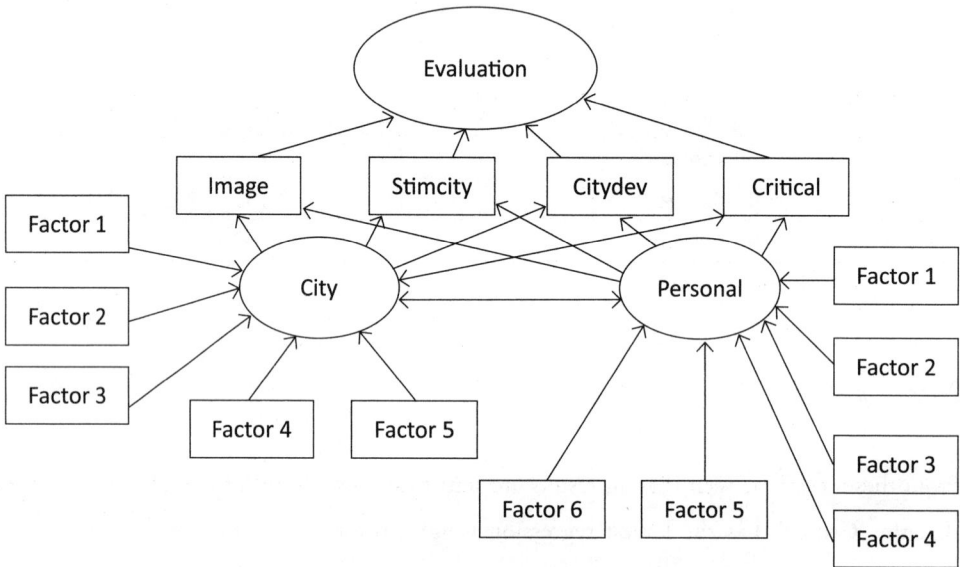

Figure 8.2   Path Analysis for Evaluating MICE Policies

For this model the CFI was 0.73, while the RMSEA was 0.17: both statistics indicate that the model failed the usual criteria as producing a good fit between model and data set. The squared multiple correlation for the 'Critical' factor was very low at 0.049 compared to, say, 'Stimcity' at the other extreme, which was 0.823. Given that the weakest part of the model, at least statistically, was the linkage between city and personal perspectives and the 'Critical' factor, this 'Critical' factor was deleted. At first sight, this looked good in that the CFI was equal to 1.0, but the RMSEA was far worse at 0.26, and indeed on closer examination, it was found that the regressions could not be calculated. It can be concluded thus far that the results are in the desired direction, that the economic and city development elements dominate, but that when the 'social cost' components are removed, the model fails to calculate, implying that they do have a certain role, however weak, to play in the equation.

As with the regression analysis, attention then was turned to the use of what were considered to be 'key' items in the data set. These were selected from the results of the regression analysis. As each stage of the model was developed with AMOS, it was separately tested for statistical rigour. The steps and items were:

The City's Economic Stimulation

Items: Relationship between government and local residents

Tourism's relationship with local businesses

City's pollution level

City's image in China

Entertainment opportunities

CFI=0.98, RMSEA=0.048

The City's Wider Development

Items: Success of events

Public services

City's economy as a whole

City's comparative position compared to similar cities

CFI=0.99, RMSEA=0.06

The City Image

Items: Event facilities

Success of events

Entertainment opportunities

Business cooperation

CFI=0.98, RMSEA=0.12

In the next step, the combining of these three latent factors when determining resident evaluation of MICE in Hangzhou produced a CFI equal to 0.78 and a RMSEA of 0.13. Yet again the results tend to, but do not achieve a desired result. Such results can occur for any number of reasons, including Type I and Type II errors, namely errors in data collection and problem specification. Given the exploratory nature of the research, both of these sources of error need to be considered in any consideration of the limitations of the research, and this is undertaken in the final chapter.

The full set of results associated with Figure 8.2 are thus shown in Table 8.8.

Table 8.8   Maximum Likelihood Estimates Related to Figure 8.2

(a)

Regression Weight	Estimate	S.E.	C.R.	p
Toomch ← Evaluation	1.000			
Selbig ← Evaluation	4.282	2.822	1.517	0.129
Stimcity ← Evaluation	8.243	5.579	1.477	0.140
Aware ← Evaluation	4.475	2.960	1.512	0.131
Cityfac5 ← City	1.000			
Cityfac4 ← City	0.890	0.064	13.872	***
Cityfac3 ← City	0.996	0.069	14.503	***
Cityfac2 ← City	0.919	0.080	11.450	***
Cityfac1 ← City	0.970	0.059	16.424	***
Persfac5 ← Personal	1.000			
Persfac6 ← Personal	0.901	0.057	15.739	***
Persfac4 ← Personal	1.001	0.056	17.957	***
Persfac3 ← Personal	0.966	0.060	16.008	***
Persfac1 ← Personal	0.985	0.049	20.140	***
Persfac2 ← Personal	0.883	0.060	14.615	***
Aware ← City	0.926	0.200	4.637	***
Stimcity ← City	1.004	0.189	5.322	***
Selbig ← City	0.985	0.179	5.492	***
Toomch ← City	0.446	0.205	2.177	0.029
Aware ← Personal	−0.369	0.181	−2.040	0.041
Stimcity ← Personal	−0.318	0.169	−1.879	0.060
Selbig ← Personal	−0.275	0.160	−1.715	0.086

(continued)

Regression Weight	Estimate	S.E.	C.R.	*p*
Toomch ← Personal	−0.130	0.189	−0.688	0.491

Note: ***p<0.001.

(b)

Intercept	Estimate	S.E.	C.R.	*p*
Toomch	6.250	0.077	80.688	***
Selbig	6.482	0.070	92.708	***
Stimcity	6.214	0.073	85.570	***
Aware	6.477	0.075	86.116	***
Cityfac5	5.957	0.063	94.247	***
Cityfac4	7.058	0.056	124.966	***
Cityfac3	6.468	0.061	106.821	***
Cityfac2	5.174	0.071	73.147	***
Cityfac1	6.759	0.052	130.204	***
Persfac5	6.275	0.062	101.766	***
Persfac6	6.023	0.060	100.593	***
Persfac4	6.474	0.060	107.782	***
Persfac3	5.867	0.063	92.864	***
Persfac1	6.381	0.054	117.617	***
Persfac2	5.025	0.062	80.597	***

Note: ***p<0.001.

(c)

Variance	Estimate	S.E.	C.R.	*p*
Evaluation	0.019	0.025	0.759	0.448
City	0.841	0.104	8.097	***
Personal	0.951	0.103	9.265	***
Error term 4	2.234	0.161	13.873	***
Error term 3	1.121	0.105	10.635	***
Error term 2	0.374	0.256	1.464	0.143
Error term 1	1.559	0.133	11.721	***
Error term 9	0.676	0.058	11.612	***
Error term 8	0.567	0.047	11.949	***
Error term 7	0.568	0.050	11.371	***

(continued)

Variance	Estimate	S.E.	C.R.	p
Error term 6	1.127	0.091	12.413	***
Error term 5	0.233	0.027	8.584	***
Error term 14	0.536	0.046	11.758	***
Error term 15	0.578	0.049	11.828	***
Error term 10	0.211	0.024	8.777	***
Error term 11	0.727	0.059	12.298	***
Error term 12	0.676	0.055	12.251	***
Error term 13	0.451	0.040	11.291	***

Note: ***$p<0.001$.

8.7 Chapter Summary

This chapter attempted to develop causal links between the items and variables identified in the previous chapters, and so build upon the text from Chapter Five to Chapter Seven. While not entirely failing, it cannot be claimed that the results represented an unqualified success. One significant problem relates to the role played by any evaluation of the opportunity costs of Hangzhou's MICE policies. It seems appropriate to consider such costs within any evaluation of MICE, but it does appear to be problematical. Residents tended to support the MICE policies for economic, image, and city development reasons, and certainly as shown in Chapter Five, the overall scores on questions related to environmental and social issues are not as high as those related to economic considerations, but they still get scores above the mid-point of the scale. Equally, there are some respondents for whom these items possess importance. There seems to be some ambiguity in the respondents' considerations of these questions, and it might be that the statistical modeling, which assumes a tight logicality between variables, fails to achieve the normally desired criteria of a good fit because the data contains this sense of ambiguity. One way of checking the degree of ambiguity that may, or may not exist, is to visit the lead questions of the questionnaire. These asked respondents to provide answers to open-ended items about the negative and positive aspects of MICE, and this forms the subject matter of the next chapter.

Chapter Nine

Residents' Opinions and Behaviours

➡ 9.1   Introduction

In the light of the results derived from Chapter Eight and the suggestion that the data contain responses that reflect some ambiguity within the data set, this chapter reverts to the opening section of the questionnaire. In this section respondents were asked to describe their history of past attendance at MICE and also to identify four possible positive and four negative impacts of the MICE policies in Hangzhou. These questions were at the beginning of the questionnaire in the hope that items mentioned subsequently would not influence the aspects that would be mentioned by the respondents. The chapter commences with a description of the results and then describes past attendance patterns.

➡ 9.2   Possible Positive and Negative Impacts of the MICE Industry in Hangzhou

Table 9.1 presents a summary derived from the respondents' comments. In total there are 541 positive comments. Of the respondents, 10 were able to name 4 positive impacts, 35 listed 3 possible positive impacts, 118 listed 2 and 159 listed just 1 item. There were 83 respondents who made no response to the questions.

Given the previous analysis it is of no surprise that the three main categories are those of city branding (196 mentions), the economy (135 mentions) and business development (113 mentions). The environment achieves a fourth place, but the answers mainly relate to issues such as better traffic flow and a general improvement in the urban environment. The latter perhaps relates to the category 'Quality of life' which attracts 28 mentions, leaving improvements to tourism to take the next place with 21 mentions.

Table 9.1   Positive Impacts Associated with MICE

Positive Impact	Number of Mentions
Tourism	**21**
-Attract talents	2
-Attract more people	3
-Attract more tourists	8
-Tourism development	7
-Develop MICE industry	1
Business Development	**113**
-Improve city's competitiveness	2
-Business opportunities	106
-Increase local event industry	1
-Information communication and gathering	4
Branding	**196**
-City's image	186
-City construction and development	2
-Showing city's capabilities	7
-Introduce Hangzhou to the world	1
Economy	**135**
-Economy	126
-Employment opportunities	7
-Foreign investment	1
-Get economic information	1
Environment	**46**
-Environment	17
-Road construction	3
-Traffic	2
-City appearance	23

(continued)

Positive Impact	Number of Mentions
-Transportation service improvement	1
Quality of Life	**28**
-Life more interesting/Improve quality of life	4
-Cultural development	5
-More entertainment/recreation	11
-More places for shopping	1
-Convenience	1
-Promote the image of 'leisure'	1
-Learning more from the outside world	2
-Leisure concept popularizing	1
-Create pride in the city	2
Others	**2**

Table 9.2 provides the list of 331 negative impacts listed by the respondents. In this case the list is shown by frequency of mentions as primarily the majority of items fall into three categories. First, 'Quality of life'—inconvenience to daily lives caused by crowding, traffic congestion, noise, pollution, and increased living costs. Second, 'Poor MICE managment'—low quality of MICE brings in some bad overseas cultures, which wastes money and other resources. Third, 'Government involvement'—negative impacts on government issues relate to many items under city public services like road development, too much construction, business opportunity, and city safety level.

Table 9.2   Negative Impacts Associated with MICE

Negative Impact	Number of Mentions
Quality of life	**297**
-Traffic conditions worsened	107
-Environment	78
-Inconvenient public transportation/Higher prices	29
-Crowded	22
-Resources/money wasted	16
-Cost of living increased	15
-Real estate price increased	9
-Pollution	9

(continued)

Negative Impact	Number of Mentions
-Noise	1
-Disrupts residents' normal schedule	3
-Adversely affects quality of life	2
-City congestion	3
-Public parking is difficult	3
Poor MICE management	17
-Some attendee companies are not qualified	4
-Too many tourists	4
-Quality of events are low	3
-Poor event quality causes complaints	2
-Too much business atmosphere rather than relaxation	1
-Brings in some bad overseas cultures	1
-Some tourists' actions negatively impact the city	1
-High prices trouble tourists	1
Government involvement	17
-Corruption	2
-Business opportunities	1
-Chaotic city	1
-Too much construction	1
-Shows the weakness of city construction	1
-Reduces the foreign tourists' passion	1
-Increased tourism prices	1
-Uncontrolled land usage	1
-Shows city's weakness	1
-Road development negatively affected	3
-Public services negatively affected	2
-Crime level/Safety	2

In view of the discussion in Chapter Eight, neither list provides a surprise, nor are these items quite consistent with the initial literature reviewed in Chapter Two and the subsequent chapters. However, the very number of negative items mentioned by respondents does support the contention of a possible ambiguity within the statistical analysis, with strong support being provided for the economic and wider development of the city, while complaints were primarily about personal inconvenience that was suffered with minor but potentially important concerns about inflationary pressures and waste of money.

9.3 Past Behaviours of the Sample

In total approximately 363 MICE were attended by the sample—it's 'approximately' because some respondents mentioned separate shows that were part of a large event and thus there was a problem of double counting in the list. Table 9.3 lists the most frequently mentioned items, and a few conclusions can be drawn from this. It should also be noted that a very wide range of meetings, exhibitions, and shows were listed, including exhibitions on sanitation, IT shows, railway products, pregnancy and baby wear—in short a great variety of interests were being met. Three main categories can be discerned— conferences and business meetings, home-oriented shows that meet the interests of a growing affluent middle class with interests in real estate, home improvements and car purchases, and then a mix of shows and exhibitions that reflect a wider range of leisure and recreational pursuits that include art shows, cartoon festivals, cultural concerns, and general educational interests including science.

The fact that the most frequently mentioned item was the company organised trip is consistent with the current Chinese business practice where, as previously mentioned, the official business trip is often associated with attending exhibitions. While this has an element of gathering information, it is also important for networking. The fact that car shows and real estate shows were the next most frequently mentioned items is, as previously noted, quite consistent with the development of Hangzhou as described in Chapter Two.

Table 9.3   Most Popular Past MICE Attended

Past MICE Attended	Number of Mentions
Company organised trip	45
Car show	31
Real estate show	30
West Lake Expo	21

(continued)

Past MICE Attended	Number of Mentions
Cartoon festival	19
Annual conference	17
Fashion show	11
Kitchen and bathroom show	11
World Leisure Expo	11
Business meeting	10
Canton Fair	10
Home design show	10
Furniture show	8
Arts and crafts show	7
Agricultural show	6
Lots of MICE	6
Wedding show	5

It can also be argued that these preferences for MICE also throw some light on the analysis of Chapter Eight, and here one can again refer to the situation of Hangzhou. Like many other cities in China, Hangzhou has undergone two significant decades of development that has led to the emergence of a new educated middle class experiencing a better quality of life, at least in material things, unknown to the previous generations.

⇒ 9.4 Chapter Summary

Given this, there is little surprise that the economic and urban development of Hangzhou and the contribution that MICE makes to that development remain large in any analysis of resident attitudes. The residents have benefitted from these changes and have a vested interest in them over time. Yet there is a growing realisation for many that these gains have come at a cost, it can be argued that, as in other parts of China, there exists such a tension. For many, there is no recognition of these costs to the environment and the growing divides of income and wealth among people. For others, there is such a recognition, but an acceptance of these costs are necessary for achieving and sustaining the growth that has brought so many benefits to so many people. And then there is a growing number of people who question whether, in the longer term, such costs are sustainable, but they have uncertainty as to what to do about these issues—what is the balance that will permit more to gain economically while not sacrificing too much, so that in the longer term the economic gains will not be undermined. It is also perhaps considerations such as these that give rise to the poor fit of the path analysis noted in Chapter Eight.

Chapter Ten

Discussion and Conclusion

⇒ 10.1 Introduction

The previous chapters provided a literature review of MICE and residents' attitudes to MICE with some reference to China, a brief description of MICE developments in Hangzhou, and then findings related to residents' reactions to the hosting of MICE in Hangzhou. The initial impetus for this study was the responses of residents in Hangzhou to the development of MICE in the city as part of its tourism promotion, and this led to the objective of looking at residents' perceptions of the role of MICE in the city. An underlying assumption of the study is that the concept of MICE represents a legitimate framework for measuring residents' perceptions of MICE-hosting in a Chinese regional city on the basis that MICE-hosting forms part of wider tourism policies that are adopted for purposes of economic and social benefits. Given that basic perceptions of MICE hosting are socio-psychological, it was also thought important to classify what would otherwise be a heterogeneous mix of residents.

This final chapter will briefly provide some implications and suggestions that will also be outlined for future research and tourism planning. The chapter will also consider the existing limitations of the thesis as well as the theoretical and practical contributions in this field of featured tourism in China.

⬄ 10.2   Role of Government

In order to attract more investment for, and generate more management skills within the event industry, local government currently acts as a coordinator and not the sole organiser or operator. Playing this role can avoid many financial risks and permit time for other government affairs, but often officials find themselves in somewhat of a quandary when it comes to planning for event development with a private sector MICE management organisation. One reason is the differing sets of objectives and conflicts of interest frequently arise over how an event will be developed in the future. For the private sector profit-making may be the only purpose, but this may cause some negative aspects in residents' daily lives with reference to, for example, land usage, environmental damage, etc. Governments may have sets of motives related to wider economic and social development, but those motives may sometimes be dominated by individual operators which, however, may fail to deliver the promised returns to the wider community. In general this situation 'puts the cart before the horse', and governments should act as the more important authority in the event planning and operation process, especially when public resources are used. Governments need to establish relevant regulations and policies before events, provide supervision and guidance during events, and examine and monitor success and impacts after events. Since there are direct relationships between residents' perceived impacts of MICE on their daily life and their attitudes toward local government's role in event development, governments must be sensitive to residents' concerns to retain authority. However, the public do realise that attracting more local businesses and event planners into the event industry is a good means for future development. It might also be claimed that more competitors are better than an exclusive operator on the grounds that competition can stimulate the quality of event operation.

Hangzhou's government probably has also realised that, in fact, global recognition of Hangzhou's image is not high enough. As one of China's most famous tourism cities, Hangzhou is not as well known as it should be. A redefinition of the city's image is important for Hangzhou to stand out in the international tourism market. There is perhaps the need for a suitable and easily memorised slogan to help attract foreign tourists. For example, Malaysia has been promoting itself as 'Truly Asia', the Republic of Korea is

'Sparkling' and at city level, Venice has been known as the 'City of Water' and Vienna 'The City of Music'. It is not easy to find a perfect name or slogan to represent a city image, but if done successfully it can enhance city tourism development in the world market. In addition, in order to improve the city's international tourism brand, governments need to improve the city's environment, public service, infrastructure, tourism service, and cultural attractions to meet the international tourism city's standard. Doing this would be quite consistent with the public demand represented by the sample in this study.

Local governments are also responsible for the city's daily operation during event hosting. This study suggests that governments put specific attention to traffic congestion during the events for this would be perceived as an effective benefit by residents when considering event impacts. It may be useful to provide an effective event schedule to residents, provide traffic directions through the transportation department, and suggest special timetables for local residents to avoid the bad congestion periods. As the natural environment is another important aspect mentioned by the residents, not only governments but also event planners need to pay more attention to environmental protection and utilise the best sustainable practices.

Use eye-catching signs at busy travel sites that warn tourists not to damage any attractions, especially at some historical sites can be helpful. Providing enough public sanitation facilities like public rubbish bins can help keep the city clean. Therefore, it is most important that governments identify areas at risk from environmental damage and provide suitable policies to avoid or mitigate such damage. Providing sufficient public transportation is also a necessity, and reducing the number of cars on the road is another major contributor to limiting greenhouse gas emissions, and the use of odd/even car number plate days as during the Beijing Olympics represents one effective policy. Other policies include car lanes for vehicles carrying more than one single passenger.

The challenge for government planners is to understand local residents' real concerns. The increasing cost of living and employment pressure were two frequently mentioned negative impacts by respondents, and the issue is not whether these two negative impacts do or do not have a direct relationship with any events held in the city, but the existence of a perception that MICE policies are seen to have a role. In practice most events' duration is short and it is difficult to see how one event can impact the cost of living, but the summation of such event impacts may be measurable. In addition, in China, Hangzhou is a famous tourism city and its cost of living index is really high, while its real estate prices are also among the highest in the country. The reason behind this situation is complicated by the city's primary features: its tourism attractions, safe environment, and good education system, etc. But residents appear to be worried that, if the city brand and image is enhanced through hosting events, more people will be attracted to the city and further increase the current property prices. Similarly, some residents may have concerns about employment. Is the extra employment directed at local people or migrants attracted to the city by its growth? Is employment becoming too vulnerable to demand fluctuations of MICE in the city and tourism more generally? Taking together these issues can create a very difficult situation. However, government's decisions do influence the local market by, for example, making land available or not for construction, and by permitting or not permitting different types of development. There is a need for residents to feel confident about their government and trust that the government has the capability to find solutions.

10.3 Better Event Management

The question arises: Has Hangzhou got the capability to host large international major events? It appears that many limitations remain in Hangzhou's tourism and event markets. Some can be simply addressed. For example, one respondent stated that the map of Hangzhou was quite old and some newly added and developed areas were still not shown on even the newest map. More seriously there appears to be a lack of experience and lack of research in regard to MICE impacts on Hangzhou, and there are a number of implications for the management of events.

The important point for event planners is to understand that the event market is not homogeneous, and planners also need to understand what elements really attract local residents to become involved. This study has found that residents possess different socio-psychological profiles and may have similar or different characteristics in their socio-demographics, living areas, transportation modes as well as perceptions of the MICE policies. This study also suggests that promoting an inexpensive attendance package and more free access to some events would be an effective strategy to respond to the low levels of resident attendance. For example, visiting the Leisure Park in Hangzhou during the Leisure Expo cost 90 RMB, which is even higher than the cost of visiting the Forbidden City in Beijing. This was only one park's entry price, if residents wanted to attend more events it would cost more. There is little doubt that there is an important relationship between ticket price, revenue, and profit. The ticket price is often the main source of income for the event operator but the high prices also inhibit a large number of potential visitors. The high entry ticket price greatly eradicate the enthusiasm of many residents, especially among low income groups. Providing different entry prices for different people like elders, students, or low income residents can attract more people, and lower prices can be used for the less popular time slots if concerns about over-crowding exist. Some family price packages can also reduce family financial burdens to enter the event. In that sense, attempts by the city to make free entry are supported, although noted previously, it is recognised that the policy is controversial.

As discussed above, long travel distances and difficulty of transport accessibility might be two of the major reasons for the poor attendance by residents. It is important to notice that residents are more likely to attend when travel distances are shorter. However, a lack of enough space or big event areas in the urban city maybe the major reason for seeking areas for MICE development further away from Hangzhou's central business districts (CBDs). An event planner needs to consider seriously what acceptable distances within different cities are. For example, a one-hour drive to the event venue is common for residents of Beijing and Shanghai, but might not be accepted by Hangzhou residents. Too many similar events have been hosted in neighbouring cities, which have caused residents' confusion and antipathy. A more cooperative and selective use of one or two hosting destinations and MICE themes would better promote cities' unique features and make them more attractive to visitors.

➡ 10.4   Public's Understanding of 'Events'

The meaning of 'event' in people's mind has changed dramatically in recent years. In previous decades, event attendance was more like a 'job' rather than a leisure activity. People always attended events with a work purpose, and most events were related to an industry or business. However, in recent years many cities have started to promote their event industry with various themes of events hosted, and thus people have started to rethink the nature of MICE. Although some events' attendances were very high, most of these were related to the specific themes of real estate, cars, and home furnishings. Cultural and other leisure events still remained largely ignored by the Chinese public. Currently, people still think event attendance is an 'accessorial or self improvement activity' and so improving awareness of the nature of public events is important. Official promotion needs to be conducted to let people know that attending events is not only a learning opportunity but also a leisure activity.

10.5 Competition Awareness

Recently MICE has become a new force in Chinese regional economic development. Yet, as previously noted, it remains largely an uncoordinated activity. For example, in 2009, the Second Fine Furniture Exposition was hosted in Ningbo in March, the 15th China International Furniture Exposition was hosted in Shanghai in September, and the 11th West Lake Exposition of International Furniture and Building Material was hosted in Hangzhou in October. These three cities are all located in the Yangtze River Delta, and are only one hour's drive away from each other. Attendees have more opportunities to choose among the sites, but for the host organisations the tough competition cannot be ignored. How to attract more attendees and businesses and survive the competition is the toughest task faced by MICE organisers. Differentiation, integrating new elements into the exposition, and cooperation will enhance competitive advantages and help find a way out of competition. Attracting more attendees requires differentiation. Similarly-themed MICE simply will cause indifference in the marketplace. Each exposition must have its own characteristics and organisations need to promote the differences to distinguish one from others and avoid homogenisation. Operational rigidity is another hindrance that impacts competitive advantages. Learning from best domestic practice and international experience can enhance the MICE service levels in what is still a comparatively embryonic Chinese MICE industry. In addition, choosing good locations, providing sufficient support services, and having strong functionality will continue to provide benefits.

10.6 Public Involvement

What the research indicates is that the general public in Hangzhou tends to regard MICE initiatives as being the responsibility of government, or of government in partnership with big businesses. There appears to be little awareness of the community-based festivals that can be found in Western countries. From a practical perspective, the marginalisation of public involvement may be reinforced by the 'think big' policies that lead to the investment in conference centres referred to in Chapter Two.

10.7 Research Contributions

As noted in Chapter Two, research into the Chinese MICE industry is embryonic, a fact that reflects the recent history of both the Chinese MICE industry itself and the emergence of tourism research as a field of academic study only in recent decades. Indeed, it might be argued that tourism itself in China is quite new, only starting to attract a large number of people in the last decades. In this sense, the study has a contribution to make.

From a conceptual viewpoint, the research project is primarily descriptive and exploratory given the nature of this Chinese research, but there is, of course, a Western tradition of research to drawn upon, including the major works of Don Getz and Mike Hall and later Australian works by researchers such as Margaret Deery, Leo Jago, and others. Drawing on such literature, a model was conceived that established a difference in residents' perceptions of MICE based on two perspectives—the first, an evaluation of MICE and MICE policies from a city or community perspective, and the second, an assessment of impacts on personal daily life. From the literature, and from a pilot study based on a series of open-ended conversational interviews, various items were identified for use in a questionnaire. Statistical tests of reliability showed that the scales used met the usual criteria for subsequent analysis. The results confirmed the literature in that residents perceived advantages of MICE to include economic progress, wider city development including infrastructure development and also an enhancement of Hangzhou's image and brand within China and in the world. However, within the pilot study a latent theme of questioning emerged—could the investment in MICE be spent better elsewhere, were there any disadvantages involved, and concerns were expressed that not only was there the possibility of environmental costs but the demand for resources, land, and properties might also add to inflationary pressures, thereby adding to the increases in the cost of living, particularly of housing.

A model was therefore proposed in Figure 3.2, and in Chapter Eight this was operationalised for statistical testing as Figure 8.2. This was subjected to path analysis, but the goodness of fit indices fell below the criteria usually thought to be appropriate.

Examination of the regression weights indicated that while the individual components of the model generally recorded high Comparative Fit Indices and in some cases good RMSEA scores, on the whole the model failed because of low causal links between the factor 'Critical' and the other variables. For this, it is suggested several possible explanations can be advanced. As discussed above, Chinese public concepts of what constitutes MICE were still bound by recent attitudes that (a) they are issues for government, (b) they relate to work-based interests, and (c) not wholly related to leisure, while they do reflect the growing interests of a materially oriented middle class wishing to own cars, homes, and consequently nice home furnishings. All of these things are understandable within the social and economic development of China—where only recently has the public discourse begun to consider wider issues of environmental sustainability.

In that sense, it might be argued the model has not wholly failed, and that it is more appropriate for a developed rather than developing nation. Its use stands as a benchmark against which future research might be able to trace changes in scores and a better fit as the 'critical voice' becomes more confident and established within general thinking and policies.

10.8 Concluding Comments

Like many other pieces of research, the project is completed in a way that raises as many questions as the answers the research provides. This was, perhaps, unavoidable, given the nature of the research which was exploratory due to a previous lack of research about China's MICE industry at the commencement of this project. In spite of the growing attention being given to China's tourism in the academic literature and the establishment of specialist journals in English directed at China's tourism such as the *Journal of China Tourism Research*, China's MICE industry still remains an underdeveloped area of featured tourism—especially with reference to residents' views and perspectives.

References

Abbey, J. R. & Link, C. K. (1994). The convention and meetings sector—its operation and research needs. In J. R. B. Ritchie & G. Goeldner (Eds.), *Travel, Tourism, and Hospitality Research: A Handbook for Managers and Researchers* (2nd ed., pp. 273-284). New York: John Wiley & Sons.

Active Ingredient Design Ltd. (2009). Getting ready—Map of Hangzhou. Retrieved October 2, 2009, from http://whitner.wordpress.com/2008/10/05/getting-ready/.

Al-Masroori, R. S. (2006). *Destination Competitiveness: Interrelationship Between Destination Planning and Development Strategies and Bolder's Support in Enhancing Oman's Tourism Industry* (Doctoral dissertation). Brisbane: Griffth University.

Andereck, K. L. & Vogt, C. A. (2000). The relationship between residents' attitudes toward tourism and tourism development options. *Journal of Travel Research, 39* (8), 27-36.

Andersson, T. D. & Lundberg, E. (2013). Commensurability and sustainability: Triple impact assessments of a tourism event. *Tourism Management, 37*, 99-109.

Anwar, S. A. & Sohail, M. S. (2003). Festival tourism in the United Arab Emirates: First-time versus repeat visitor perceptions. *Journal of Vacation Marketing, 10* (2), 161-170.

Armstrong, J. (1986). International events and popular myths. In Travel and Tourism Research Association (Canadian Chapter) (Ed.). *International Events: The Real Tourism Impact* (pp. 7-37). Proceedings of the 1985 Canada Chapter Conference. Edmonton: Travel and Tourism Research Association.

Asian Association of Convention and Visitor Bureaus (AACVB). (2014). *Newsletter.*

Retrieved July 28, 2016, from http://www.asiacvbs.com/new5.html.

AsianInfo.org. (2000). Tourism in China. Retrieved July 2, 2006, from http://www.asianinfo.org/asianinfo/china/pro-tourism.htm.

Association of Corporate Travel Executives (ACTE). (2010). Australian perspective: Corporate travel and MICE travel in the post global economy. 15th April Executive Forum, Sydney, 15 April, 2010.

Australian Tourist Commission (ATC). (1997). International visitor survey, 1997. Retrieved July 2, 2006, from http://www.tourism.australia.com/statistics/international-visitor-survey.aspx.

Ayres, R. (2000). Tourism as a passport to development in small states: Reflections on Cyprus. *International Journal of Social Economics, 27*(2), 114-133.

Babbie, E. (1992). *The Practice of Social Research* (6th ed.). Belmont, CA: Wadsworth Publishing Company.

Bai, H. (2006). Brief discussion on the development of Internet television industry (浅论网络电视产业的发展). *Journal of Fujian Provincial Committee Party School of CPC, 12,* 60-61.

Bao, J. G. & Dai, G. Q. (2003). Western event and event tourism development, research progress and international organisation (西方会议会展与会议旅游——发展简况、研究简介与国际机构). *China Conference and Exhibitions, 7* (14), 57-59.

Bauer, M. (2000). Classical content analysis: A review. In M. Bauer & G. Gaskell (Eds.), *Qualitative Researching with Text, Image and Sound* (pp. 131-151). Thousand Oaks, CA: Sage Publications.

Bazeley, P. (2004). Issues in mixing qualitative and quantitative approaches to research. In R. Buber, J. Gadner & L. Richards (Eds.), *Applying Qualitative Methods to Marketing Management Research* (pp. 141-156). London: Palgrave Macmillan.

Bedford, P. (2008). The global financial crisis and its transmission to New Zealand—an external balance sheet analysis. *Reserve Bank of New Zealand: Bulletin, 71*(4), 18-28.

Bendibao.com. (2008). Hangzhou's tourism had big development in 2007, with total revenue over 60 billion RMB (2007年的杭州旅游大发展，总收入突破600亿). Retrieved October 20, 2008, from http://hz.bendibao.com/news/2008125/25254.shtm.

Bentley, T. A. & Page, S. J. (2001). Scoping the extent of adventure tourism accidents.

Annals of Tourism Research, 28, 705-726.

Berg, L. V. D. & Braun, E. (1999). Urban competitiveness, marketing and the need for organizing capacity. *Urban Studies, 36*(5-6), 987-999.

Biesta, G. J. J. & Burbules, N. C. (2003). *Pragmatism and Educational Research*. Lanham, MD: Rowman & Littlefield Publishers.

Bingham, A. (1993). China's phenomenal growth has environmental tag. *Pollution Prevention (Asia/Pacific edition), 1*(4), 10-22.

Borrett, N. (1991). *Leisure Services UK*. London: Macmillan.

Bowden, J. A. (1994). The nature of phenomenographic research. In J. A. Bowden & E. Walsh (Eds.), *Phenomenographic Research: Variations in a Method*. The Warburton Symposium. Melbourne: Royal Melbourne Institute of Technology.

Bowdin, G., McDonnell, I., Allen, J. & O' Toole, W. (2001). *Events Management*. Oxford: Butterworth-Heinemann.

Bramezza, I. (1996). *The Competitiveness of the European City and the Role of Urban Management in Improving the City's Performance*. Amsterdam: Thesis Publishers.

Breen, H., Bull, A. & Walo, M. (2001). A comparison of survey methods to estimate visitor expenditure at a local event. *Tourism Management, 22*, 473-479.

Buck, R. C. (1977). Making good business better: A second look at staged tourist attractions. *Journal of Travel Research, 15*(3), 2-30.

Buhalis, D. (2000). Marketing the competitive destination of the future. *Tourism Management, 21*(1), 97-116.

Bull, C. & Lovell, J. (2007). The impact of hosting major sporting events on local residents: An analysis of the views and perceptions of Canterbury residents in relation to the Tour de France 2007. *Journal of Sport & Tourism, 12*, 229-248.

Bulter, R. W. (1980). The concept of a tourist area cycle of evolution: Implications for management of resources. *Canadian Geographer, 24*(1), 5-12.

Burns, J. P. A. & Mules, T. J. (1986). *A Framework for the Analysis of Major Special Events*. Adelaide: The Center for South Australian Economic Studies.

Burrell, G. & Morgan, G. L. (1979). *Sociological Paradigms and Organisational Analysis: Elements of the Sociology of Corporate Life*. Farnham, Surrey: Ashgate Publishing.

Canniffe, M. (1998). Big events, big businesses. *Accountancy Ireland, December*, 10-11.

Carey, C. (1994). Research needs for developing established events and attractions. In

J. R. B. Ritchie & C. Goeldner (Eds.), *Travel, Tourism, and Hospitality Research: A Handbook for Managers and Researchers* (2nd ed., pp. 285-313). New York: John Wiley & Sons.

Carlsen, J. (1999). A review of MICE industry evaluation and research in Asia and Australia 1988–1998. *Journal of Convention & Exhibition Management, 1*(4), 51-66.

CCTV Financial Channel. (2016). China's top ten cities in economy, Hangzhou on the list (中国经济最强10大城市出炉！杭州上榜). Retrieved May 10, 2016, from http://zj.zjol.com.cn/news/409597.html.

CCTV News. (2012). 2011 China's event economy report issued, China's number of MICE ranks second in the world (2011中国会展经济蓝皮书发布 我国展会数量居世界第二). Retrieved May 10, 2013, from http://www.cntv.cn/pinpai/20120601/111044.shtml.

Cheney, S. & Ryan, C. (2009). Eco-tourism and luxury—the case of AI Maha, Dubai. *Journal of Sustainable Tourism, 17*(3), 287-301.

China Convention and Exhibition Economy. (2016). 2015 China's exhibition industry development analysis report (2015年中国会展业发展报告). Retrieved July 28, 2016, from http://wenku.baidu.com/view/19699c7e1a37f111f1855bc9.html.

China Council for the Promotion of International Trade (CCPIT). (2009). Statistics. Retrieved May 10, 2013, from http://data.mofcom.gov.cn/SWSJDomestic/DomesticTrade.action.

China Exhibition. (2007). Beijing's real estate exposition is too 'hot' and needs cooling down (京城房展会过热，需降温). Retrieved October 1, 2012, from http://www.people.com.cn/BIG5/channel3/26/20000519/69916.html.

China International Trade Promotion Committee. (2007). *Report on the Development of China's Convention & Exhibition Economy 2006* (中国会展经济发展报告2006). Beijing: China Economic Press.

China Internet Network Information Center (CNNIC). (2008). The 22nd China Internet development statistics report (第22次中国互联网络发展状况统计报告). Retrieved October 1, 2008, from http://wenku.baidu.com/view/b5951075a417866fb84a8ebd.html.

China IRN.com. (2006). Analysis of China's auto growth (中国汽车增长态势分析). Retrieved October 1, 2012, from http://www.chinairn.com/doc/70270/92897.html.

China National Tourism Administration (CNTA). (2000). Strategic thinking on China's hospitality industry—series one: The basic development trend (中国酒店业的战略思考系列一：基本发展趋势). *China Tourism News*, March 6, 3.

China National Tourism Administration (CNTA). (2007). Suggestions on facilitating tourism development (关于进一步促进旅游业发展的意见). Retrieved July 2, 2006, from http://www.chinalawedu.com/falvfagui/fg22598/250880.shtml.

China National Tourism Administration (CNTA). (2015). Foreign visitor arrivals by purpose, JAN–SEP 2015 (2015年1—9月入境外国游客人数：按目的分). Retrieved May 18, 2016, from http://en.cnta.gov.cn/Statistics/TourismStatistics/201511/t20151104_750748.shtml.

China News Network. (2008). Deputies 'questioned' mayor of Hangzhou: Housing prices are not a little high, but too high (人大代表"质疑"杭州市长：房价不是有点高 是太高). Retrieved October 1, 2012, from http://news.xinhuanet.com/house/2008-02/21/content_7641155.htm.

China News Service. (2011). Hangzhou's residential land price became China's highest, reaching 22,800 RMB per square metre (杭州成中国住宅地价最高城市 每平米已达2.28万). Retrieved May 16, 2016, from http://gz.house.163.com/11/0328/08/707IOS2I00873C6D.html.

China-Window. com. (2015). Hangzhou economy. Retrieved July 28, from 2016, http://www.china-window.com/china_economy/china_economy_guide/hangzhou-economy.shtml.

Chinese Academy of Social Sciences (CASS). (2008). Year book of Chinese Academy of Social Sciences (中国社会科学院年鉴). Beijing: CASS.

Chinese International Airline Agency. (2000). Abstract of China Eastern Airline's annual report 2000 (中国东方航空股份有限公司2000年年度报告摘要). Retrieved December 18, 2012, from http://wenku.baidu.com/view/103fde6bddccda38376baf2d.html.

Chongqing Municipal People's Government. (2007). Chongqing governmental statistical analysis (重庆市统计年鉴). Retrieved October, 27, 2013, from http://www.cqtj.gov.cn/tjnj/2007/menu.htm.

Chor, D. & Manova, K. (2012). Off the cliff and back? Credit conditions and international trade during the global financial crisis. *Journal of International Economics*, *87*(1), 117-133.

Clark, C. D. (2004). *Quantitative Psychological Research: A Student's Handbook* (2nd ed.). Philadelphia: Psychology Press.

Cnnb.com.cn. (2006). More specialized volunteers, Ningbo's MICE industry owns a 'first' in the country (志愿者越分越细 宁波会展业催生了一个全国第一). Retrieved March 5, 2012, from http://news.cnnb.com.cn/system/2006/10/16/005193540. shtml.

Commonwealth Department of Tourism. (1995). *A National Strategy for the Meetings, Incentives, Conventions and Exhibitions Industry*. Canberra: Australian Government Publishing Service.

Cooke, K. (1982). Guidelines for socially appropriate tourism development in British Columbia. *Journal of Travel Research*, *21*(1), 22-28.

Cooper, M. (1999). Prediction and reality: The development of the Australian convention industry 1976–1993, and beyond. *Journal of Conventions & Exhibition Management*, *1*(4), 3-15.

Corben, R. (1990). Sobering times ahead. *Asia Travel Trade*, *22*(6), 34-40.

Cousineau, C. (1991). Festivals and events: A fertile ground for leisure research. *Journal of Applied Recreation Research*, *16*(1), 1-2.

Creswell, J. W. (1994). *Research Design: Qualitative and Quantitative Approaches*. Thousand Oaks, CA: Sage Publications.

Creswell, J. W. (2003). *Research Design: Qualitative, Quantitative, and Mixed Methods Approaches*. London: Sage Publications.

Crompton, J. L. (1979). An assessment of the image of Mexico as a vacation destination and the influence of geographical location upon that image. *Journal of Travel Research*, *17*(Spring), 18-23.

Crompton, J. L. & McKay, S. L. (1997). Motives of visitors attending festival events. *Annals of Tourism Research*, *24*(2), 425-439.

Crouch, D. (2000). Places around us: Embodied lay geographies in leisure and tourism. *Leisure Studies*, *19*(2), 63-76.

Crouch, G. (1992). Effect of income & price on international tourism. *Annals of Tourism Research*, *19* (3), 643-644.

Crouch, G. I. & Ritchie, J. R. B. (1998). Convention site selection research: A review, conceptual model, and propositional framework. *Journal of Convention & Exhibition*

Management, 1(1), 49-69.

Cui, J. (2006). Chinese mainland's resident income gap and government's financial policy improvement (中国大陆城镇居民收入差距研究分析与政府财政调节机制之完善). The 2nd Cross-Strait Conference on Public Administration: Policy Challenges in the 21st Century.

Cui, Y. H. & Wen, J. (2006). Construction of the appraisal index system of Chinese enterprises' internationalization based on dynamic evolution (基于动态演进的中国企业国际化程度评价指标体系构建). *Journal of Hubei University of Economics, 6*, 86-89.

Dai, G. Q. (2005). *Impacts Evaluation of Mega Events: A Case Study of the 1999 Kunming Expo* (重大事件对城市发展及城市旅游的影响研究：以1999昆明世界园艺博览会为例). Beijing: China Tourism Press.

Dai, X. F. (2002). Chinese event tourism's current situation and future trend (中国会展旅游的现状及发展趋势). Retrieved December 18, 2012, from http://www.china.com.cn/chinese/zhuanti/234971.htm.

Dall'Alba, G. (1994). Reflections on some faces of phenomenography. In J. Bowden & E. Walsh (Eds.), *Phenomenographic Research: Variations in a Method*. The Warburton Symposium. Melbourne: Royal Melbourne Institute of Technology.

Darlington, R. B. Weinberg, S. & Walberg, H. (1973). Canonical variate analysis and related techniques. *Review of Educational Research, 43*(4), 453-454.

Davidson, R., Hertrich, S. & Schwandner, G. (2004). How can Europe capture Chinese MICE? Research Paper of APTA Conference 2004, Globalization and Tourism Research: East Meets West. Nagasaki, Japan, 4–7 July, 2004.

DeCoster, J. (1998). Overview of factor analysis. Retrieved October 1, 2009, from http://www.stat-help.com/notes.html.

Decrop, A. (1999). Triangulation in qualitative tourism research. *Tourism Management, 20*, 157-161.

Deery, M. & Jago, L. (2010). Social impacts of events and the role of anti-social behavior. *International Journal of Event and Festival Management, 1*, 8-28.

Deery, M., Jago, L., Fredline, L. & Dwyer, L. (2005). *National Business Events Study: An Evaluation of the Australian Business Events Sector*. Melbourne: Common Ground.

Della Bitta, A. J., Loudon, D. J., Booth, G. G. & Weeks, R. R. (1977). Estimating the economic impact of a short-term tourist event. *Journal of Travel Research, 16*, 10-15.

Denzin, N. K. (1978). *The Research Act* (2nd ed.). New York: McGraw-Hill.

Denzin, N. K. & Lincoln, Y. S. (1994). *Handbook of Qualitative Research*. Thousand Oaks, CA: Sage Publications.

Di Giovanni, J. (2005). What drives capital flows? The case of cross-border M & A activity and financial deepening. *Journal of International Economics, 65*(1), 127-149.

Dong, J. (2003). China's auto demand will continue its rapid growth (中国汽车需求将持续高速增长). Retrieved October 1, 2012, from http://info.hktdc.com/report/mkt/chinese/mkt_c031103.htm.

Dootson, S. (1995). An in-depth study of triangulation. *Journal of Advanced Nursing, 22* (1), 183-187.

Du, H. Y. (2006). *A Brief History of China* (中国简史). Dalian: Liaoning Normal University Press.

Dwyer, L. & Mistilis, N. (1997). Challenges to MICE tourism in the Asia-Pacific region. In M. Oppermann (Ed.), *Pacific Rim Tourism* (pp. 219-229). Wallingford, Oxon: CAB International.

Dwyer, L. & Mistilis, N. (1999). Tourism gateways and regional economies: The distributional impacts of MICE. *International Journal of Tourism Research, 1*, 441-457.

Dwyer, L., Forsyth, P. & Spurr, R. (2005). Estimating the impacts of special events on an economy. *Journal of Travel Research, 43*(5), 351-359.

Dzurec, L. C. & Abraham, J. L. (1993). The nature of inquiry: Linking quantitative and qualitative research. *Advances in Nursing Science, 16*, 73-79.

Easterling, D. S. (2005). The residents' perspective in tourism research: A review and synthesis. *Journal of Travel & Tourism Marketing, 17*(4), 45-62.

Edgell, D. L. Sr. & Harbaugh, L. (1993). Tourism development: An economic stimulus in the heart of America. *Business America, 114*(2), 17-18.

Egypt, C. (2009). The global financial crisis: Impact, responses and way forward. Meeting of the Committee of Experts of the 2nd Joint Annual Meetings of the AU Conference of Ministers of Economy and Finance and ECA Conference of Ministers of Finance, Planning and Economic Development. Cairo, 2–5 June, 2009.

Embassy of the People's Republic of China in the United States of America. (2005). 37 Cities' real-estate price ranking (全国37大城市房价排行榜). Retrieved October 1,

2012, from http://www.china-embassy.org/chn/xw/t188862.htm.

Ennew, C. (2005). The future of tourism in Asia Pacific: A global perspective. Retrieved June 28, 2012, from http://www.u21global.com/portal/corporate/docs/EnnewTheFut ureofTourisminAsiaPacific.pdf.

Exhibition Liaison Committee (ELC). (1995). The exhibition industry explained. UK: Exhibition Liaison Committee.

Fenich, G. G. (1995). Convention center operations: Some questions answered. *International Journal of Hospitality Management, 14*(3/4), 311-324.

Fenich, G. G. (1998). Convention centre operating characteristics. *Journal of Convention and Exhibition Management, 1*(2/3), 1-25.

FFW Topic. (2008). Xiamen: Event industry drives the real estate price (厦门：会展经济带动周边房价一路狂飙). Retrieved October 1, 2012, from http://topic.ffw.com.cn/zt/newHouse/2007/20071122hzzx/.

Fidrmuc, J. & Korhonen, I. (2010). The impact of the global financial crisis on business cycles in Asian emerging economies. *Journal of Asian Economics, 21*(3), 293-303.

Fontana, A. & Frey, J. H. (2000). The interview: From structured questions to negotiated text. In N. K. Denzin & Y. S. Lincoln (Eds.), *Handbook of Qualitative Research* (pp. 645-672). Thousand Oaks, CA: Sage Publications.

Francisco, V. T., Butterfoss, F. D. & Capwell, E. M. (2001). Key issues in evaluation: Quantitative and qualitative methods and research design. *Health Promotion Practice, 2*(1): 20-23.

Fredline, E. & Faulkner, B. (2002a). Resident's reactions to the staging of major motorsport events within their communities: A cluster analysis. *Event Management, 7*, 103-114.

Fredline, E. & Faulkner, B. (2002b). Variations in residents' reactions to major motorsport events: Why residents perceive the impacts of events differently. *Event Management, 7*, 115-125.

Fredline, L., Jago, L. & Deery, M. (2003). The development of a generic scale to measure the social impacts of events. *Event Management, 8*, 23-37.

Fu, G. H. (2005). *Event and Festival Conspectus* (会展与节事旅游管理概论). Beijing: Peking University Press.

Fu, Y. Q. & Zheng, X. M. (2014). Integration of tourism and convention and exhibition industry: Industry value chain analysis, path and countermeasures (旅游与会展产业

的融合：产业价值链分析、路径与对策). *Journal of Northwest A & F University (Social Science Edition), 14*(2), 146-153.

Getz, D. (1989). Special events defining the product. *Tourism Management, 10*(2), 125-137.

Getz, D. (1991). *Festivals, Special Events and Tourism*. New York: Van Nostrand.

Getz, D. (1997). *Event Management and Event Tourism*. New York: Cognizant Communication Corporation.

Getz, D. (2007). Event tourism: Definition, evolution, and research. *Tourism Management, 29*(8), 403-428.

Getz, D. & Frisby, W. (1988). Evaluating management effectiveness in community-run festivals. *Journal of Travel Research, 27*(1), 22-27.

Getz, D. & Wicks, B. (1993). Policy report: Cultural tourism studies in Australia and Canada. *Festival Management & Event Tourism, 1*(4), 163-170.

Ghitelman, D. (1995). Convention centre development: Never enough? *Meeting & Conventions, 30*(2), 48-58.

Gibson, H. (1998). Sport tourism: A critical analysis of research. *Sport Management Review, 1*(1), 45-76.

Glancey, J. (1984). *Bright Lights, Big City*. New York: Vintage.

Go, F. M. & Govers, R. (1999). The Asian perspective: Which international conference destinations in Asia are the most competitive? *Journal of Convention & Exhibition Management, 1*(4), 37-50.

Grabmeier, J. (1997). New research shows what makes cities visually appealing. Retrieved January 6, 2012, from http://researchnews.osu.edu/archive/cityimg.htm.

Grado, S. C., Strauss, C. H. & Lord, B. E. (1998). Economic impacts of conferences and conventions. *Journal of Convention & Exhibition Management, 1*(1), 19-33.

Guangzhou Daily. (2007). 2008 will become the watershed in history as the world's urban population will outnumber rural population (2008成历史分水岭 世界城市人口将首超农村人口). Retrieved, June 1, 2012, from http://news.xinhuanet.com/world/2007-06/28/content_6300729.htm

Guba, E. G. (1990). *The Alternative Paradigm Dialog*. In E.G. Guba (Ed.), *The Paradigm Dialog* (pp. 17-30). Newbury Park, CA: Sage Publications.

Guba, E. G. & Lincoln, Y. S. (1985). Naturalistic inquiry. Beverly Hills, CA: Sage

Publications.

Guba, E. G. & Lincoln, Y. S. (1989). Fourth generation evaluation. Newbury Park, CA: Sage Publications.

Guba, E. G. & Lincoln, Y. S. (1994). Competing paradigms in qualitative research. In N. K. Denzin & Y. S. Lincoln (Eds.), *Handbook of Qualitative Research* (pp. 105-117). Thousand Oaks, CA: Sage Publications.

Gubrium, J. & Holstein, J. (2000). Analyzing interpretive practice. In N. K. Denzin & Y. S. Lincoln (Eds.), *The Handbook of Qualitative Research* (2nd ed.) (pp. 487-508). Thousand Oaks, CA: Sage Publications.

Gunn, C. A. (1972). *Vacations Cape: Designing Tourist Regions.* Austin, TX: University of Texas Press.

Hair, J. F. Jr., Anderson, R. E., Tatham, R. L. & Black, W. C. (1992). *Multivariate Data Analysis with Readings* (3rd ed.). New York: Macmillan.

Hair, J. F., Anderson, R. E., Tatham, R. L. & Black, W. C. (1995). *Multivariate Data Analysis* (4th ed.). Englewood Cliffs, NJ: Prentice Hall.

Hair, J. F., Anderson, R. E., Tatham, R. L. & Black, W. C. (1998). *Multivariate Data Analysis* (5th ed.). Englewood Cliffs, NJ: Prentice Hall.

Hall, C. M. (1989). The definition and analysis of hallmark tourist events. *GeoJournal, 19*(3), 263-268.

Hall, C. M. (1992). *Hallmark Tourism Events: Impacts, Management and Planning.* London: Belhaven Press.

Hall, C. M. (1994). *Tourism in the Pacific Rim: Development, Impacts and Markets.* South Melbourne: Longman Cheshire.

Hall, C. M. & Selwood, H. J. (1987). Cup gained, paradise lost? A case study of the 1987 America's Cup as a hallmark event. Palemerston North, NZ: Department of Geography, Massey University.

Hall, D., Roberts, L. & Mitchell, M. (2003). *New Directions in Rural Tourism.* Aldershot: Ashgate Publishing Limited.

Hangzhou.com.cn. (2010). For national day holiday this year, hotel prices of the Yangtze River Delta have increased, Hangzhou's hotel prices have increased the most, and budget hotel prices have increased 30%. (今年国庆长三角酒店价格普涨, 杭州涨幅最大, 经济型酒店上涨三成). Retrieved June, 3, 2012, from http://hznews.

hangzhou.com.cn/jingji/content/2010-09/23/content_3464358.htm.

Hangzhou.gov.cn. (2016a). Hangzhou statistics (杭州统计). Retrieved November 1, 2016, from http://www.hangzhou.gov.cn/col/col805740/index.html.

Hangzhou.gov.cn. (2016b). Statistical report on Hangzhou's economy and social development 2015 (2015年杭州市经济和社会发展统计公报). Retrieved May 18, 2016, from http://www.hangzhou.gov.cn/art/2016/3/24/art_805865_663727.html.

Hao, H., Li, X., Tan, M., Zhang, J. & Zhang, H. (2015). Agricultural land use intensity and its determinants: A case study in Taibus Banner, Inner Mongolia, China. *Frontiers of Earth Science, 9*(22), 308-318.

Higham, J. E. S. & Ritchie, B. (2002). The evolution of festivals and other events in rural southern New Zealand. *Event Management, 7*, 39-49.

Hiller, H. H. (1995). Conventions as mega-events: A new model for convention–host city relationships. *Tourism Management, 16*, 375-379.

Hing, N., McCabe, V., Lewis, P. & Leiper, N. (1998). Hospitality trends in the Asia-Pacific: A discussion of five key sectors. *International Journal of Contemporary Hospitality Management, 10*(7), 264-271.

Hochschild, A. (1983). *The Managed Heart.* Berkeley, CA: University of California Press.

Hoffman, M. (1987). Critical theory and the inter-paradigm debate. *Millennium: Journal of International Studies, 16*(3), 231-249.

Hoffman, M. (2000). Critical theory and the inter-paradigm debate. In H. C. Dyer et al. (Eds.), *The Study of International Relations* (pp. 60-86). London: Palgrave Macmillan UK.

Holcomb, B. (1999a). Marketing cities for tourism. In D. R. Judd & S. Fainstein (Eds.), *The Tourist City* (pp. 54-70). New Haven, CT: Yale University Press.

Holcomb, B. (1999b). Re-visioning place: De- and re-constructing the image of the industrial city. In G. Kearns & C. Philo (Eds.), *Selling Places* (pp. 133-143). Oxford: Pergamon Press.

Hong Kong Trade Development Council (HKTDC). (2008). Chinese mainland's economy will maintain strong momentum in 2008. Retrieved October 1, 2012, from http://economists-pick-research.hktdc.com/business-news/article/Economic-Forum/Mainland-China-s-Economy-Will-Maintain-Strong-Momentum-in-2008/ef/en/1/1X000000/1X0034VT.htm.

Hong, Y. & Zhao, M. (2006). Developing MICE industry, Hangzhou Heping Exhibition Center became a treasure cornucopia (发展会展经济 杭州和平会展中心成为财富聚宝盆). Retrieved October 1, 2012, from http://www.chinaqw.com/news/2006/0704/68/35129.shtml.

Hu, C. & Hiemstra, S. J. (1996). Hybrid conjoint analysis as a research technique to measure meeting planners' preferences in hotel selection. *Journal of Travel Research, 35*(2), 62-69.

Hudson, L. A. & Ozanne, J. L. (1988). Alternative ways of seeking knowledge in consumer research. *Journal of Consumer Research, 14* (4), 508-521.

Humphreys, L. M. & Plummer, M. K. (1995). Economic impact of hosting 1996 Summer Olympics. *Georgia Business and Economic Conditions, 56*(1-2), 8-16.

International Business Daily. (2005). On the educational function of MICE (浅析会展的教育功能). Retrieved July 18, 2012, from http://xuewen.cnki.net/CCND-GJSB20050216T006.html.

International Congress and Convention Association (ICCA). (2004). ICCA Statistics 2003. Retrieved July 18, 2012, from http://www.iccaworld.org/knowledge/industrylinks.cfm.

International Congress and Convention Association (ICCA). (2006). ICCA Statistics 2005. Retrieved July 18, 2012, from http://www.iccaworld.com/spps/sitepage.cfm?catid=88&expNav=1.

International Congress and Convention Association (ICCA). (2008). ICCA statistics 2007. Retrieved July 18, 2012, from http://www.iccaworld.com.

International Congress and Convention Association (ICCA). (2013). A modern history of international association meetings: 1963–2012. Retrieved November 1, 2016, from www.iccaworld.org/dcps/doc.cfm?docid=1626.

Jackson, J. (2006). Developing regional tourism in China: The potential for activating business clusters in a socialist market economy. *Tourism Management, 27*(4), 695-706.

Jafari, J. (1986). On domestic tourism. *Annals of Tourism Research, 13*(30), 491-496.

Jago, L. K. & Shaw, R. N. (1998). Special events: A conceptual and definitional framework. *Festival Management & Event Tourism, 5*(1/2), 21-32.

Janiskee, R. L. (1990). History-themed festivals: A special events approach to rural recreation and tourism. Proceeding of Applied Geography Conferences, *13*, 111-117.

Janiskee, R. L. (1994). Some macro scale growth trends in America's community festival industry. *Festival Management & Event Tourism, 2*(1), 10-14.

Janiskee, R. L. (2006). Event management and event tourism. *Annals of Tourism Research, 33*(3), 872-874.

Janiskee, R. L. & Drews, P. (1998). Rural festivals and community reimaging. In R. Butler, C. M. Hall & J. Jenkins (Eds.), *Tourism and Recreation in Rural Areas* (pp. 19-42). Chichester, Sussex: John Wiley & Sons.

Jansen-Verbeke, M. (1986). Inner city tourism. *Annals of Tourism Research, 13*(10), 79-100.

Jenning, G. (2001). *Tourism Research*. Milton: John Wiley & Sons Australia, Ltd.

Jick, T. J. (1979). Mixing qualitative and quantitative methods: Triangulation in action. *Administrative Science Quarterly, 24*(1), 602-611.

Jin, X., Weber, K. & Bauer, T. (2010a). The state of the exhibition industry in China. *Journal of Convention and Event Tourism, 11*, 2-17.

Jin, X., Weber, K. & Bauer, T. (2010b). China's second-tier cities as exhibition destinations. *International Journal of Contemporary Hospitality Management, 22*, 552-557.

Jin, X., Weber, K. & Bauer, T. (2012). Impact of clusters on exhibition destination attractiveness. *Tourism Management, 33*, 1429-1439.

Johnson, P. S. & Thomas, B. (1993). *Perspectives on Tourism Policy*. London: Mansell.

Ju, H., Tian. J. X., Wang, L. J. & Huang, G. L. (2006a). Research on development distribution and innovation model of convention and exhibition industry. *China Soft Science, 11*, 131-136.

Ju, S. L., Lu, L., Yang, X. Z. & Zhu, T. X. (2006b). Research on the spatial structure of China's exhibition economy based on urban system. *Urban Planning Forum, 1*, 93-97.

Judd, D. R. & Fainstein, S. (1999). *The Tourist City*. New Haven, CT: Yale University Press.

Kay, A. L. K. (2005). China's convention and exhibition center boom. *Journal of Convention and Event Tourism, 7*, 5-22.

Kenneth, R. & Howe, S. (1988). Against the quantitative-qualitative incompatibility thesis or dogmas die hard. *Educational Researcher, 17*(8), 10-16.

Kim, D. Y., Morrison, A. M. & Mills, J. E. (2003). Tiers or tears? An evaluation of the web-based marketing efforts of major city convention centers in the U.S. *Journal of Convention & Exhibition Management, 5*, 25-49.

Kim, K., Uysal, M. & Chen, J. S. (2002). Festival visitor motivation from the organizers' point of view. *Event Management*, 7(1), 127-134.

Kim, N. S. & Chalip, L. (2003). Why travel to the FIFA World Cup? Effects of motives, background, interest, and constraints. *Sport Management Program*, 25, 695-707.

Kim, S. S., Prideaux, B. & Chon, K. (2010). A comparison of results of three statistical methods to understand the determinants of festival participants' expenditures. *International Journal of Hospitality Management*, 29, 297-307.

Kim, S. S. & Sun, H. L. (2008). Is there competition in the exhibition market in Asia?—Analysis of the positioning of major Asian exhibition host cities. *Asia Pacific Journal of Tourism Research*, 13(3), 205-227.

Klein, R. B. (2004). *Principles and Practice of Structural Equation Modeling*. New York: The Guilford Press.

Kolb, B. M. (2006). Tourism marketing for cities and towns: Using branding and events to attract tourists. Oxford: Butterworth-Heinemann.

Kuhn, T. S. (1970). *The Structure of Scientific Revolutions* (2nd ed.). Chicago: University of Chicago Press.

Kunming Expo Garden Co., Ltd. (2006). 1999 Kunming International Horticultural Exposition (1999中国园艺博览会). Retrieved March 05, 2012, from http://www.expo99km.gov.cn/expo/Wpublisher/DisplayPages/ContentDisplay_15.aspx?contentid=126.

Kunming Expo Garden Co., Ltd. (2006). How to survive after the event period: Innovation is the key to theme park's survival (展会后如何生存：创新是主题公园生存的关键). Retrieved October 1, 2012, from http://www.expo99km.gov.cn/expo/Wpublisher/displaypages/ContentDisplay_17.aspx?contentid=133.

Kunming Scientific and Technological Bureau. (2005). Building sewage treatment systems in the urban ecological park (在城市生态公园内建立污水处理系统). Retrieved March 5, 2012, from http:// www.kmsti.net.cn/gwt200405.htm.

Lane, B. (1994). What is rural tourism? *Journal for Sustainable Tourism*, 2, 7-21.

Law, C. M. (1987). Conference and exhibition tourism. *Built Environment*, 13(2), 85-95.

Law, C. M. (1993). *Urban Tourism: Attracting Visitors to Large Cities*. London: Mansell.

Lawson, F. (2000). *Congress, Convention and Exhibition Facilities: Planning, Design and Management*. London: Architectural Press.

Laybourn, P. (2004). Risk and decision making in events management. In I. Yeoman, M. Robertson, J. Ali-Knight, S. Drummond & U. McMahon-Beattie (Eds.), *Festival and Events Management: An International Arts and Culture Perspective*. Oxford: Elsevier Limited.

LeBlanc, M., Robinson, M., Picard, D. & Long, P. (2004). Tourist characteristics and their interest in attending festivals and events: An Anglophone/Francophone case study of New Brunswick, Canada. *Event Management, 8*, 203-212.

Lee, M. J. & Back, K. J. (2007). Effects of destination image on meeting participation intentions: Empirical findings from a professional association and its annual convention. *The Service Industries Journal, 27*(1), 59-73.

Lew, A. A., Yu, L., Ap, J. & Zhang, G. (2003). *Tourism in China*. Binghamton: The Haworth Hospitality Press.

Li, D. J. (2004). Event and tourism, who promotes whom? (会展　旅游　谁推动谁). Retrieved July 28, 2012, from http://news.xinhuanet.com/expo/2004-02/18/content_1319572.htm.

Li, J. (2003). Who will be the leader of MICE industry—Beijing, Shanghai, or Guangzhou? (谁领风骚？京、沪、穗会展业). *Economy World, 03*, 45-47.

Li, J. Q., Li, K. Y. & Zhang, Y. F. (2003). The time-space analysis of unexpected incident's influence on Chinese inbound tourism and suggestion on regional responses. *World Regional Studies, 12*(4), 78-83.

Li, S. & Luo, C. L. (2007). Re-estimating the income gap between urban and rural households in China. *Procedia—Social and Behavioral Sciences, 236*, 1-384.

Lian, Y. M. (2006). China city life quality report (中国城市生活质量报告). Beijing: China Time and Economy Press.

Lindberg, K. & Johnson, R. L. (1997). Modeling resident attitudes toward tourism. *Annals of Tourism Research, 24*(2), 402-424.

Ling, K., Wang, W. C. & Liu, T. (2001). The statistical research on the relationship between urban economic development and environmental pollution: The case of Nanjing city (城市经济发展与环境污染关系的统计研究——以南京市为例). *Statistical Research, 10*, 46-52.

Listokin, D. (1985). The convention trade: A competitive economic prize. *Real Estate Issues, 10*, 43-46.

Liu, C. J. & Var, T. (1986). Resident attitudes toward tourism impacts in Hawaii. *Annals of Tourism Research*, *13*(2), 193-214.

Liu, D. Y. (2004). *Event Destination Image Design* (会展胜地形象策划). Shanghai: Lixin Accounting Publishing House.

Liu, D. K. (2004). *China MICE Industry: Theory, Situation, and Policy* (中国会展业：理论、现状与政策). Beijing: China Commerce and Trade Press.

Liu, J., Longstaff, F. A. & Pan, J. (2003). Dynamic asset allocation with event risk. *The Journal of Finance*, *LVIII*(1), 231-259.

Lombardi, R. (1990). Communicating with the public about major accident hazards. In H. Gow & H. Otway (Eds.), *Communicating with the Public about Major Accident Hazards: Commission of the European Community*. London: Elsevier Science.

Ma, C. L. (2006). Problems and solutions of tourism and festival sponsor development (旅游节庆赞助商开发的难点和出路). Retrieved March 05, 2012, from http://macongling.blog.sohu.com/1165278.html.

Manning, F. (1983). Cosmos and chaos: Celebration in the modern world. In F. Manning (Ed.), *The Celebration of Society: Perspectives on Contemporary Cultural Performance* (pp. 3-30). Bowling Green, OH: Bowling Green University Popular Press.

Mansfeld, Y. (1992). Group-differentiated perceptions of social impacts related to tourism development. *Professional Geographer*, *44*, 377-392.

Marcouiller, D. W. (1997). Toward integrative tourism planning in rural America. *Journal of Planning Literature*, *11*(3), 337-357.

May, V. (1995). Environmental implications of the 1992 Winter Olympic Games. *Tourism Management*, *16* (4), 269-275.

Mazanec, J. (2009). Unravelling myths in tourism research. *Tourism Recreation Research*, *34*(3), 319-323.

McCabe, V., Poole, B., Weeks, P. & Leiper, N. (2000). *The Business and Management of Conventions*. Milton: John Wiley & Sons Australia Ltd.

McIntosh, A. J. (1998). Mixing methods: Putting the tourist into the fore-front of tourism research. *Tourism Analysis*, *3*(2), 121-127.

Merton, R. K., Sills, D. L. & Stigler, S. M. (1984). The Kelvin dictum and social science: An excursion into the history of an idea. *Journal of the History of the Behavioral Science*, *20*, 319-331.

Meyer, A. D., Tsui, A. S. & Hinings, C. R. (1993). Configurational approaches to organisational analysis. *Academy of Management Journal, 36*(6), 1175-1195.

Mihalik, B. J. & Simonetta, L. C. (1998). Resident perceptions of the 1996 Olympic Games. *Festival Management & Event Tourism, 5*(1/2), 9-19.

Mihalik, B. J. & Simonetta, L. C. (1999). A midterm assessment of the host population's perceptions of the 1996 Summer Olympics: Support, attendance benefits, and liabilities. *Journal of Travel Research, 37*(3), 244-248.

Mill, J. S. (1866). *Auguste Comte and Positivism.* Philadelphia: J. B. Lippincott and Co.

Miller, D. & Friesen, P. H. (1984). A longitudinal study of the corporate life cycle. *Management Science, 30*(10), 1161-1182.

Miller, J. G. & Roth, A. (1994). A taxonomy of manufacturing strategies. *Management Science, 40* (3), 285-304.

Mills, E. S. (1991). Should governments own convention centers? Retrieved January 6, 2012, from http://www.heartland.org/Article.cfm?artId=10796.

Mitchell, E. S. (1986). Multiple triangulation: Methodology for nursing science. *Advances in Nursing Science, 8*(3), 18-26.

Mok, C. & DeFranco, A. L. (1999). Chinese cultural values: Their implications for travel and tourism marketing. *Journal of Travel & Tourism Marketing, 8*(2), 99-105.

Morgan, D. L. (1998). Practical strategies for combing qualitative and quantitative method: Application to health research. *Qualitative Health Research, 3*, 362-376.

Morgan, D. L. (2007). Paradigms lost and pragmatism regained: Methodological implications of combining qualitative and quantitative methods. *Journal of Mixed Methods Research, 1*, 48.

Morgan, N. & Pritchard, A. (1998). *Tourism Promotion and Power: Creating Images, Creating Identities.* Chichester: John Wiley and Sons.

Morris, P. W. G. (1994). *The Management of Project.* London: Thomas Telford.

Mullins, P. (1992). Cities for pleasure: The emergence of tourism urbanization in Australia. *Built Environment, 18*(3), 187-198.

Murphy, P. E. (1985). *Tourism: A Community Approach.* London: Methuen.

Murray, J. S. (1999). Methodological triangulation in a study of social support for siblings of children with cancer. *Journal of Pediatric Oncology Nursing, 16*, 194-200.

National Bureau of Statistics of China. (2008). Comparison of urban residents' disposable income in four places including Shanghai (上海等四省市城市居民可支配收入比

较图). Retrieved October 1, 2012, from http://www.stats.gov.cn/tjsj/.

National Bureau of Statistics Research Group. (2004). An empirical analysis of China's regional development gap (我国区域发展差距的实证分析). Retrieved October 1, 2012, from http://www.cpirc.org.cn/yjwx/yjwx_detail.asp?id=3570.

Neuman, W. L. (1997). *Social Research Methods: Qualitative and Quantitative Approaches.* Boston: Allyn and Bacon.

Newman, H. K. (1999). Neighbourhood impacts of Atlanta's Olympic Games. *Community Development Journal, 34*(2), 151-159.

Notzke, C. (2004). Indigenous tourism development in Southern Alberta, Canada: Tentative engagement. *Journal of Sustainable Tourism, 12*(1), 29-54.

Office of National Afforestation Committee. (2015). National Afforestation Condition Report 2014 (2014年中国国土绿化状况公报). Retrieved May 18, 2016, from http://www.forestry.gov.cn/main/72/content-745999.html

Oppermann, M. (1996a). Convention cities—Images and changing fortunes. *Journal of Tourism Studies, 7*(1), 10-19.

Oppermann, M. (1996b). Convention destination images: Analysis of meeting planners' perceptions. *Tourism Management, 17*, 175-182.

Oppermann, M. & Chon, K. S. (1997). Convention participation decision making process. *Annals of Tourism Research, 24*, 178-191.

Pearce, P. L. & Stringer, P. F. (1991). Psychology and tourism. *Annals of Tourism Research, 18*(2), 136-154.

Perdue, R. R., Long, P. T. & Allen, L. (1987). Rural resident tourism perceptions and attitudes. *Annals of Tourism Research, 14*, 420-429.

Perdue, R. R., Long, P. T. & Allen, L. (1990). Resident support for tourism development. *Annals of Tourism Research, 17*, 586-599.

Perdue, R. R., Long, P. T. & Kang, Y. S. (1995). Resident support for gambling as a tourism development strategy. *Journal of Travel Research, 34*(2), 3-11.

Peters, M. & Pikkemaat, B. (2005). The management of city events: The case of "BERGSILVESTER" in Innsbruck, Austria. *Event Management, 9*, 147-153.

Peters, M. & Weiermair, K. (2000). Tourist attractions and attracted tourists: How to satisfy today's 'fickle' tourist clientele? *Journal of Tourism Studies, 11*(1), 22-29.

Pike, S. (2002). Destination image analysis: A review of 142 papers from 1973 to 2000.

Tourism Management, 23, 541-549.

Policy Studies Institute (PSI). (1992). Arts festivals. *Cultural Trends, 15,* 1-20.

Polo, M. (1913). *The Travels of Marco Polo* (马可·波罗游记). Beijing: Zhengmeng Publishing.

Professional Convention Management Association (PCMA). (2003). Annual Survey. Retrieved July 18, 2012, from http://www.pcma.org/resources#.

Qian, M. X. (2006). Analysis and suggestion on accelerating the development of exhibition economy in Jiangsu (加快推进江苏会展经济发展的分析与建议). *Jiangsu Science & Technology Information, 9,* 28-31.

Qian, Z. H. & Wong, T. C. (2000). The rising urban poverty: A dilemma of market reforms in China. *Journal of Contemporary China, 9*(23), 113-125.

Rack, J., Wichmann, O., Kamara, B., et al. (2005). Risk and spectrum of diseases in travelers to popular tourist destinations. *Journal of Travel Medicine, 12*(5), 248-253.

Raybould, M. & Fredline, L. (2012). An investigation of measurement error in visitor expenditure survey. *International Journal of Event and Festival Management, 3*(2), 201-211.

Research and Markets. (2006). China tourism industry. Retrieved July 18, 2012, from http://www.researchandmarkets.com/reportinfo.asp?report_id=220246.

Richards, G. & Wilson, J. (2004). The impact of cultural events on city image: Rotterdam, cultural capital of Europe 2001. *Urban Studies, 41*(10), 1931-1951.

Richardson, S. & Long, P. (1991). Recreation, tourism, and quality of life in small winter cities: five keys to success. *Winter Cities, 9*(1), 22-25.

Richtmyer, R. (2005). Study finds convention centre forecasts overly rosy. Retrieved January 6, 2012, from http://www.adn.com/front/story/6032921p-5922415c.html.

Riley, R. (1996). Revealing socially constructed knowledge through quasi-structured interviews and grounded theory analysis. *Journal of Travel & Tourism Marketing, 5*(1/2), 21-40.

Ritchie, B. (1984). Assessing the impacts of hallmark events: Conceptual and research issues. *Journal of Travel Research, 23*(1), 2-111.

Ritchie, J. R. B. & Aitken, C. (1985). Olympulse II—Evolving resident attitudes towards the 1988 Olympic Winter Games. *Journal of Travel Research, 23*(Winter), 28-33.

Ritchie, J. R. B. & Beliveau, D. (1974). Hallmark events: An evaluation of a strategic response to seasonality in the travel market. *Journal of Travel Research, 14*(2), 14-20.

Robert, J. S. (2000). Wild ontology: Elaborating environmental pragmatism. *Ethics and the Environment, 5*(2): 191-209.

Robinson, M. & Phipps, A. (2003). World passing by: Journeys of culture and cultural journeys. *Journal of Tourism and Cultural Change, 1*(1), 1-10.

Robinson, M., Picard, D. & Long, P. (2004). Festival tourism: Producing, translating, and consuming expressions of cultures. *Event Management, 8*, 187-189.

Rod, D. (2003). Branding Asian tourist destinations—A series. Retrieved June 28, 2012, from http://www.asiamarketresearch.com/columns/tourism-branding.htm.

Rogers, T. (1998). *Conferences: A Twenty-First Century Industry*. Harlow Essex: Addison Wesley Longman.

Rogerson, C. M. (2005). Conference and exhibition tourism in the developing world: The South African Experience. *Urban Forum, 16*(2-3), 176-196.

Rolfe, H. (1992). *Arts Festivals in the UK*. London: Policy Studies Institute.

Ross, A. & Fang, V. (2009). Critical eye on Hangzhou: An ancient capital is poised to make a high-tech leap. *The China Business Review*. Retrieved January 6, 2012, from http://www.chinabusinessreview.com/public/0409/fang_ross.html.

Rossman, G. & Rallis, S. (2003). *Learning in the Field: An Introduction to Qualitative Research* (2nd ed.). Thousand Oaks, CA: Sage Publications.

Rubin, H. J. & Rubin, I. S. (2005). *Qualitative Interviewing: The Art of Bearing Data* (2nd ed.). Thousand Oaks, CA: Sage Publications.

Rummel, R. J. (1970). *Applied Factor Analysis*. Evanston, IL: Northwestern University Press.

Runder, R. S. (1966). *Philosophy of Social Science*. Englewood Cliffs, NJ: Prentice Hall.

Rurakdee, N. (1991). The impact of the Visit Malaysia Year on Thai tourism. *Bangkok Bank Monthly Review, 32*(May), 182-198.

Ryan, C. (1997). Tourism: Mature subject discipline?. *Pacific Tourism Review, 1*, 3-5.

Ryan, C. (1998). Economic impacts of small events: Estimated and determinants—A New Zealand example. *Tourism Economics, 4*(4), 339-352.

Ryan, C. (2002). Tourism and cultural proximity: Example from New Zealand. *Annals of Tourism Research, 29*(3), 631-647.

Ryan, C. (2004). Ethics in tourism research—Objectivities and personal perspectives. In

B. W. Ritchie, P. Burns & C. Palmer (Eds.), *Tourism Research Methods: Integrating Theory and Practice*. Wallingford, Oxon: CAB International.

Ryan, C. (2005). The ranking and rating of academics and journals in tourism research. *Tourism Management, 26*(5), 657-662.

Ryan, C. (2009). Thirty years of tourism management. *Tourism Management, 30*(1), 1-2.

Ryan, C. & Carland, R. (1999). The use of a specific non-response option on Likert-type scales. *Tourism Management, 20*(1), 107-113.

Ryan, C. & Gu, H. M. (2009). *Tourism in China: Destination Cultures and Communities*. New York: Routledge.

Ryan, C. & Lockyer, T. (2001). An economic impact case study: The South Pacific Masters' Games in New Zealand. *Tourism Economics, 7*(3), 267-275.

Ryan, C. & Montgomery, D. (1994). The attitudes of Bakewell residents to tourism and issue in community responsive tourism. *Tourism Management, 15*(5), 358-367.

Ryan, C. & Saleh, F. (1993). Jazz and knitwear—Factors that attract tourists to festivals. *Tourism Management, 14*(4), 289-297.

Ryan, C., Scotland, A. & Montgomery, D. (1998). Resident attitudes to tourism development—A comparative study between the Rangitikei, New Zealand and Bakewell. *Progress in Tourism and Hospitality Research, 4*(2), 115-130.

Ryan, C., Smee, A. & Murphy, S. (1996). Creating a database of events in New Zealand: Early results. *Festivals Management & Event Tourism, 4*(3/4), 151-155.

Ryan, M. J. & Bristor, J. M. (1987). The symbiotic nature of hermeneutical vs. classically generated knowledge. In R. W. Belk et al. (Eds.), *1987 AMA Winter Educators' Conference* (pp. 191-194), Chicago: American Marketing Association.

Safavi, F. (1971). A cost benefit model for convention centres. *Annals of Regional Science, 2*, 221-237.

Sarantakos, S. (1998). *Social Research* (2nd ed.). South Yarra, Australia: Macmillan Education Australia Pty. Ltd.

Sassen, S. & Roost, F. (1999). The city: Strategic site for the global entertainment industry. In D. R. Judd & S. Fainstein (Eds.), *The Tourist City* (pp. 143-154). New Haven, CT: Yale University Press.

Schofield, P. (1996). Cinematographic images of a city: Alternative heritage tourism in Manchester. *Tourism Management, 17*(5), 333-340.

Sears, D. W. & Reid, J. N. (1992). Rural strategies and rural development research: An assessment. *Policy Studies Journal, 20*, 2, 301-309.

Selby, M. (2004). *Understanding Urban Tourism: Image, Culture & Experience.* New York: I. B. Tauris.

Shao, S. P. (2004). From "return the lake to the people" to "Forbidden City raised admission fees" (从 "还湖于民" 到 "故宫门票提价"). *Workers' Daily.* Retrieved October 1, 2012, from http://www.people.com.cn/GB/guandian/1034/3038769.html.

Shen, Z. J. (2016). China's events number accounts for a quarter of the world's, exhibitors' capability ranks second in the world (中国展会数量占全球四分之一 展商实力排名世界第二). Retrieved May 1, 2016, from http://finance.ifeng.com/a/20160114/14166978_0.shtml.

Sherwood, P. (2007). *A Triple Bottom Line Evaluation of the Impact of Special Events: The Development of Indicators* (Doctoral dissertation). Melbourne: Victoria University.

Sherwood, P., Jago, L. & Deery, M. (2004). Sustainability reporting: An application for the evaluation of special events. In C. Cooper, C. Arcodia, D. Solnet & M. Whitford, (Eds.), Proceedings of creating tourism knowledge: 14th International Research Conference of the Council for Australian University Tourism and Hospitality Education. Brisbane: CAUTHE.

Shone, A. & Parry, B. (2001). *Successful Event Management: A Practical Handbook.* London: Continuum.

Shone, A. & Parry, B. (2004). *Successful Event Management.* London: Thomson Learning.

Sohu News. (2007). Hangzhou employees' average annual income in 2006 has increased 936 RMB over 2005 to 23,581 RMB (去年杭州市职工平均工资23581元 比前年增936元). Retrieved October, 1, 2012, from http://news.sohu.com/20070816/n251622253.shtml.

Soutar, G. N. & McLeod, P. B. (1989). The impacts of the America's Cup on Fremantle residents: Some empirical evidence. In G. J. Syme, B. J. Shaw, D. M. Fenton & W. S. Mueller (Eds.), *The Planning and Evaluation of Hallmark Events* (92-102). Aldershot: Avebury.

Soutar, G. N. & McLeod, P. B. (1993). Residents' perceptions on impacts of the America's Cup. *Annals of Tourism Research, 20*(4), 571-582.

Spickard, S. E. (1996). Economic impact of convention and conference centers. Retrieved

January 6, 2012, from http://www.beachbrowser.com/conference-center/economic-impact-OF-convention-and-confenrence-centers.htm.

Standeven, J. & DeKnop, P. (1999). *Sport Tourism*. Champaign Ill: Human Kinetics.

Start Soft. (2008). Cluster analysis. Retrieved March 1, 2012, from http://www.statsoft.com/textbook/stcluan.html

Statistics Canada. (2002). Canadian travel survey—2001. Ottawa: Government of Canada.

Sternberg, R. J. (1990). The geographic metaphor. In R. J. Sternberg, *Metaphors of Mind: Conceptions of the Nature of Intelligence* (pp. 85-111). New York: Cambridge University Press.

Su, Z. F. & Hu, R. D. (2007). The dynamic analysis of the relationship between urbanization and consumption growth in China—An empirical study based on VAR model (中国城镇化发展与居民消费增长关系的动态分析——基于VAR模型的实证研究). *Shanghai Economic Review, 5*, 58-65.

Swanson, K. E., Kuhn, R. G. & Xu, W. (2001). Environmental policy implementation in rural China: A case study of Yuhang, Zhejiang. *Environmental Management, 27*, 481-491.

Swarbrook, J. & Horner, S. (2001). *Business Travel and Tourism*. Butterworth: Heinemann.

Teerarat, S. (2013). Thailand MICE Tourism. Retrieved October 10, 2016, from https://www.amchamthailand.com/asp/view_doc.asp?DocCID=4026.

The Asian Association of Convention and Visitor Bureaus (AACVB). (2014). 7th Asia for Asia: Rock the Generation. Retrieved July 8, 2014, from http://www.aacvb.org/ASIAFORASIA.html.

The Global Association of the Exhibition Industry (UFI). (2004). UFI 71st congress—A success in Thailand's city of Angels: Exhibition professionals from 53 nations to meet at annual session. Retrieved July 18, 2012, from http://www.ufi.org/archive/media-releases/48-PR_-L1-1032-L2-1032-3840.pdf.

Thomas, R. & Wood, E. H. (2004). Event-based tourism: A survey of local authority strategies in the UK. *Local Governance, 29*(2), 127-136.

Thompson, A. (1999). Security. In R. Cashman & A. Hughes (Eds.), *Staging the Olympics: The Event and Its Impact* (pp. 106-120). Sydney: University of New South Wales Press.

Tuchman, G. (1994). Historical social science. In N. K. Denzin & Y. S. Lincoln (Eds.),

Handbook of Qualitative Research (pp. 306-323). Thousand Oaks, CA: Sage Publications.

Turco, D. M. & Kelsey, C. W. (1992). Determining the economic impact of recreation special events. Alexandria, VA: National Recreation and Park Association.

Turner, V. (1969). *The Ritual Process*. Chicago: Aldine.

United Nations World Tourism Organization (UNWTO). (2006). *Tourism 2020 Vision*. Madrid: World Tourism Organisation.

United Nations World Tourism Organisation (UNWTO). (2012). Why Tourism?. Retrieved July 18, 2012, from http://unwto.org/en/content/why-tourism.

Usher, R. (1996). A critique of the neglected epistemological assumptions of educational research. In D. Scott & R. Usher (Eds.), *Understanding Educational Research* (pp. 9-32). London: Routledge.

Uysal, M., Gahan, L. & Martin, B. (1993). An examination of event motivations: A case study. *Festival Management & Event Tourism, 1*, 5-10.

Wagen, L. V. D. & Carlos, B. R. (2005). *Event Management: For Tourism, Cultural, Business, and Sporting Events*. New Jersey: Pearson Education, Inc.

Walker, M., Kaplanidou, K., Gibson, H., Thapa, B., Geldenhuys, S. & Coetzee, W. (2013). Win in Africa, with Africa: Social responsibility, event image, and destination benefits. The case of the 2010 FIFA World Cup in South Africa. *Tourism Management, 34*, 80-90.

Walmsley, T. L., Dimaranan, B. V. & McDougall, R. A. (2000). A baseline scenario for the dynamic GTAP Model. Purdue University: Center for Global Trade Analysis.

Wang, B. (2004). Thoughts and suggestions on the rapid and healthy development of city exhibition economy (对城市会展经济快速健康发展的思考及建议). *Market Research, 3*, 45-46.

Wang, B. L. (2003). Event tourism development model discussion (会展旅游发展模式之探讨). *Tourism Tribune, 18*(1):35-39.

Wang, D. (2007). *China's Outbound Travel Market* (中国出境旅游市场). Beijing: Ivy Consulting and China Outbound Tourism.

Wang, D. Q. & Li, T. (2014). Study on the brand positioning of MICE in the perspective of ecological niche—A case study of the International Fair of China Western International White Spirit Exposition (生态位视域下会展品牌定位研究——以中

国西部国际博览会白酒专业博览会为例). *Enterprise Economy, 5,* 12-15.

Wang, F. C. & Wang, Q. Y. (2015). Analysis on the present development situation and development model of China's Internet Exhibition (我国网络会展发展现状及发展模式分析). *Manager's Journal, 3,* 168-169.

Wang, J. H. & Qi, F. H. (2006). Analyzing China's MICE status quo and future actions based on the SCP model (基于SCP模型分析中国会展旅游的现状和应采取的行为). *Market Modernisation, 17,* 170-171.

Wang, Y., Zhuang, G. S., Xu, C. & An, Z. S. (2006). The air pollution caused by the burning of fireworks during the Lantern Festival in Beijing. *Atmospheric Environment, 41,* 417-431.

Warnick, R. B., Bojanic, D. C. & Xu, F. (2015). Using a trade market analysis technique to refine measurements for economic impact analysis of special events. *Journal of Travel Research, 54*(1), 52-65.

Watt, D. C. (1998). *Event Management in Leisure and Tourism.* New York: Addison Wesley Longman Publishing.

Weber, K. (2001). Meeting planners' use and evaluation of convention and visitor bureaus. *Tourism Management, 22,* 599-606.

Weber, K. & Ladkin, A. (2003). The convention industry in Australia and the United Kingdom: Key issues and competitive forces. *Journal of Travel Research, 42*(2), 125-132.

WebFinance Inc. (2005). Incentive definition. Retrieved July 18, 2012, from http://www.investorwords.com/2394/incentive.html.

Wei, F. (2004). Analysis of China's convention industry: Problems and countermeasures. *Chinese Business Review, 3*(6), 12.

Wei, L. C. & Qu, X. Y. (2007). Some thoughts on China's MICE economy development (对我国会展经济发展的思考). *Information on Economic and Technical Cooperation, 10,* 10.

Wen, J. J. & Tisdell, C. A. (2001). *Tourism and China's Development: Policies, Regional Economic Growth and Ecotourism.* New Jersey: World Scientific.

Williams, S. (2001). *Emotions and Social Theory.* London: Sage Publications.

Wilson, S., Fesenmaier, D., Fesenmaier, J. & Vanes, J. (2001). Factors for success in rural tourism development. *Journal of Travel Research, 40,* 132-138.

Wirtz, R. A. (2001). Stadium and convention centers as community loss leaders. Retrieved January 6, 2012, from http://www.zianet.com/nmiri/e_stadiums_081004.htm.

Wood, H. (1982). Festivity and social change. London: Polytechnic of the South Bank, Dept. of Social Sciences, Leisure in the Eighties Research Unit.

World Economic Forum. (2016). The travel & tourism competitiveness index 2015: T & T as a resilient contribution to national development. Retrieved October 10, 2016, from http://reports.weforum.org/travel-and-tourism-competitiveness-report-2015/the-travel-tourism-competitiveness-index-2015-tt-as-a-resilient-contribution-to-national-development/.

World Leisure Expo. (2006). 2006 Hangzhou World Leisure Expo. Retrieved July 2, 2006, from http://www.worldleisure.org/expo2006/overview.html.

World Leisure Exposition Office. (2006). Statistical analysis. Retrieved July 2, 2012, from http://cn.wl-expo.com/en/news02.html.

World Trade and Tourism Council (WTTC). (2017). Travel & tourism economic impact 2017. Retrieved January 25, 2017, from http://www.wttc.org/-/media/files/reports/economic-impact-research/countries-2017/egypt2017.pdf.

Wu, A. & Weber, K. (2005). Convention center facilities, attributes and services: The delegates' perspective. *Asia Pacific Tourism Association, 10*(4), 399-410.

Wu, H. L. (2005). Reflections on China's MICE tourism development (中国会展旅游发展的思考). *Enterprise Economy, 5*, 103-105.

Xiao, L. (2010). China's exhibition: Crisis and hopes (中国会展：危机与希望同在). Retrieved October 1, 2012, from http://finance.sina.com.cn/roll/20100227/10167469581.shtml.

Xiaoshan Statistical Information Net. (2006). The fifth research analysis of the Leisure Exposition (休博会调查分析之五). Retrieved October 1, 2012, from http://www.tj.xs.zj.cn/main/I/_6f399q65o87.htm.

Xinhua News Agency. (2003). Event tourism's current situation and development trend (会展旅游的现状及发展前景). Retrieved July 18, 2012, from http://news.xinhuanet.com/expo/2003-03/18/content_784524.htm.

Xinhua News Agency. (2006). Media's comment: China is entering a 'car society' (媒体评说：中国正在步入"汽车社会"). Retrieved July 18, 2012, from http://news.xinhuanet.com/auto/2006-12/01/content_5417583.htm

Xinhua News Agency. (2007). Hangzhou: 'Future World' theme park faces challenges (杭

州："未来世界"主题公园面临挑战). Retrieved November 4, 2007, from http://
www.js.xinhuanet.com/zhuanti/2007-05/09/content_9978472.htm.

Xu, F. (2002). On the conception connotation and marketing promotion of MICE
tourism (会展旅游的概念、内涵与市场开发). *Tourism Tribune*, *17*(4), 56-59.

Yang, L. X. (2009). Analysis on the development of convention and exhibition industry
in China (我国会展业发展研究). *Journal of Shanxi University of Finance and
Economics*, *1*, 57-62.

Yang, M. & Zhang, J. H. (2006). How to avoid the huge cost of construction being wasted
(百亿元建筑浪费如何避免). *Builders Monthly*, *6*, 57.

Yeoman, I., Robertson, M., Ali-Knight, J., Drummond, S. & McMahon-Beattie, U. (2004).
Festival and Events Management: An International Arts and Culture Perspective. Oxford:
Elsevier Limited.

Yin, R. K. (1994). *Case Study Research: Design and Methods* (2nd ed.). Newbury Park, CA:
Sage Publications.

Yoon, S., Spencer, D. M., Holecek, D. F. & Kim, D. K. (2000). A profile of Michigan's
festival and special event tourism market. *Event Management*, *6*, 33-44.

Yoon, Y. S., Lee, J. S. & Lee, C. K., (2010). Measuring festival quality and value affecting
visitors' satisfaction and loyalty using a structural approach. *International Journal of
Hospitality Management*, *29*, 335-342.

Zelinsky, W. (1994). Convention land USA: The geography of a latter-day phenomenon.
Annals of the Association of American Geographers, *84*, 68-86.

Zhang, C. & Liang, W. T. (2008). Macau talent shortage and talent trend (澳门人才短缺
与人才需求趋势). *International Talent*, *1*, 54-55.

Zhang, F. G., Hao, J. M., Jiang, G. H., Ding, Z. Y., Li, X. B. & Li, T. (2005). Spatial-
temporal variance of urban land use intensity (中国城市土地利用集约度时空变异
分析). *China Land Science*, *1*, 23-29.

Zhang, G. R. (1989). Ten years of Chinese tourism: Profile and assessment. *Tourism
Management*, *10*(1), 51-62.

Zhang, H. C. (2005). China's TV customer market (中国电视受众市场). Retrieved
October 1, 2012, from http://www.iguanzhong.com/uch/space.php?uid=6&do=blog
&id=6514.

Zhang, H. Q., Pine, R. & Lam, T. (2005). *Tourism and Hotel Development in China: From*

Political to Economic Success. Binghamton: The Haworth Press, Inc.

Zhang, Q. H., Jenkin, C. L. & Qu, H. (2003). *Inland Chinese Outbound Travel to Hong Kong and Its Implications.* Binghamton: The Haworth Hospitality Press.

Zhang, W. (2009). Financial crisis hit the United States' casino city: Hotel prices and casino visitors decreased (金融危机重创美国赌城 游客减少酒店价格下跌). Retrieved May 10, 2010, from http://news.163.com/09/0211/23/51TL3JM7000120GU.html.

Zhang, X. Y. (2002). Hangzhou: Paradise on Earth (杭州：人间天堂). Retrieved July 2, 2006, from http://www.chinatoday.com.cn/English/e20026/hangzhou.htm.

Zhejiang Asia-Pacific Exhibition Industry Research and Development Centre. (2007). 2006 Zhejiang exhibition industry development report (2006年浙江会展业发展报告). Retrieved July, 18, 2012, from www.zftec.gov.cn/main/zt/zlyxh/xh-06bg.html.

Zhejiang Online. (2014). Hangzhou's inbound tourists only accounted for 3.2%, the city lacks big international events (杭州入境旅游人数仅占3.2% 国际性会展数量少规模小). Retrieved July 20, 2015, from http://zjnews.zjol.com.cn/system/2014/06/17/020085388.shtml.

Zhejiang Tourism Bureau. (2006). Zhejiang Province had more than 10 million visitors during the May 1 Golden Week in 2006 (2006年浙江省"五一"黄金周旅游人数突破千万大关). Retrieved July 18, 2012, from http://www.tourzj.gov.cn/zww/ShowNew.aspx?type=56&id=308.

Zhejiang.com. (2006). Hangzhou West Lake Exposition's past and now (杭州西湖博览会的过去和现在). Retrieved July 18, 2012, from http://xbh.zjol.com.cn/05xbh/system/2002/05/10/001021285.shtml.

Zheng, L. N. (2015). Hangzhou's domestic tourist number reached 106 million in 2014 (2014年杭州全年国内旅游人数1.06亿人次). Retrieved July 26, 2015, from http://www.zj123.com/info/detail-d300631.htm.

Zheng, S. H. & Liu, J. L. (2005). *Leisure: An Introduction* (休闲概论). Tianjin: Nankai University Press.

Zhengzhou Evening. (2006). Urban construction: No more blindly following the foreign styles (城市建设"崇洋风"该刹一刹了). Retrieved March 2, 2012, from http://www.ha.xinhuanet.com/add/2006-10/25/content_8344327.htm.

Zhou, C. & Ryan, C. (2008). Resident perception of expo host cities—the case of the World Leisure Expo. *Journal of Hospitality Application and Research*, 3(1), 5-21.

Zhou, W. (2007). Eco-Olympics started to appear in Beijing (绿色奥运图景初现北京). *Journal of Environment Education*, *10*, 36-38.

Zhou, Y. G. (2006). Cultural background of Hangzhou's 'Zen Buddhism' brand (杭州 "禅都" 品牌的文化背景). Retrieved October 10, 2007, from http://www.sociology.cass.cn/shxw/zxwz/P020070731311790159474.pdf.

Zhu, H. M. (2006). Empirical analysis of Hangzhou's major newspaper coverage on the 2005 West Lake Expo (杭州主要报纸媒体对2005年第七届西博会报道之实证分析). Retrieved October 1, 2012, from http://www.chinamediaresearch.cn/article/4802/.

Zou, L. (2005). Service! The key to MICE competition (服务!展会竞争的筹码). Retrieved March 5, 2012, from http://hzpd.newssc.org/system/2006/10/26/010169037.shtml.

Appendix

(English version of the questionnaire)

The purpose of this questionnaire is to discover YOUR attitudes towards conferences and events held in Hangzhou. Your name and address are not required and you have every right to not answer all questions. Your answers will be kept confidential and any report will be of aggregating data only.

It will take about 20 minutes to complete the questionnaire.
If you have any questions about the questionnaire, please do not hesitate to contact Zhou Chao (Nicole).

Section one:

1. Have you attended any meetings, conferences, exhibitions, and had incentives opportunities in the last five years? (If yes, what kinds of events have you attended? If no, please give the reason why you did not attend any events)

   Yes ☐ _____

   No ☐ _____

2. Have you attended any events/exhibitions during the Hangzhou World Leisure Expo?

   Yes ☐ If yes, which ones? _____

   No ☐

3. What was the main reason of your attendance? (You can tick more than one)

   Work related ☐   Business related ☐   Study ☐   Leisure purposes ☐

   Family related ☐   It is interesting ☐   Accompanying friends ☐

   To acquire new knowledge ☐   Shopping ☐   Travel related ☐

   Others ☐   Please specify: _____

4. Whether you have, or have not, attended any MICE in Hangzhou, please describe in your own words what you think **the most positive impacts** of the MICE policies in Hangzhou are.

5. What do you think are **the most negative impacts** of the MICE policies in Hangzhou?

Section Two: Impacts of MICE on Hangzhou

In this section we would like you to use the following scale:

1   Has gotten really bad/Things are now very bad

2   Has gotten significantly worse

3   Has gotten quite a bit worse

4   Has gotten a little worse

5   Has neither improved nor gotten worse/No change

6   Has improved just a little

7   Has improved quite a bit

8   Has improved considerably/significantly/quite a lot

9   Has improved vastly

0   No opinion/Don't know/Not applicable

PLEASE CIRCLE THE NUMBER THAT BEST REPRESENTS YOUR OPINION

* First (On the left)—Please consider the following items from the overall perception of the city.

* Second (On the right)—Using the same scale—this time from your own personal perspective and consider how they have impacted on your normal daily life.

Because of MICE in Hangzhou …

	For the whole city	For my personal daily life
—Event facilities (event centres, event parks, etc.)	1 2 3 4 5 6 7 8 9 0	1 2 3 4 5 6 7 8 9 0
—Related facilities (hotels, restaurants, shopping places, etc.)	1 2 3 4 5 6 7 8 9 0	1 2 3 4 5 6 7 8 9 0
—Entertainment opportunities	1 2 3 4 5 6 7 8 9 0	1 2 3 4 5 6 7 8 9 0
—Maintenance of public facilities like parks and roads	1 2 3 4 5 6 7 8 9 0	1 2 3 4 5 6 7 8 9 0
—Traffic congestion in the city	1 2 3 4 5 6 7 8 9 0	1 2 3 4 5 6 7 8 9 0
—Quality of road infrastructure (highways, etc.)	1 2 3 4 5 6 7 8 9 0	1 2 3 4 5 6 7 8 9 0
—Public services (medical, law, logistics, security, etc.)	1 2 3 4 5 6 7 8 9 0	1 2 3 4 5 6 7 8 9 0
—Damage to the natural environment	1 2 3 4 5 6 7 8 9 0	1 2 3 4 5 6 7 8 9 0
—City's pollution level	1 2 3 4 5 6 7 8 9 0	1 2 3 4 5 6 7 8 9 0
—Employment rate and opportunities	1 2 3 4 5 6 7 8 9 0	1 2 3 4 5 6 7 8 9 0
—Unemployment rate	1 2 3 4 5 6 7 8 9 0	1 2 3 4 5 6 7 8 9 0
—City's safety level and crime rate	1 2 3 4 5 6 7 8 9 0	1 2 3 4 5 6 7 8 9 0
—Number of tourists	1 2 3 4 5 6 7 8 9 0	1 2 3 4 5 6 7 8 9 0
—Property values and rental costs	1 2 3 4 5 6 7 8 9 0	1 2 3 4 5 6 7 8 9 0
—Price of goods and services	1 2 3 4 5 6 7 8 9 0	1 2 3 4 5 6 7 8 9 0
—Total living costs	1 2 3 4 5 6 7 8 9 0	1 2 3 4 5 6 7 8 9 0
—Tourism's relationship with local businesses	1 2 3 4 5 6 7 8 9 0	1 2 3 4 5 6 7 8 9 0
—Business cooperation level (both domestic and international)	1 2 3 4 5 6 7 8 9 0	1 2 3 4 5 6 7 8 9 0
—Local business opportunities	1 2 3 4 5 6 7 8 9 0	1 2 3 4 5 6 7 8 9 0
—City's economy as a whole	1 2 3 4 5 6 7 8 9 0	1 2 3 4 5 6 7 8 9 0

(continued)

Item	For the whole city	For my personal daily life
Pride in and satisfaction with the city	1 2 3 4 5 6 7 8 9 0	1 2 3 4 5 6 7 8 9 0
Government involvement in the event business	1 2 3 4 5 6 7 8 9 0	1 2 3 4 5 6 7 8 9 0
Level of promotion and media involvement	1 2 3 4 5 6 7 8 9 0	1 2 3 4 5 6 7 8 9 0
Control of the city's event economy and business	1 2 3 4 5 6 7 8 9 0	1 2 3 4 5 6 7 8 9 0
Government promotion to business participants	1 2 3 4 5 6 7 8 9 0	1 2 3 4 5 6 7 8 9 0
Price levels and management of prices for events	1 2 3 4 5 6 7 8 9 0	1 2 3 4 5 6 7 8 9 0
Event risk control level	1 2 3 4 5 6 7 8 9 0	1 2 3 4 5 6 7 8 9 0
Success of the events	1 2 3 4 5 6 7 8 9 0	1 2 3 4 5 6 7 8 9 0
Suitability of policies and regulations related to tourism	1 2 3 4 5 6 7 8 9 0	1 2 3 4 5 6 7 8 9 0
Suitability of policies and regulations related to events	1 2 3 4 5 6 7 8 9 0	1 2 3 4 5 6 7 8 9 0
Relationship between government and local businesses	1 2 3 4 5 6 7 8 9 0	1 2 3 4 5 6 7 8 9 0
Efforts to stimulate local business involvement in events	1 2 3 4 5 6 7 8 9 0	1 2 3 4 5 6 7 8 9 0
Relationship between government and local residents	1 2 3 4 5 6 7 8 9 0	1 2 3 4 5 6 7 8 9 0
Level of local government's interest in events	1 2 3 4 5 6 7 8 9 0	1 2 3 4 5 6 7 8 9 0
Providing suitable plans for the city's event tourism development	1 2 3 4 5 6 7 8 9 0	1 2 3 4 5 6 7 8 9 0
City's image in China	1 2 3 4 5 6 7 8 9 0	1 2 3 4 5 6 7 8 9 0
City's image in the world	1 2 3 4 5 6 7 8 9 0	1 2 3 4 5 6 7 8 9 0
City's level of attraction to people from other cities in China	1 2 3 4 5 6 7 8 9 0	1 2 3 4 5 6 7 8 9 0
City's level of attraction to foreign people	1 2 3 4 5 6 7 8 9 0	1 2 3 4 5 6 7 8 9 0
City's competitive position compared to similar cities	1 2 3 4 5 6 7 8 9 0	1 2 3 4 5 6 7 8 9 0

Section Three: Events, Conferences, and General Promotion of Them

This section asks you your level of agreement with the following statements. Please refer to the following scale and circle the numbers to the questions:

1	2	3	4	5	6	7	8	9	0
Very strongly disagree	Strongly disagree	Moderately disagree	Slightly disagree	Neither agree nor disagree	Slightly agree	Moderately agree	Strongly agree	Very strongly agree	No opinion/ Not applicable

Hosting big events can increase recognition of the city in the world	1	2	3	4	5	6	7	8	9	0
Hosting big events is the best way to show to the world the city's capabilities	1	2	3	4	5	6	7	8	9	0
Hosting big events can quickly stimulate the city's economic development	1	2	3	4	5	6	7	8	9	0
Hosting big events can quickly stimulate local business development	1	2	3	4	5	6	7	8	9	0
I believe hosting big events will directly give Hangzhou's tourism and hospitality industry a positive impact	1	2	3	4	5	6	7	8	9	0
Hosting big events can always have long-term benefits for city development	1	2	3	4	5	6	7	8	9	0
I believe my personal economic status will be better	1	2	3	4	5	6	7	8	9	0
Because of hosting big events, poorer people can no longer afford living in the urban area	1	2	3	4	5	6	7	8	9	0
I think the government is spending too much money hosting events	1	2	3	4	5	6	7	8	9	0
I think the government should use the money for education and medical care	1	2	3	4	5	6	7	8	9	0
Because of hosting big events, the property values and rental costs will increase	1	2	3	4	5	6	7	8	9	0
Because of hosting big events, life in Hangzhou will be more interesting	1	2	3	4	5	6	7	8	9	0

(continued)

	1	2	3	4	5	6	7	8	9	0
Because Hangzhou is hosting big events, I like living here	1	2	3	4	5	6	7	8	9	0
I think distance to the event venue is the most important factor that inhibits me from attending an event	1	2	3	4	5	6	7	8	9	0
The price of the entrance ticket is the most important factor for attending an event	1	2	3	4	5	6	7	8	9	0
An event should fit the city's culture and history	1	2	3	4	5	6	7	8	9	0
Hosting big events can entertain local residents and give them the opportunity to attend major international events	1	2	3	4	5	6	7	8	9	0
Hosting big events is a good way to know about cultures of other countries	1	2	3	4	5	6	7	8	9	0
I would love to have an opportunity to be involved in the event process	1	2	3	4	5	6	7	8	9	0
Building event theme parks is worthwhile	1	2	3	4	5	6	7	8	9	0
I will also consider some important events in other cities	1	2	3	4	5	6	7	8	9	0
An event that relates to the people's lives is more interesting and valuable	1	2	3	4	5	6	7	8	9	0

Section Four: Background Information

1. Where do you live?

Centre of the city ☐   A little distant from the centre of the city ☐

On the city periphery ☐   Outside the city ☐

2. What is the main transportation that you use daily?

Private car ☐   Public bus ☐   Bicycle ☐   On foot ☐   Taxi ☐

Company car ☐   Others: _____

3. Your gender: Male ☐   Female ☐

4. Your age:

18 and under ☐   19–25 ☐   26–30 ☐   31–35 ☐   36–40 ☐   41–45 ☐

46–50 ☐   51–55 ☐   56–60 ☐   61–65 ☐   66 and above ☐

5. What is your monthly salary range?

1,000 RMB and less ☐   1,001–3,000 RMB ☐   3,001–5,000 RMB ☐

5,001–7,000 RMB ☐   7,001–10,000 RMB ☐   More than 10,000 RMB ☐

6. What is your education level?

Primary school ☐   Middle school and high school ☐   Associate degree ☐

Bachelor's degree ☐   Master's degree ☐   Doctor's degree ☐

7. What is your employment status?

Employed ☐   Unemployed ☐   Retired ☐   Student ☐

Engaged in part-time work ☐   Engaged in home duties ☐

8. What is your occupation? _____

* If you have any comments you may wish to make about Hangzhou's hosting MICE or other future big international events, please write down: _____

_____

Index

图书在版编目(CIP)数据

　　中国会展产业发展：居民的感知研究 = The Meetings, Incentives, Conferences, and Exhibitions (MICE) Industry in China: Residents' Perceptions：英文 / 周超著. — 杭州：浙江大学出版社，2017.8
　　ISBN 978-7-308-17001-7

　　Ⅰ. ①中… Ⅱ. ①周… Ⅲ. ①展览会－产业发展－研究－中国－英文 Ⅳ. ①G245

中国版本图书馆CIP数据核字(2017)第132319号

中国会展产业发展：居民的感知研究

The Meetings, Incentives, Conferences, and Exhibitions (MICE) Industry in China: Residents' Perceptions

周　超　著

策　　划	陈丽勋
责任编辑	杨利军
文字编辑	董　唯
责任校对	刘序雯　仲亚萍
封面设计	项梦怡
出版发行	浙江大学出版社
	（杭州市天目山路148号　　邮政编码　310007）
	（网址：http://www.zjupress.com）
排　　版	杭州林智广告有限公司
印　　刷	杭州日报报业集团盛元印务有限公司
开　　本	710mm×1000mm　1/16
印　　张	15
字　　数	349千
版 印 次	2017年8月第1版　2017年8月第1次印刷
书　　号	ISBN 978-7-308-17001-7
定　　价	45.00元